WHY I LOVE BLACK WOMEN

Why I Love Black Women

Michael Eric Dyson

Basic *Civitas* Books

A MEMBER OF THE PERSEUS BOOKS GROUP

Designed by Lovedog Studios

A CIP catalog record for this book is available from the
Library of Congress.

ISBN 0-465-01763-0
03 04 05 / 10 9 8 7 6 5 4 3 2 1

To My Dear Friends

Freda Sampson, Gilda Keith, Coody Garrett,
Sharon Kirkland, Ruth Booth, the late Lovelene Earl,
Ruth Allen, Brenda Joyce Dyson, Dominique Royce,
D. Soyini Madison, Liz Maguire, Delphinia Smith,
Maisha Dyson, Torkwase Dyson, Barbara Perkins,
Linda Malone-Colon, Debra Langford,
Vanessa Lloyd-Sgambati, Evelyn Sample-Oates

And

Carolyn Moore-Assem and Marcia L. Dyson

Contents

Acknowledgments

I want to thank Liz Maguire, my editor, for her wonderful and unfailing support. Liz, this is number seven together, and we're still going strong! I also want to thank Will Morrison for his attention to all the details, and for his daily grind, that helped this book come into being. I especially want to thank Christine Marra and Marco Pavia, whose expert managing of production and copyediting for the book has made it even stronger.

I want to thank Janet Moore, my sweet and efficient friend, and the daughter and personal assistant to her father, and our pastor, the Rev. Dr. Jeremiah A. Wright, Jr. Her unfailing supply of sermons and other materials helped me at crucial times in the writing of this book. I want to thank Walidah Bennett, a bright professor and thinker who also makes a wonderful breakfast. Thanks for the psychic sanctuary and the meals that fed my body — and my mind and soul. I also want to thank Akilah Zuberi, a brilliant healer, educator and metaphysician whose insight and wisdom are already a blessing to our lives.

I want to thank the lovely women who spoke to me over the years, forming the basis for this book: Madame Black; Toni Morrison; Aunt Lila; Aunt Mary; Mrs. Wise; Pat and Pam Nash; Vanessa Bell Armstrong; Kiratiana Freelon (thanks for all your help); Kimberly Levy (thank you for your incredible diligence in helping me with names and descriptions); Senator Dianne Wilkerson; Ruth Hill; Michelena Jester; Mipe Okunseinde; Jetta Grace Martin; Akuorkor Ablorh; Yadani Beyene; Alliah Agostini; Margaret Anadu; Jennifer Sunami; Myrlie Evers-Williams; Mamie Till-Mobley; Coretta Scott King; the late, great Dr. Betty Shabazz; Christine King Farris; Bernice King; Dr. Barbara King; Oprah Winfrey; Attilah Shabazz; Ruth Simmons; Maya Simmons; Deborah Bethea; Barbara Perkins; Angela Davis; Assata Shakur; Susan Taylor; Maxine Waters; Barbara Lee; Kimberle Crenshaw; Patricia Williams; Vicky Free; Maggie Anderson; Ingrid Saunders Jones; Vanessa Bell Calloway; Darlene Clark Hine; Jamie Foster Brown; Rosa Smith; Beverly Dukes; Elaine Johnson; Heather Hill; Linda Johnson Rice; Margena Christian; Pam Cash (thanks for all the research help!); Dona Robertson; Kelly Spurlin; Joyce Ladner; Denise Nicholas; Mary Wilson; Judy Pace; Nichelle Nichols; Freda Payne; Star Jones; the late, great Barbara Christian, and her wonderful daughter, Najuma; Gabrielle Foreman; Elaine Kim; Suzette Spencer; Brenda Dyson (I'm

so proud of you, you are a gifted, amazing woman!);
Torkwase Dyson (an amazing artist, poet and seer); Diedre
Harris-Kelley (a great artist); Eleeza Harris-Kelley (a bril-
liant young lady); and of course, my wonderful mother,
Addie Mae Dyson.

I also want to thank the following publications, Web Sites,
outlets and television programs from which I have drawn
some of the quotes and research used in this book: *Jet*; *Ebony*;
The Other Side; *Stanford News*; *The Associated Press*; *Brown Daily
Herald*; *Brown University News Service*; *Texas Journal of Ideas,
History and Culture*; *Critical Inquiry*; *Australian Broadcasting
Corporation*; *AfroCubaWeb.com*; *Souls*; *Essence*; *The Vigil*; *Times-
Delphic*; *CNN*; *NBC News*; *ABC 20/20*; *The MacNeil/Lehrer
NewsHour*; www.house.gov/waters; *Hannity & Colmes*;
Newhouse News Service; *Chicago Sun-Times*; *www.house.gov/lee*;
www.BlackElectorate.Com; *Politically Incorrect*; www.daveyd.com;
San Francisco Chronicle; *Charlie Rose Show*; *The Nation*; *New
York Times*; *This Week*; *National Review*; *Equal Time*; *The Daily
Bruin*; *Newsday*; *The World & I*; *The Atlanta Journal and
Constitution*; *Sister 2 Sister*; *Journal of Blacks in Higher Education*;
Chronicle of Higher Education; *Sun Reporter*; *Annual Reviews Inc.*;
Essence.com; *Black Enterprise*; *Chicago Tribune*; *CBS This Morning*;
Crain's Chicago Business; *Folio: The Magazine for Magazine
Management*; *The Record*; *Fortune*; *The Boston Globe* and *Dallas
Morning News*.

Finally, I want to thank my family: my son, Michael Eric
Dyson, II, my main man and a good hearted person and very
bright college student; Dr. Mwata Dyson, a great physician in

the making and a good man; and Maisha Dyson, a determined woman and an actress honing her considerable skill. I also want to thank my steadfast brothers: Anthony, Everett, Jr. (hang in there, soldier), Gregory and Brian (you're going to be very successful).

Finally, I want to thank my lovely wife Marcia, whose love and devotion—and her incredibly hard work, and her reading of every word of this book—have largely made my work possible.

"Because I'm a
Black Woman in America"

"Why are you taking a photograph?" the attractive, white, middle-aged woman asked me as she trimmed my beard. She was the owner of a Philadelphia salon to which the photographer for this book took me.

"For a cover shot session," I replied. "I'm writing a book about my love for black women."

"Well, it's about time," she enthused. "I'm so tired of black women being verbally assaulted, especially by their own children."

She was undoubtedly referring to the seemingly endless stream of epithets against females that flow from the mouths of some of hip-hop culture's biggest stars, but she had local fish to fry as well.

"I see these young black men in the neighborhood, and they spew the vilest things you can imagine to young black girls. I just don't understand it. I'm an old activist from the sixties, and I thought that the principles that black women fought for would have gained them more respect than this from their kids."

I nodded in agreement. Indeed, I had often stated in my lectures and sermons across the nation that black women who worked with tireless devotion to free their race from economic want and racial oppression must be horrified to hear some of the vicious remarks that roll effortlessly off the tongues of their children.

"Yes, it is pretty awful," I admitted. "That's part of the reason why I'm writing my book, because even though I've examined—and often defended—hip-hop culture in a number of books and speeches, I can't justify the hateful beliefs that too many males hold."

"Well, what are we going to do about this horrible situation?" she plaintively demanded, with a touch of righteous anger in her voice. "How can we stop this madness?"

I didn't have an adequate response then, and I'm not sure that a single answer even exists. The salon owner's comments and questions conjured the hurt expressed to me by black women across the country as they labor to love their men and themselves in the face of extraordinary odds. A year ago, I decided the least I could do was write about black women's situation in my column for the *Chicago Sun-Times*. I wanted to ease the load of sisters and let them know that I had their back. I wanted them to realize that there are indeed many black men who cherish and adore black women for the very traits that seem to only win them cruel put-downs or unfair criticism. I expressed my love for every shape and sort of sister in our community: from the working class to professionals, from light-skinned women to deep chocolate divas, and from diminutive ladies to larger-than-life lovelies.

After my column was printed, I heard from sisters thanking me for my words and thinking out loud about the condition in which they find themselves, especially as single black women looking for healthy relationships. One sister said that she had been happily married for fifteen years and that she "would have only done one thing differently…marry earlier in life. There are beautiful black men out there that make you soooo proud of them. I think a lot of sisters are just looking in the wrong places and settling for all the wrong things…money and cars. If they only knew the best man to find is one that truly loves God, because if he does, he can't help himself but love you."

A college sophomore from the South wrote, "I'm currently a single black female, and since you broke it down for me, I know why I'm single: because many black men are intimidated by me because I'm going to do something with my life…I'm not going to be another statistic. I'm nineteen years old and I'm not someone's 'baby-mama.'"

A sister wrote, "I am a proud BLACK sister who loves our strong BLACK brothers, even though there are so few of them who feel the same about us." She pursued her master's degree, something that appeared to intimidate many black men. Unfortunately, "so many of our brothers want a woman only to be a doormat or a punching bag. This is not the way I chose to live, so I live alone. So many people think that living without a man is lonely. I tried living with a man (two years), and I have never been as lonely as during that time. I am now wiser, and know that 'alone' does not mean 'lonely.'"

Another black woman wrote that "so many times we sisters feel as though there's something wrong with the way we are, that we get such low respect, or no respect, from our own men, regardless of how we try to better our lives and our bodies. We either make too much money or not enough, are too fat or too skinny, too tall or too short, too light or too dark, it's always something." She had learned to love herself, which protected her from vulnerability to men who sought to "disrespect, reject, or misuse" her.

These letters from black women, like the questions of the white stylist, pose a considerable challenge to black men: how to answer the destructive forces that have been unleashed on black women, often at our hands. While black men are surely not responsible for the economic, social, and racial devastation that black women endure—and which is rooted in the history of black oppression more generally—we are accountable for those attitudes, beliefs, and behaviors we exhibit that undermine our women. I am sure that we need to undergo a profound transformation in how we think about gender, and how we conceive of women's lives and their role in our race and world.

Such a transformation, I believe, begins in love, the greatest force in the world.

Loving black women is a crucial way to combat the forces that bring stigma and demonization to black women's doors. This book is a small effort to love black women in all of their remarkable beauty and wonderful complexity, their intellectual brilliance and their spiritual genius, and their soulfulness and sensuality.

I think it is undeniable that we live in a society that has failed to acknowledge the full extent of our debt to black women's gifts. We have often absorbed their wisdom, sucked their lives, appealed to their insight, depended on their strength, desired their beauty, fed on their hope, hungered for their affirmation, sought their approval, and relied on their faith. And yet we have not paid sufficient tribute to how central black women are to our race, our nation, indeed, our globe, as they have fought for freedom with their hearts, minds, and souls. Those of us who have benefited from black women's love ought to love them back, in the presence of the world.

Why I Love Black Women is my small but heartfelt testimony to how black women's gifts have shaped my life, making me a better man, son, father, brother, minister, professor, worker, friend, and member of the race and human family. This is my love letter to black women, an unapologetic rebuttal of the vicious stereotypes that have dogged black women—as jezebels, sapphires, and mammies—and the lies that slandered their character. I embrace and celebrate professors and preachers, domestics and divas, writers and widows, mentors and

mystics, politicians and prophets, singers and speakers, revolutionaries and readers, and mothers and mates. These black
women and others like them have forever marked my life and
the lives of countless men and women. I sing my song with
pride and offer my witness to black women's worth with joy.
In a word, black women are extraordinary.

I was recently reminded of just *how* extraordinary sisters are
when Felicia Brown-Haywood, an administrator at a university where I lectured, told me the story of her five-year-old
daughter, Regilynn.

"I had enrolled Regilynn in the childcare center on campus," Brown-Haywood recalled. "The students were predominantly white, as were the teachers." She said that when she
went to pick up Reginlynn one day, her daughter's teacher
asked to speak to her.

"Today our class had, as one of its activities, the chance to
string beads," the teacher told Brown-Haywood. "In the middle of doing this, the yarn we were using to string the beads
became entangled, and as a result, we had to put it aside and
pursue other activities. Regilynn asked if she could untangle
the yarn, because she really wanted to make a necklace. I told
her to go ahead, thinking she would become frustrated
because it seemed like an impossible task." To the teacher's
surprise, Regilynn was able to straighten out the yarn.

"Regilynn, how did you do this?" the teacher asked the
five-year-old.

"Because I'm a black woman in America," the little girl
replied without missing a beat.

Brown-Haywood said that she shared the story with her colleagues, all white women, and that whenever they overcame a barrier or successfully faced down an arduous task, they adopted the saying to explain their accomplishment, "Because I'm a black woman in America."

If my book can help others see the intelligence, strength, beauty, and determination of black women—and more, help to affirm little black girls who believe that they can do anything because they are black women in America—then *Why I Love Black Women* is as good an answer as I can give to that salon owner in Philadelphia.

Part 1

Heads and Hearts

I. You Were Always
on My Mind

1

A Perfect Grade

I can still see her face: a honey chocolate, pie-shaped visage framed by a shock of dark curls and lit by bright eyes that were lanterns of learning through which her students illuminated for the first time the dark corners of black history. Mrs. James was my fifth-grade teacher at Wingert Elementary School in a ghetto on Detroit's near west side, the same ghetto I lived and played in—and sometimes fought and fled from—during the first eighteen years of my life. She was my homeroom teacher, which meant that she was the teacher who would guide and ground my educational journey that year. She was my intellectual anchor in the windswept sea of ideologies and interpretations dressed up as facts that washed against my nine-year-old mind.

Although I didn't know it then, I lived in a deeply segregated world, a world as black as coffee with no cream but, as

I was to discover, still full of sugar. The sweetest treat was Mrs. James's demand that her students know who they were. Today, her appeal seems awfully uncontroversial, given the rise of multicultural curricula and the belief that black kids—and not them alone—ought to know something about black culture. This, however, was 1967, before black pride had fully gripped the nation's blacks and re-kinked their hairstyles from artificially straightened manes to defiant Afros and resplendent cockleburs.

This was when blacks were still Negroes, when the riot of the summer of '67 had burned Detroit's ghettoes to baleful cinder, leaving scores of people dead, and sending whites scrambling to the suburbs. Baseball had been integrated for over two decades, but the nation's pastime permitted just three black baseball players to darken Tiger Stadium, heartily disproving the adage in the Negro leagues that only the ball was white. Martin Luther King, Jr., had not yet died, but his philosophy had. Nonviolence was the ideological relic of a veritable ethnosaur. And while I had never heard of him before he perished, King might as well have been Cecil B. DeMille trying to sell Moses from *The Ten Commandments* to northern urban blacks starving for Gordon Parks and *Shaft*.

It was by no means apparent that Mrs. James should teach us about ourselves by teaching us the majestic cadences of Margaret Walker's "For My People," which I can still hear in the girlish bravado of the two young ladies Mrs. James inspired to learn the poem by heart. But her motivation and influence didn't end there—I won my first blue-ribbon for public recitation when I spoke from memory Paul Laurence Dunbar's vernacular poem "Little Brown Baby." Long before the rise of hip-hop, Mrs. James taught me the value of black speech wrung from the common diction of the folk. But more than that, she turned the classroom into a laboratory, figuring how to construct a pedagogy that conveyed the splendor of our neglected black past in all its shocking brilliance—shocking to all, it seemed, except to Mrs. James, who with effortless recall and bright confidence regaled us with story after story of a black genius we should treasure and enlarge.

There were stories of black cowboys like "Deadwood Dick" and Bill Pickett, opera stars like Marian Anderson, performers and activists like Paul Robeson, intellectuals like W. E. B. Du Bois, educators like Mary McCloud Bethune, inventors like Garret T. Morgan and Jan Matzeliger, musicians like Duke Ellington and Louis Armstrong, leaders like Ida B. Wells and Mary Church Terrell, and on and on and on.

For one year, and in stark contrast to what we learned before, we breathed black, thought black, saw black, learned black, believed black—and for the first time for many of us, *felt* black.

I got that same feeling when I took Madame Black's French course at Northwestern High School. Lola Black was an energetic bundle of sweet brown sugar, a shapely young woman with cinnamon-colored skin, a pretty round face, big eyes, an infectious smile, layered tresses and lovely legs. I had a huge crush on Madame Black, just as I had on Mrs. James, and on many of my instructors, including my eighth-grade typing teacher, Mrs. Click, a woman of enchanting beauty whose deep chocolate skin and commanding but sweet spirit often kept me after school seeking her attention and affection. Madame Black made learning fun. She was perpetually in motion and eternally optimistic, bolstering her black students' confidence in mastering a difficult subject. I loved the way my name rolled sensuously off her lips. "Mee-shell," Madame Black called me, refusing, once we grasped the basics, to speak anything but French to us, inspiring us to conjugate our verbs and translate our desires in our fledgling efforts at speaking a foreign language.

But Madame Black was speaking a third language besides French and English: the language of black self-esteem through rigorous study and linguistic excellence. Unlike the scurrilous stereotypes of the black classroom as a theater for therapy— where black people compensated for their social wounds by inflating their intellectual importance in history—Madame Black's schoolroom was a laboratory for intense investigation of black intelligence and black skill. Day after day, Madame Black chipped away at the nefarious beliefs deposited into young black minds about our inability to learn and to compete academically with white kids. Unlike Mrs. James, Madame Black didn't have a frontal assault. Rather, she worked through image and implication, placing before us—in her own body and mind—a powerful example of the gratifications and rewards of being sharp and smart. By that point in our lives, she didn't have to tell us that lethal lies about black intelligence had undermined the race and spread as poisonously as the noxious fumes that were fanned under Jim Crow's vicious wings a generation earlier. She knew that the greatest defense against persistent bigotry was a strategic offense. Madame Black convinced us through demanding work that we were worthy of our own best efforts at academic excellence.

Madame Black identified me as a hungry student, and she fed my appetite for learning beyond the curriculum. She answered my after-school inquiries about how I could improve my accent, deepen my knowledge and practically use my skills in helping my people. She taught me that the first step in enabling black folk to learn was to enable my fellow students to learn. Toward that end, she encouraged my burgeoning intellectual inclinations by having me tutor my peers in French. Outside her classroom, in a small hallway hidden from the main traffic, I opened my textbook to help students in their conjugations, their translations and their pronunciations. As I taught, I learned. As I gave them a sense that they could do things well, I got an even firmer belief in my ability to do well. All along, Madame Black smiled at me, giving me pep talks and lavishing me with praise for my performance.

Madame Black must have known that I was in love with her, although she never embarrassed me by naming my desire as anything but an insatiable urge to learn. She used whatever means were at hand to buttress her black students' will to renounce ignorance, even our deep affection for her. Madame Black gave us a sense that language was a doorway into new and different cultures, and into new and different ways of understanding our own history. I got most of these lessons from speaking with her after class, when formal pedagogy had ceased but, in a sense, an even more authentic teaching began. Madame Black supported my interest in learning as much as I could about black life and culture by directing me to books by authors like James Baldwin and Ralph Ellison. Our informal learning sessions were often enlivened by the presence of my friendly competition—Madame Black's husband, Dr. Cordell Black, a professor of French at a local university. He came by after school to fetch his winsome bride, and he too must have sensed the longing beyond the learning that burned inside me. Dr. Black effortlessly and discretely redirected eros into epistemology and gave me a thrilling sense of the wide range of the black intellectual tradition. One day, he spotted me with Jean Paul Sartre's massive tome, *L'Etre et le Neant*.

"Look, Lola," Dr. Black exclaimed in French, "look at him, look at his aspiration and ambition. He's reading Sartre's *Being and Nothingness* in French! My, what a student."

As he laughed a laugh of wonderment and encouragement, Dr. Black directed me to Du Bois's other works beyond his classic *Souls of Black Folk*, including his magisterial tome, *Black Reconstruction*, and to the work of Frantz Fanon, including *Black Skin, White Masks*, and *The Wretched of the Earth*. Even after I left Northwestern, Madame Black and Dr. Black continued to nurture my love of black learning and gave me a strong sense of my connection to a grand tradition of erudition that was within my grasp. Even though our curriculum was not nearly as explicitly tied to the black pedagogy engaged by Mrs. James, Madame Black's style of teaching and loving her students was no less critical to our intellectual growth.

But even Mrs. James's approach to teaching, as important as it was to her young students' intellectual lives and sense of self, wasn't uncontroversial or universally applauded. It was not until years later that my mother told me that Mrs. James endured a great deal of criticism—surprisingly, to me, from parents and even from her fellow black teachers—for teaching us a curriculum we would never be able to use, for learning facts and figures and features of our culture that were irrelevant to us "making it" in the world. By invoking such a narrow measure to judge the effectiveness of our education, many of our other teachers, as wonderful as they were, missed Mrs. James's message: that you really don't have a purpose for your facts if you don't know the facts of your purpose.

Mrs. James gave us such facts and, in so doing, gave us a sense of our purpose: we were black people fighting to free our minds from the destructive intellectual bleaching that results when official education seeks to whitewash our story. This lone, lovely, determined black woman, this unique and fearless teacher, reached deep into my soul and shaped a planet of black imagination that continues to orbit my intellectual universe. Like all those nameless, faceless, often un-thanked black women who have taught and continue to teach our children, sometimes at risk to their own physical well-being, Mrs. James did far more for me and countless others than she could possibly know.

I never spoke to Mrs. James after leaving the fifth grade. Back then, we didn't know our teachers' first names, and no one has been able to put me in contact with her since. But Mrs. James's and Madame Black's belief in the value and beauty of black people informs every sentence I write, every thought I think, every sermon I give, every speech I make, every lesson I teach, every breath I breathe.

2

I Believe I Can Fly

I first met Toni Morrison in 1987, when I was a graduate student at Princeton. The encounter meant much more to me than meeting a great writer—in reality, I was coming into contact with a woman whose words had helped to shape and even save my life. Of course, that's just the sort of melodramatic statement that you'd never catch in a Morrison novel. Morrison has too skilled a pen and too watchful an eye ever to indulge in petty observations.

And yet, the truth is, her writing came to me just as the word of God came to John, the forsaken apostle of Jesus on the lonely island of Patmos. The biblical book that John wrote, *Revelation*, bears the title of the lonely prophet's apocalyptic visions, urging readers to remain faithful during times of suffering and persecution. That gives me license in appealing to my preacher's vocation to describe Morrison's impact on me. After all, revelation and rebirth are never far apart.

Unlike John, I wasn't exiled to an island as the political consequence of my religious beliefs. Mine was more a spiritual isolation. I married my twenty-six-year-old actress girlfriend Terrie when I was eighteen because I had got her pregnant. We were both members of the same church, sang in the same choir, and, I thought, had the same kind of love for each other. It was not until two months after our shotgun wedding that I discovered that Terrie was shooting blanks. As we lay on the mattress plumped directly on the floor of our dilapidated two-room flat, Terrie let on that the thrill was gone and that we never should have married.

Earlier in our relationship, however, we had shared a love of reading. I moved into her efficiency apartment when she got in the family way, and soon we joined a book club. We might have been poor, but we were determined to be literate. Our lives were organized around books and work. Terrie worked as a waitress in a suburban restaurant that demanded she serve food in a micro-mini skirt that barely covered her route to pregnancy. When she began to show, she was forced to quit.

My work was less steady. I worked for a while as a manager trainee at a fast-food restaurant. Prior to that, for less than three months, I was a clerk-typist in a shop at a Chrysler plant. And for an even shorter period, I was an arc-welder in the wheel-brake and drum factory where my father had worked for thirty-three years. I also worked as an emergency substitute janitor for the Detroit public schools.

In between jobs, I worked as an all-around utility man: painting houses, cutting lawns, shoveling snow, demolishing buildings as a construction worker, and cleaning hotel floors as a maintenance man. Generally, I did whatever I had to do to make ends meet. For a long spell, we had to go on welfare, even as Terrie was enrolled in the W.I.C. (Women, Infants, and Children) healthcare program. I stood in long and embarrassing lines to collect food stamps and retrieve powdered eggs and milk to nourish our growing seed.

Through it all, our reading kept us intellectually stimulated. Perhaps it also kept me ignorant to her steeply declining affection. We waded through a riveting biography of legendary actress Vivien Leigh, learning of her manic-depression and its damaging effect on her marriage to Sir Laurence Olivier. We inhaled the juicy memoir of Evelyn Keyes, the actress who found minor fame as Suellen O'Hara in *Gone With the Wind* and major fun in bedding actors like Anthony Quinn.

Our most powerful and momentous book arrived one afternoon as we struggled against joblessness: Toni Morrison's *Song of Solomon*. It was a rush of pure poetry full of brutal yet beautiful imagery. The book not only spelled out black suffering, but it captured the transcendent possibilities of black imagination. It transplanted me to a spot deep in the black psyche created through the sheer force of rightly ordered words. *Song of Solomon* supplied for me a language of moral yearning and manly struggle in a world that could be cruel from within and beyond black life.

Of all the tomes we collected from our book club membership, it was Morrison's volume more than any other that grabbed me by the tongue. *Song of Solomon* infused my fledgling literary efforts—a poem here, an essay there, and a sermon when I started preaching—with a love of black language's sensuality, its signifying qualities, its splendid idioms and vernaculars, and its accommodation of high intelligence.

Morrison gained a spot on my shelf beside two of my favorite writers, James Baldwin and Ralph Ellison, and, from my reading of the Harvard Classics, next to Lord Tennyson, Matthew Arnold, Herman Melville, and Abraham Lincoln. Long before I learned what magical realism was, Morrison made me peer into the heart of what couldn't be seen by the naked eye. And years before explanations of her art squiggled beneath the microscopic scrutiny of literary theory, I caught a glimpse through Morrison's work of how language behaves.

I tucked *Song of Solomon* beneath my arm when we were evicted from our apartment—on Christmas Day. If it was not a strict example of life imitating art, it was nonetheless Morissonian because the tragic hibernated and then awakened in ordinary life. I didn't feel altogether disrobed or unarmed. That's because Morrison's unblinking engagement with evil helped prepare me for the worst. And her insistence on bending language until it broke the seams of rationality helped me to take refuge in the saving power of symbols and metaphors. The writer can conjure the gift to see ourselves and our moral possibilities from a different angle than the one suggested by whatever reality we confront.

During that celebration of Christ's birth in 1977—a day that was both meteorologically and metaphysically cold—something new was born in me: the determination to rise on the wings of language from the ashes of my personal defeat. I owe a large part of that drive to Morrison's eloquent writing and to her tapping the wellsprings of human survival through memory and desire.

The most poignant words from our black women writers have often convinced us that the ghastly horrors of our personal predicaments must finally give way to our shrewd reinventions in the womb of language. Black women writers have dipped their pens in the blood of ancestors to narrate our tribal griefs. But they have also drawn from personal experience to paint mirrors of self-reflection on our collective imagination. Black women writers have furiously willed worlds of creative expression into existence. They have inscribed on the world's consciousness the complex and explosive black identities that flow from their souls. For me, Morrison was a poignant messenger of their healing and uplifting art.

When Terrie and I were kicked out on that Christmas Day, things got far worse before they got better. We found a vacant flat in which we squatted, but it hardly felt like home—the man with whom we shared the bathroom pulled a pistol on me. Squirrels regularly scurried in and out of a hole in the wall of our unit. We were often too poor to eat every day, although occasionally a friend from church would leave groceries on our front steps. Our son was born with Medicaid, because I'd been fired from my clerk's job a month before he was born. In little more than a year's time, our marriage dissolved. But my resolve to live and to be fed by language's gifts was undiminished.

I eventually went to college at twenty-one, working in factories and pastoring churches to put myself through school. At twenty-six, I entered Princeton to work on my doctorate in religion. Two years later, I met Toni Morrison when she visited Princeton to determine if she wanted to teach there. At fifty-six, she still cut a strikingly beautiful figure, making as ferocious an impression in person as her prose made on page. Toni's shock of naturally and intricately braided gray dreadlocks sprang from her head like the majestic mane of a mighty lioness. Her rich golden brown face was centered by a perfectly shaped African nose and anchored by gorgeous lips carved from sweet chocolate hues. Her penetrating eyes fixed in a gaze that was at once cerebral and sensual. Toni was simply sexy, and I saw for myself the appeal that lay behind Houston Baker's animated testimony to me: at Howard, where Morrison once taught and where Baker was a student, he and his fellow students jockeyed to sit at the front of the class to be near their buxom and brainy instructor. If I hadn't been fortunate enough to sit at Morrison's feet as her student, at least I was able to see her weave her verbal magic in a special audience of her admirers. In a talk given in an intimate setting in the dormitory where I served as a graduate student assistant, I closed a circle begun a decade earlier when Morrison's language leapt from print and landed in my heart. She sat down, and like her memorable novels, her words rose in my soul.

"Beginnings must do so much more than start," she said in a voice at once incandescent and incantatory. She was talking about the mechanics of literary craft. But she may as well have been speaking about my relationship with her, one established through the word, through *her* words, a relationship unknown to her but as familiar to me as my own speech. My relationship to Morrison revealed the power of black women's writing: we embrace their words, expanding upon them, taking them to rather personal places, and thus, opening our imaginations and giving birth to our creative souls. When *Jet* reported on Morrison's seventieth birthday gala at the New York Public Library, the magazine unwittingly helped me to measure the evolution of a kinship begun in deprivation and anonymity a quarter of a century earlier when it noted those "on hand to help Morrison celebrate her big day included: Kathleen Battle, Angela Davis, Phylicia Rashad, Geoffrey Holder and wife Carmen deLavallade, Nikki Giovanni, Sonia Sanchez, and Michael Eric Dyson."

For me, the love of black women writing blackness into being, and narrating the pains and raptures of black identity through story, began with *Song of Solomon*. But true to Morrison's sentiment, her novel did so much more than start my love for a given writer. It ignited in me the daring hope that I could write myself into existence with bold and colorful strokes. From then on, like Milkman Dead, I believed I could fly.

3

Can We Talk!

"Stop talking under my clothes," my friend Rhonda playfully admonished me. I had just given her a compliment, one that, to be sure, was a trifle tacky, but a compliment nonetheless.

"Girl, you got a great future, and it's all behind you," I had proudly blurted when I noticed that her form-fitting knit-dress clung for life to her glorious gluteus maximus, with emphasis on *maximus*.

I'd heard that line used by a homeless man on the streets of Detroit. I was so taken that I quickly searched my youthful pockets for a dollar and offered it to him as a reward for his intriguing pavement doggerel. More than likely it was a royalty payment of sorts, since I knew immediately that I'd repeat his line to many women, those sisters on whom I could get away with using a phrase that, in retrospect, seemed both time-bitten and a tad politically incorrect.

But Rhonda, a beautiful, brown-skinned woman with big eyes and, well, an even bigger premise on which to rest her voluptuous frame, shot me down as only sisters can. She conquered me with a turn of phrase I'd never encountered.

"Talking under your clothes?" I only half protested. "What does that mean?"

Before she could answer, I'd figured it out. I followed the image of my words leaping from my mouth onto Rhonda's hands and legs, slowly creeping up her skin, lifting ever so subtly the sleeves and hem to her dress, and tracing their way around her anatomy. I was being too familiar, too fresh. Rhonda made me feel just enough embarrassment to wince, but not enough shame to quench any appropriate praise I might offer in the future. It was the language of social limits dressed up as banter and delivered with flawless timing. Talk about moral skill mixed with cultural diplomacy and a crash course in gender etiquette!

That was a memorable lesson in the vivid, imaginative, colorful, and signifying ways that black women speak. But in many ways, it wasn't a new lesson at all, and quickly reminded me just how much I loved to hear black women talk. It really didn't matter what they were saying—and don't get me wrong, often what they were saying was serious, humorous, edifying, insightful, wise, and the like—so long as they occasionally fell back on the linguistic conventions they gleaned from their Mamas, or some black woman who ripely possessed the full arsenal of black female *talk*.

I used to love to hear my aunts talk because of their

Southern accents and colloquialisms. Even though my Mama was the youngest of five farm-raised Alabama siblings—three boys and two girls—she had virtually cleansed her rhetorical palette of any traces of her Coosa County upbringing in the little town of Hissop. But Aunt Lila Mae and Aunt Mary were deeply twanged.

"Ur-ruh, Mye-kel, haynd me that are-run," Aunt Lila asked me one morning on a visit she made when I was eight years old. Anything she asked me to do I did with great glee and dispatch, something my Mama must have noted with humor. I suppose I had a crush on Aunt Lila because she reminded me of the television detective Honey West, played by Anne Francis, on whom I also had a big crush. Like Francis, Aunt Lila had a mole on the side of her lips that oozed sexiness, although to me it was more pretty than sensuous. Her yellow skin glowed, while her diminutive stature brought her nearer to me and made her seem less formidable than other adults.

But what I loved most was Aunt Lila's uncut, unfettered, thick-as-Alaga-syrup Alabama brogue that poured deliciously and slowly out of her adorned mouth. Even when she was angry, she snapped her speech in Southern italics. "Ahsker," she commanded my cousin Oscar, who was a year older, "you *betta* sit yo'self down on that couch and behave like you got some sense, you *heah* me boy?" When she returned to her home in Cleveland, it was always a sad day, since she filled our house with her fragrantly authentic country talk.

When Aunt Lila wasn't around, I cherished visits from my Aunt Mary, who'd moved with my mother's brother Edgar and their three children to Detroit in the mid-sixties. Aunt Mary was a tall, statuesque, ebony-hued woman with a friendly face and mischievous smile. She was always full of good humor. I loved how she got tickled and let roll off her lips, "boy, *huuush* yo' mouth." Or how she asked me to find the "do-hickey" she was searching for, which, more than likely, was "over yonder." She and my Uncle Edgar called me "cut buddy," which I figured out much later referred to the fact that Uncle Edgar was for years the official family barber. And I loved how Aunt Mary remarked on my love for Gladys Knight, circa 1967, when I watched her on television and talked about her for days afterward. "Ooh, you just be lovin' you up some Ms. Gladys, don't you?" Yes, Ma'am!

Of course, as I got older, I was introduced to different sides of black women's talking. Black female signifying, I soon learned, was a special art that seemed to be almost genetically transmitted from one generation to the other. To get the full effect of how black women talk, you've got to "be there" to see the hand gestures, the head movements, the flicks of the wrists, the snaps of the fingers, the shifting of the hips, the turning of the back, the rolling of the eyes and the like.

For instance, you've got to see the black female imitation of Diana Ross and the Supremes' "Stop in the Name of Love" freezing of the five fingers in the air accompanied by the request to "talk to the hand, boyfriend." The gesture suggests that all conversation has stopped, all nonsense has been shelved, and Harry Truman's "the buck stops here" mantra has been reformed in the black female palm placed squarely in your face. And you've got to witness firsthand what is known in the vernacular as the "Z formation": the Zorro-like pantomime created when a sister snaps her fingers three times in the signature style of the masked swordsman, supplying a black female exclamation point to the ultimate dis of a verbal opponent or errant mate.

As meaningful as these signifying performances are, they attain their ultimate impact when accompanied by a black woman's verbal jabs. "Oh *no* she didn't," a black woman is often heard repeating in disbelief at a comment made by a peer as she snaps her fingers, squints her eyes, stretches her eyebrows, furrows her brow, or places her hands on her hips, sometimes in dramatic combinations of some or all of the above. "Humh, he *thinks* he can," a woman might say as she snaps her fingers once in a wide, circular fashion and gives a withering look of utter disdain in dismissing the rumored advances of a man who's bragged about his ability to woo her. "Girl, him and what *man*," I've heard a woman say as she exchanges hand-slaps with her girlfriend, signifying that a potential suitor is full of himself and doesn't possess the necessary romantic skills to stoke her interest.

Black female talk that is irreverent is equally intriguing. Can anyone truly curse—no, *cuss*—like a black woman, especially one from whom you might not expect such disquieting dispatches? I've seen black women dressed to the nines, hair immaculately "did" as they say in the 'hood, nails painted and polished to perfection, with briefcase in hand, break off a string of expletives that would make Rudy Ray Moore blush.

But the sisters do it with such panache and abandon that it gives cussing an edifying register it might not otherwise obtain. "Honey, his *simple a—* never even noticed that I had left the room," a corporate executive might offer of a self-absorbed colleague. "*Day-umh*," another sister, a lawyer perhaps, might observe after hours about a contract dispute at work. "The *sonuvab—* never even looked me in my eyes."

And I've heard full-fledged feminists—feminists who knew that I knew I was privileged to hear such communication in mixed company, and therefore wouldn't ever dare think of joining in—say of another female who sabotaged a business meeting by failing to show up, "The *b—* didn't even have the decency to let me know she didn't have my back." After the publication of my controversial book on Martin Luther King, Jr., the wife a famous black figure received me into their home while feigning paranoia, exclaiming half-jokingly, "*Muthaf—*"—and that's not the normal epithet enunciated with the first two syllables stressed, but a Southern articulation that smothers and stretches the first and third syllables—"you bettuh not stand next to me 'cause niggahs are gunnin' for yo' a—."

Certainly, black female variations of the N word are quite fascinating as well, and no one can stop you in your tracks with a "Nig-guh, *pleeeeze*" the way a black woman can who wields that linguistic taboo like an ancient grudge. But some of the most inventive and humorous and spontaneous verbal ejaculations fly from the lips of sisters giving color commentary at the movies. I think back a few years to the black woman behind me who belted out, "kick his *buh-lack a,* Tina"—that's right, sisters can wrench two syllables from one—referring to a scene in the film *What's Love Got to Do with It* when Angela Bassett, playing Tina Turner, finally retaliates against the violent assaults of her husband Ike, menacingly portrayed by Laurence Fishburne. (I know sisters to this day who can't bear to look at Fishburne because of his dead-on inhabitation of Ike Turner's implacably ominous persona.)

Among the most hurtful words that black women can utter, at least as far as black men are concerned, are those wrapped around the proportions of our sexual prowess—or our sore lack of it. Black female crotch talk can be unnerving, demoralizing, and infuriating. Such talk persistently renders us vulnerable, no matter how confident we might otherwise be. In hip-hop music, the lyrics of female artists testify to the withering indictment of sexual underperformance in songs like Missy Elliot's "One-Minute Man."

Away from the recording studio, real-life slights can be just as brutal. "Girl, he 'bout this big," a sister can say, holding her thumb and forefinger no more than an eighth of an inch apart. Perhaps the most disintegrating assault on the legendarily upright black phallus that I've heard raced from the mouth of a black woman who said to a would-be lothario, "Your thang is so small, that if you put it on the edge of a razor-blade it would look like a BB on a four-lane highway."

Above all, I have taken refuge in the yearning and solicitous speech of black women, who condense a world of affection in dulcet tones and sweet turns of phrase, none more delightful than that single-word poem of edification, "baby." There's something singularly redeeming about the way black women speak the word, elongating its initial syllable into a symphony of soulful affirmation, as Anita Baker does on, say, "Lead Me Into Love," when she purrs, "bay-*ay*-bee." Or think of the rush of staccatos that open Aretha Franklin's "Since You've Been Gone," as the Queen of Soul rains down her thrice-repeated affection while sliding up the scale and into our hearts with "Bay-bee, *bayyy*-bee, sweet bay-bee…"

In the thrall of erotic ecstasy, I have felt the heat of black women's passion framed in a verbal gesture of trust and surrender that floats gently on the words, "Oh, bay-bee." Ironically, in another context, with different accents, those very words can signify an entirely different emotional register. Perhaps no voicing of black affection surpasses the tenderness of a mother correcting the mistaken impression of disfavor, or a female lover lavishing undeserved forgiveness, both in a lilting, "Oh-h-h-h, *bay*-beeee," a comforting flourish that lifts spirits, dispels fears, and restores hope.

Rhonda offered me those very words when I apologized for "talking under her clothes." But I've heard them countless times again as one black woman or another—a teacher, lover, friend, colleague, wife, or mentor—has favored me with her pithy blessing. And even when I didn't deserve it, perhaps especially then, I marveled at just how good a simple phrase spoken by a black woman could make me feel. In ways too wonderful for words, I still do.

II. When the Spirit Moves

4

_____

You Better Think

I learned at an early age that black females often exhibit a level of sophisticated thinking for which they are rarely credited. I got a keen glimpse of their critical inventiveness one summer morning in a stately neighborhood building that had quickly become my second home. In my Sunday School class at the Tabernacle Missionary Baptist Church, I squirmed in my fold-up metal chair before my classmates as we sat in a semicircle, poring over the meaning of a scripture that stumped most of us. I was surely no biblical scholar, but I had listened as attentively as any ten-year-old might to the sermons preached by our eloquent if long-winded pastor.

Ours was a "silk-stocking" church where well-to-do Negroes drove a fair distance to mix with congregants who hailed from the west-side Detroit ghetto in which Tabernacle was ensconced. As usual, I hiked the fifteen-minute jaunt to church with my older brother Anthony as our fifty-cent offering jangled in our neatly pressed pants. Often, we made it to church, even if our offering didn't. There were times when we couldn't resist dipping into our pockets at the ghetto market to buy cookies. Despite showing remarkable discipline in sometimes not shedding our tithe before church, we usually succumbed to temptation in short order. Even Stevie Wonder saw our sin when he charged on his song "I Wish" that "you trade yours for candy after Sunday School."

As our teacher Mrs. Wise led us systematically through the lesson for the morning, it might have been the wine-candy I had just bought that had me all abuzz and unable to duly concentrate. We were parsing the meaning of the Twenty-third Psalm, but I couldn't get past the first verse: "The Lord is my shepherd; I shall not want." I couldn't understand why we wouldn't want the Lord. Him not wanting us, of course, was a different matter, something we were taught in church to believe was our sinful fate until Jesus stepped in to take our punishment and save us from the hell to which we were sure to be condemned. Augustine had as sure a grip on our theology as the richer folk in our congregation had on their crisp twenty-dollar bills. This was a wrenching paradox for me: here we were in church—in a classroom beneath the sanctuary where Tabernacle members in our chanted doxology praised God "from whom all blessings flow"—denying our need for God, going so far as to state with the Bible's help that we didn't even *want* him.

It's not that I was immune to such scatological thoughts, but they wouldn't erupt until years later when as a teen reading Sartre and Pascal I denied the existence of God. It wasn't so much Pascal's doctrine that bothered me—after all, he argued that we should wager belief in God so as not to come up short in case heaven is real—as it was his self-inflicted wounds from a barbed-wire belt that discouraged my feeling that the deity who inspired such sacrifice was worth serving.

But Sartre got my adolescent self good. He lured me with his insistence that human beings should make their own choices in a godless universe where our existence precedes our essence, where the only design is the one we furnish. That, and exotic tales of Parisian cafes on the Left Bank, where thinkers like him and De Beauvoir and Camus gathered to hash out the intellectual stakes of a full-fledged humanism. Enough with God, I thought, even though I didn't leave the church and insisted on pricking the church's conscience by making arguments against God on God's own turf. To paraphrase Pascal, I was a man, and as such, a reed, the thinnest reed in nature, he claimed, but a *thinking reed*. In my mind that meant I had to spurn religion and authority and think for myself.

My mother, who at that point didn't regularly attend church, was simply mortified, since my atheism was accompanied by a sartorial rebellion that, in retrospect, may have troubled her even more than my lapsed faith. I was representing her at church, a fideistic substitute of sorts, and I could at least carry the family name with dignity and not the dingy dungarees and weathered wool sweatshirt I wrapped around my unscrubbed body beneath a bush of unkempt hair. To my pastor's credit, he encouraged me to remain in church and to run the course of my atheism. My strident disbelief was dramatically reversed a year later when I was caught in the middle of an armed robbery, and I promised the God I didn't believe in that I would use my mind to serve him if he would let me live. He did, and I have.

As a ten-year-old, however, not yet skilled in grasping complex ideas in literary form, the apparent denial of God was painful. Although I had never deconstructed the Twenty-third Psalm, I already knew it occupied precious space in the believer's heart. The sheer repetition of the psalm in church liturgy underscored its rhythmic insistence on God's care. But I had never listened for the logic behind its spiritual promise, never thought about its concepts and its philosophy of belief. Now Mrs. Wise was encouraging us to think about these matters and to critically view the claims we Christians held to be true.

To be sure, our scrutiny of the Twenty-third Psalm reminded me that analyzing what we believe is often a beneficial yet burdensome task, especially since it demands that we cross-examine our faith in the courtroom of reason. Mrs. Wise gingerly led us through the paces of critical thinking in the guise of biblical and theological study. Equally important, she taught us by example that literary criticism is a crucial art in stimulating belief. What one believes must be rendered respectable and compelling through the stories we tell each other in the household of faith. Since our knowledge derives from our beliefs—you can't really know what you doubt to be true or real—the literature we consume shapes our understanding of the world we live in.

But this was all new and somewhat abstract to me, and wouldn't be filled in completely until I learned to demythologize what I had digested. At the time, literary critique was a fuzzy art at best, and one bogged in the subtleties of crafty and clever readings, readings I couldn't execute because I was too green in matters of interpretation. So the Twenty-third Psalm lay mute beneath my literalism. And never mind the semi-colon that separated the first verse's main clauses, a clue that wouldn't have made sense to me since I didn't yet understand that grammar communicates meaning as surely as tone of voice and bodily gestures.

"Why don't we *want* the Lord?" I quizzed Mrs. Wise as she dutifully expounded on the virtues of seeing the Lord as a shepherd leading his flock and protecting them from roving wolves, which only compounded the mystery of our rejection of him. Judging by the looks on the faces of some of my fellow adolescent theologues, I must have come off like a colored "Beaver" Cleaver asking his brother Wally about some supercilious matter that in the Beave's mind had been exaggerated to cosmic proportions. But I knew intuitively their response had more to do with the fear of admitting ignorance than it had to do with their superior knowledge. Just then, my friend Pam Nash gently intervened to enlighten my classmates and me.

"It doesn't mean that we don't want *the Lord*," Pam sweetly insisted. "It means that we won't want for *anything*, that the Lord will fill all our desires."

Pam and her sister Pat were fraternal twins, always neatly dressed, well-behaved, and immensely attractive girls who radiated the confidence and noble self-possession of the conscientious black middle class. I admired them a great deal. For this instance in my tender career in biblical interpretation, Pam had brought me a gift of understanding that rivaled the pleasures of funk music and lifted me from what John Bunyan in *Pilgrim's Progress* calls the "slough of despond."

"Ohhhh," I responded, relieved that we weren't being called on to ditch God in his house. "Now I understand."

That was more than thirty years ago, but I often return to the memory of that Sunday School classroom and see in its inchoate stirrings the birth of my critical consciousness. I learned there to think sharply about my life in the light of the Biblical texts and religious themes that have shaped my career. Perhaps more uplifting is that their example reminds us that the female-fueled black church has often been the source of our greatest thinking about remedies for the social and moral ills of our culture, country, and globe. Because of Mrs. Wise and Pam Nash and literally thousands of other black women like them, we have not gone wanting for the kind of thinking that opens eyes, quickens minds—and ultimately, saves lives.

5

You Don't Hear Me!

"Giving honor to God, who is the head of my life," the elderly black woman stated in a clear, strong voice as she stood up to speak in the church's basement at the Wednesday night prayer meeting.

I had heard Mrs. Griffith and many of the other black women who frequented the weekly prayer meetings repeat that proclamation in their often powerful and moving testimonies. It was an ecclesiastical icebreaker and put hearers on notice that the speaker knew the source of her life and strength.

"He's been so good to me I don't know where to begin," Mrs. Griffith admitted. "I been strugglin' with Arthur this week"—as in arthritis, a universal code word among its largely elderly sufferers that never failed to draw groans of recognition and nods of empathy—"but the Lord gave me some

good medcin' to fight him off." Mrs. Griffith went on to cata-
logue her other blessings, including her lowered rent and an
unexpected bonus in her monthly stipend that, she said,
would allow her to increase her Sunday morning offering.

"Amen, Sis*tuh*," one of the ministers mischievously chirped
as the smallish gathering of about sixty members laughed as
on cue.

"But most of all, I wanna thank God for Jesus," Mrs.
Griffith passionately declared, signaling the end of her testimony with a rhetorical gesture just as familiar as the one with
which she had begun.

"Without him, we couldn't do nothin'," she continued as
the chorus of verbal support quickened and formed a rhythmic drumbeat to her escalating witness.

"Without him, there'd be no reason to live."

"Come on now," a male member chimed in.

"Without him, we'd be prisoners to sin."

"*Speak* Sistuh Griffith," a female voice rang out.

"I don't know about *you*," Mrs. Griffith teased us. We all
knew where she was heading. Her verbal gambit pleaded
ignorance about the content of the fellow believer's faith,
while implying that the only sure knowledge is what goes on
in one's own mind and heart. It was a climactic moment in
the public performance of black sacred speech.

"But if it wasn't for *Jeeezus*, I couldn't make it a single day,
not even a single moment." Mrs. Griffith had been standing in
place and facing forward, but now she slightly twisted her
torso to address her makeshift flock in her impromptu sermon.

"I wanna thank him for what he's *already* done for me," she thundered. "And for what he's gonna do tomorrow."

"Oh, praise the Lord," an elderly woman let loose.

"It's no secret what God can do," she intoned in a piercing crescendo as she raised her hand and lowered her frail body into her seat. In near unison, our sixty voices collectively concluded the oft-cited couplet of the song she was quoting. "What He's done for others, He'll do for you," we uttered to rousing applause.

I loved coming to prayer meetings because I got a more intimate sense of belonging to a congregation where, like the bar on the television series *Cheers*, "everybody knows your name." Our church had nearly five thousand members, making it easy to get lost in the shuffle, especially as a poor youth. Prayer meetings provided a glimpse of the church in glorious subtraction. The midweek prayer and praise service, as the Wednesday meetings were officially known, winnowed the faithful from the once-a-week-on-Sunday-morning crowd in most churches, much the way Bible study does. Beyond that, prayer meetings offered a theological ultrasound of a congregation's spiritual health by forming a picture of the hidden organs of faith and prayer that sustain the church body.

I was also drawn to prayer meeting because I was able to absorb the wisdom of the church's senior saints and gray-haired griots. In their collective testimonies and prayers and prefatory comments to the songs they requested us to sing, the elders gave a running commentary on the hidden injuries of race and class, and the enduring hope and love that propelled them over these huge obstacles. When they bore witness to the pains and pitfalls they had surmounted through faith, they gave renewed poignancy to clichés like, "God will make a way out of no way."

It was the opportunity to hear the rich and surprisingly varied voices of the sisters that was the greatest appeal of prayer meeting. At prayer meeting, old black women—or "sore-head sisters" as they sometimes called themselves in playful self-deprecation—thumbed through the Bible and unleashed from its pages golden nuggets of insight that rivaled those of most preachers I'd heard. And their homespun wisdom was endearing. "I was so green, you could plant me in the ground and I'd grow," one sister humorously remarked in recounting the naïveté that led to a youthful error.

Often, the sisters would turn to the "Gospel Pearls," a thinner collection of down-home religious tunes that, like the prayer meeting, distilled the larger Sunday-morning hymnal to the essential elements of the faith in song. Since the Gospel Pearls contained far fewer songs than the regular Sunday hymnal, I could almost tell what song different sisters would request each week. Still, I never grew tired of hearing them again and again since their choices gave sonic clues to their spiritual autobiographies.

But my favorite moments invariably came when the Spirit lighted on some sister as she bowed before her chair with head in hands and called on God with haunting folk eloquence.

"Lord, I want to thank you for wakin' me up this morning," a sister would gently begin. "I know it wasn't my alarm clock that got me up, but your sweet mercy."

"Yes, yes," the voices of her peers greeted her.

"Thank you for lettin' the golden moments roll on a little longer."

"Yes, yes."

"Oh, Lawd, I'm like an empty pitcher befo' a full fountain."

"Umh, humh, say it sister."

"I'm like clay in the potter's hands."

"Yes, Lord."

By now her rhythm grew sweeter and swifter, her speech springing into song in sweeps of tuneful cadence.

"I thank ya, Lawd, that last night wasn't my last night, and that the walls of my room was not the wall of my grave."

"Lord have mercy," another sister emoted.

"I thank ya that my bed wasn't my coolin' board," she said, referring to the practice of blacks in the Southern states of laying out the dead on a flat surface. "And that my sheets wasn't my windin' sheets."

"Oh, Jesus. Oh, Jesus."

The sister went on for several minutes. This wasn't for the faint of heart and it surely wasn't Sunday morning, where the Spirit sometimes had to be quenched in deference to the clock. On Wednesday nights, we could take our time and luxuriate in the Spirit's presence and unfettered guidance. After ten minutes of grueling, thrilling, energizing verbal calisthenics, she wound up her prayer in the fashion imbibed from her Mississippi or Alabama or Georgia roots.

"Now Lord, when my life is over, when I have to go into a room and come out no more, I pray you guide me safely from this world to the next. Amen."

"Bless his name, bless his name," some sister caught up in the spirit shouted as many of us stood to hug each other in pure Christian love.

These were delightful moments for me. In retrospect, perhaps it's because the sisters who were the back-up singers, as the poet Kate Rushin has beautifully termed it, finally came front and center to sing their songs, pray their prayers, and often, unofficially, preach their sermons. No longer hidden behind anonymous "amens" or episodic prayers in sanctuary settings that failed to vent their spiritual genius, these black women claimed full voice on Wednesday nights.

Religious rhetoric was segregated by gender in the black church. There were unspoken yet inflexible rules that governed when and where women could speak. The pulpit and the deacon's bench were strictly off limits. I had seen ministers fall into utter conniptions if a woman so much as glanced too strongly at the hallowed ground that was to be traversed only by "God's man." Thankfully, the Sunday School class, trustee board, vacation Bible school, preSunday service testimonial, and prayer meeting were acceptable arenas of female speech.

Years later, as a twenty-four-year-old pastor in Tennessee in the early eighties, I tested the black church's rhetorical and theological apartheid: I urged my congregation to ordain three women as deacons. In the Baptist church, deacons serve at the discretion of the pastor. They aid *him* in offering prayer for the congregation, visiting saints in hospitals and nursing homes, cheering depressed members through prayer and exhortation, and administering the sacrament of the Lord's Supper in church and to the sick and shut-in. There was nothing inherently masculine about such tasks, and I repeated that argument in my biblical and theological teaching for nearly a year. I aimed in these settings to erode the congregation's skepticism and its fear of violating Baptist doctrine and local church practice. I met weekly with the female candidates to bolster their confidence. I preached Sunday morning sermons promoting a feminist interpretation of scriptures. I taught Bible study with an eye to addressing those passages of scripture that seemed to frown on female authority while highlighting others that reveled in the second sex's strengths.

Things went extremely well until a few weeks before the ordination service, when word got around Johnson City that my church was about to elevate three women to a holy office reserved "for the mens." The head of the local black Baptist Association, who had befriended me on occasion—he suggested I adopt the local practice of substituting initials for my first and middle names so that my members couldn't get too familiar and call me Michael rather than Rev. M. E. Dyson—rose up in vindictive and secret alliance with many of my male deacons and their wives and other church members to oust me one Sunday morning.

"You gon' let this yellow nigguh come down here and change our ways in the blinking of an eye," I was later informed by a faithful soul of my erstwhile colleague's remonstration of my members. Of course, I thought that was the lemon calling the corn yellow. He was one of those "white, bright, damned near white" Negroes with a shock of ruler-straight salt-and-pepper hair. On occasion, like Adam Clayton Powell, Jr, he whipped his mane at will during a sweating fury in the pulpit while subtly emphasizing his prominent spot atop the color hierarchy that continued to menace black folk in our demonizing of darkness.

"If y'all don't stop him now, he'll wreck the church and ruin our traditions."

I should have known something was awry as I tried my key in the church door that morning but couldn't tumble the bolts. The same was true for my office door, but I figured that the janitors must have changed the locks for security reasons and had simply forgotten to tell me. As I greeted worshippers in my pre-sermon ritual of shaking hands, I noticed quite a few faces I had never seen before. I chalked it up to a sudden rash of out-of-town guests. When I stepped forward to the rostrum to speak, I got an eyeful of the sour faces and furrowed brows that flecked the sanctuary like a skunk's white back. If only I could have caught a whiff of the stench to come, I might have spared myself the pain and embarrassment of being tossed out of the church on the Lord's Day.

After I completed my sermon, and the choir had sung, and I had extended the invitation for the unsaved or those seeking a new church home to join our fellowship, a deacon suddenly jumped to his feet.

"We got trouble here, and it's time for us to put an end to it now," he declared. I was surprised at the interruption, especially since I had no idea that our church was suffering. I was even more stunned as he continued speaking and I quickly discovered that the source of the trouble was *me*.

"This man here come to town with a lotta praise, but he done tore this church up." He pointed at me like Emmet Till's grandfather had bravely pointed at the white man who had abducted and murdered his grandson in Money, Mississippi. Back then, Till's grandfather courageously condemned the white supremacist in the simple elegance of country dialect, "Dar he is." But now, male supremacy was at stake and one of its defenders was pointing the finger.

"He tryin' to mess thangs up and put women in places they don't belong," he nearly shouted as a gurgle of "amens" and "un-hunhs" swelled beneath his bitter indictment. "I think we oughtta take a vote *right* here, *right* now, and put an end to the matter."

The congregation agreed, and for one of the very few times in my life, I was crushed to complete speechlessness. I had "swallowed my throat," in Marcia Dyson's eloquent phrase, a state common to the female life I had deemed myself defending, but one to which I had rarely been subject.

I was grieved but not surprised to see that nearly all of the women sided with their menfolk in voting to end my tenure as pastor. After all, I was a vexing visitor about to be vanquished; they were wives, daughters, sisters, mothers, nieces, girlfriends—and yes, mistresses too—who had to live with these men and get along with them as best they could, if they were to prosper and have a good life, a life that depended too much and too predictably on these men. I was a dispensable interloper, and while it pained many of the women to see me go, it would have pained them even more for me to stay.

I was given a month's severance pay and nothing else to support my wife and five-year-old son. I cried angry tears and packed my bags and found my way back to school to complete my degree in philosophy. But the lessons I learned as pastor of Thankful Baptist Church—the irony singes me to this day—are ones that I have never forgotten: that change takes time, especially yours if you're deeply invested; that black folk who are oppressed by racism readily turn to the same arguments used to keep them down to oppress women; that many women are hard-pressed to find the moral and social support to rebel against their own suffering; and that the black church is often the ground of our liberation and the soil that nurtures our most enslaving bigotries.

As I packed my car and headed out of town, I thought of the wise and spiritually weathered sisters in prayer meeting. I felt their loving hands brushing back my tears. I heard their consoling voices encouraging me on to my next station. My journey would lead to college, then on to graduate school, where I would earn a Ph.D. in religion. I then began to teach in seminary the liberating gospel of Jesus, which included fighting against the sexism and male domination of our churches.

When I later heard the gospel colorfully and brilliantly articulated by great preachers like Prathia Hall, Carolyn Knight, Ella

Mitchell, Yvonne Delk, Barbara King, Vashti McKenzie, Leontine Kelley, and Marcia Dyson, I felt vindication in my fledgling feminist efforts. It was Hall's powerful preaching that introduced me to the genius of black female homiletical artistry. She interwove biblical narratives with stories from her pioneering career as a civil rights activist. Hall often topped off her sermons with rhetorical flourishes and stylistic gestures gleaned from her Baptist brethren and refined in her feminist crucible. Her sermons also displayed a thrilling measure of melodious speech, known colloquially as "the whoop" and more formally as the "chanted sermon." As ministers say in black church circles, she had "the learnin' and the burnin'."

Hall journeyed to Brazil in 1996 to preach to the Conference on World Mission and Evangelism. In her address, "Captivity Is a Lie," Hall argued that captivity, "no matter where and how viciously it asserts itself, is a fraud. It postures a power it does not possess. Jesus Christ has already been there. Captivity has been captured. For us, the church, there is only this task: to believe, and to then turn to the work of removing the chains—chains that have already been broken. The victory has already been won."

As the holder of the Martin Luther King, Jr., Chair in Social Ethics at Boston University, Professor Hall was equally comfortable before an academic audience. In front of 3,000 people at Stanford's interdenominational baccalaureate ceremony, she turned to the Eighty-fifth Psalm, with its anticipation of a day "when mercy and truth are met together, righteousness and peace have kissed each other, truth shall spring out of the earth, and righteousness shall look down from heaven," to encourage the Class of 1992 to "take seriously your own yearnings for justice and peace." Hall declared that there "is much talk today about the disappearance of the American dream. It may well be that the dream must disappear, that a greater vision might replace it."

Hall ended her sermon with a moving story drawn from her struggle for freedom in the South. "It was 1963. I was one of a group of students working to achieve voting rights and political empowerment in southwest Georgia. We were encouraging persons who had been prevented from participating in the political process, by a pervasive campaign of terror, to register to vote." Hall recalled that a sheriff stopped her and her comrades and asked them what they were doing. When she told him they were registering citizens to vote, the lawman became enraged. "He began to sputter and curse and tremble and literally foam at the mouth. Suddenly, he whipped out a gun and emitted a stream of exceedingly graphic expletives, and began to fire bullets in a circle around my feet." Hall stood still, fearing that any movement would have given him an excuse to murder her on the spot. "Finally, when the gun was empty, he seized us and threw us into jail. Was I frightened? My Lord, I was so terrified, I was numb. But I learned something that day about the shalom of God. I learned that the struggle for justice and peace is the shalom of God, and the shalom of God is both power and protection."

The irony, of course, is that in her fight to exercise her ministerial gifts, Hall had to combat the very black men

alongside whom she fought for racial freedom during the sixties. As she once remarked, "I stood in the total authenticity of
my being—black, preacher, Baptist, woman. For the same God
who made me a preacher, made me a woman. And, I am convinced that God was not confused on either count."

Hall was much too modest to publicly recount another
contribution she made to American history. In 1962, Martin
Luther King, Jr., and his aide James Bevel toured the embers
of the Mount Olive Baptist Church in Terrell County,
Georgia, that had been torched by the Ku Klux Klan. In a
service of commemoration, a young college student named
Prathia Hall led the congregation in prayer. She rhythmically
repeated an inspiring phrase that captured her vision for the
future: "I have a dream." King remembered Hall's phrase and
the powerful response it evoked in him and the congregation
that night. He immediately absorbed its gleaming moral hope
into his oratorical repertoire. Eventually he transformed it
into the most memorable line uttered by the most renowned
black leader of the twentieth century in his most famous
speech.

Like my own vision of the beauty and power of black
sacred speech, it all came from the mouth of a praying black
woman. As was true for King, how much greater could we be
if, instead of disciplining their speech and regulating their
authority, we listened to and learned from the lives and struggles of black women, and heard in their preaching, praying,
and testifying the very voice of God?

6

S-a-a-a-n-g, Girl!

"Listen brother, you've got to come over here right now," my friend and fellow church member James Pippin excitedly demanded after I answered the phone.

"What's wrong, Pip?" I anxiously replied. "You all right?"

"Man, I've got a copy of an album by a gospel singer who's gonna give Aretha a run for her money," Pippin goaded me. He knew Aretha Franklin, the Queen of Soul, was revered in my heart and that her pretty tones and thrilling shrieks often vibrated the walls of my small apartment. I didn't have to tell him that to me his egregious comparison was sacrilegious.

"Look, bro, you don't have to get all hyperbolic," I defensively responded. "If you want me to come over, man, just say so. I'll see you as soon as I can get there."

"Oh, by the way, she's from Detroit." He got in a final tease, chuckling as he clicked the receiver to its base.

Pippin was double-dipping in disaster. First, he had the nerve to challenge the Queen's throne. And if that wasn't bad enough, he attempted to exploit my native passions by pitting one homegirl against the next, and worse yet, a seasoned veteran—no, the reigning champion—against an untested newcomer. Nevertheless, I hopped into my wife's white mustang and made my way to Pippin's house. On the long drive over, I couldn't help but think of how big a presence Aretha had been in my life, how her voice had hovered over me and marked every stage of my transition from boy to man.

To the world beyond the church, Aretha's freakish precocity seemed to emerge fully formed from obscure origins in the Detroit neighborhood where her father, C. L. Franklin, a noted preacher, brought her up. In fact, it was in Rev. Franklin's legendary rhetorical womb that Aretha gestated before hatching her monumental talent. As a bronze gospel wunderkind, Aretha's gift poured out in a theological prescience so striking that her father, a past-master himself of the far-flung ecstasies and esoteric vibrations of the black voice, must have felt that a double portion of the Spirit, *his* spirit, had fallen on his woman-child. One can hear fourteen-year-old Aretha on her first gospel recording declaring with unforced believability that she was heading to a place where she would "Never Grow Old." Like all great artists, Aretha was not so much speaking to us as speaking for us, at least for the fortunate phalanx gathered at her father's New Bethel Baptist Church where the recording took place. In Aretha's mouth, the gospel standard temporarily dissolved its yearning for a distant heaven and seized her youthful form to embody its promise *right now*.

My love for Aretha was inherited from my mother, who frequented New Bethel when she arrived in Detroit from the South. Rev. C. L. Franklin was a "down-home" preacher, a lionized pulpiteer whose homilies spread over seventy-six recordings that found wide circulation in black communities throughout the nation. Ironically, I had to go all the way to the country—to the Alabama farm of my grandparents on which my mother was reared, and where she picked cotton— to hear for the first time the oratorical wizardry of a Detroit icon. I listened raptly and repeatedly to Franklin's rhetorical gifts churning through my grandfather's archaic portable record player. He possessed a powerful voice with a remarkably wide range. Franklin could effortlessly ascend to his upper register to squeal and squall. He was equally capable of descending to a more moderate vocal hum and pitch, and then, at a moment's notice, he could recompose in dramatic whisper. The velocity of his speech was no less impressive, too. Franklin was the greatest exemplar of "whooping," or the "chanted sermon," where ministers coarsen their articulation, deliberately and skillfully stress their vocal cords, and transition from spoken word to melodious speech. He was the shining emblem of folk poetry shaped in the mouth of a minister whose mind was spry and keen. Franklin's style rarely undercut his substance.

Mama said that often, after Franklin finished his sermons, Aretha would rise and escalate the spirit to even more frenzied highs. Years later, after searching for a style to accommodate the magnitude of her art, Aretha would do the same in the secular realm. She carried into the universe beyond revival tents and sanctuary walls a religious passion for worldly subjects, among them the flourishing and failure of love affairs, and the pleasures of the senses. When Aretha switched from gospel to rhythm and blues, she followed a path carved by such luminaries as Ray Charles and Sam Cooke. Because of their struggles, she didn't have to confront the same degree of reproach they had endured. But she encountered her share of resentment and anger among the faithful who believed that she had betrayed her first love and highest calling. These same folk didn't understand that when Aretha turned Otis Redding's song "Respect" into a quasi-feminist manifesto, she was, intentionally or not, signifying on the lack of regard she faced as a woman in all her homes, secular and sacred. While women largely filled its gospel choirs and sanctuary seats, the church remained, in its powers, discretions, and privileges, a man's world. Of course, so was the world outside the church, but at least women didn't lose their dignity or self-worth by being asked to believe that God made it so.

Not even Aretha's successful reentries into the gospel world of her youth, one in 1972, the other fifteen years later, have completely silenced the displeasure with her defection among those old enough to remember it. Since her departure, there has been an unspoken search for the next Aretha, for a successor who would stay the course and sing only for the Lord. Neither would her critics be mollified by C. L. Franklin's adroitly defensive claim on Aretha's 1972 gospel album, *Amazing Grace,* that his daughter "never really left the church."

I kept this debate in mind as I pulled up to Pippin's brick house. Pippin and I had weathered some hard times under the same umbrella. I had come to Knoxville in 1979 to begin my freshman year at Knoxville College, a month shy of my twenty-first birthday. As a newly minted minister, I sought out a church home where I could stimulate my faith and exercise my gifts, and I landed at the Mount Zion Baptist Church. Pippin, an older, wiser big brother, often gave me a lift to church since he worked nearby as a manager and disc jockey at a tiny radio station. He also occasionally played percussions in a local combo.

Still, we were both poor. I preached wherever and whenever I could. Pippin worked his various gigs to better financial effect, but it didn't take much to top the $50 I received on a good day for a guest sermon. We often dined at "all-you-can-eat" buffets, going in early, eating late breakfasts and early lunches, then remaining to read papers and shoot the bull until we got hungry again for supper. Pippin also shared with me promotional copies of forthcoming albums and tapes that he received at the radio station. That's how he came across this vaunted Aretha successor.

"Come on in, man," Pippin greeted me at the door. "Gerri took the baby to visit Mother Rosalyn, so we've got the house to ourselves."

Gerri was Pip's wife and a fantastic gospel singer and pianist in her own right. Before I'd gotten married for the second time, Gerri, Pip, and I hung out regularly, and she agreeably joined in many of our shenanigans.

"Now who's this singer you want me to hear?" I quizzed Pippin as I rested my coat but not my questions. "Is she Baptist or Pentecostal? What church did she attend? If she's so bad, how come I ain't never heard of her, and I'm from Detroit?"

"Take a chill pill and cool out, bro," Pippin calmly deflected my hazing. "I'm gonna play her for you right now. I guarantee you that you'll be blown away."

I suppose if Pippin's discovery had taken place in our more sophisticated technological era—a quick download and file sharing over the Internet—the mystery could have been quickly solved. Back then, in 1984, in a failed Orwellian future, we had to do it the old-fashioned way: stand before "The Stereo" and place the stylus over the rotating, compressed wax and allow the analog vibrations to brush across our soundscape and through our nearly busted woofers and tweeters.

As the familiar crackles and snaps surged through the speakers, and the needle rapidly unraveled the tightly configured lines on the album's black face—and no matter how expertly you cleaned your vinyl disc it was bound to emit faint noises from a sharp object impressing a moving, flat surface—the turntable gyrated the first few seconds of Pippin's latest find. I was unimpressed. It started with the synthesized sound of rushing wind. It was quickly followed by four strident, graduated chords hammered by a cheesy synthesizer, underwritten by a scaling piano smothered in the faux-symphonic bluster of organ and chimes. A hokey effect from an amateur outfit, I glibly, caustically concluded. I was slouched in my chair.

Then her voice broke in.

"Master," she began in an understated, clear alto declaration, delaying her next words so we could fix our minds on the meaning of her lyrics as the piano pounded out her deliberate pace. "The temp-*ehhhhhhhhhest* is ray-ging." Now I had straightened my posture and leaned in as if to grab every syllable as it spilled through the thinly wired netting of Pippin's stereo speakers. My delighted host was grinning like a Cheshire cat. The singer slid up the word "tempest" like a plane effortlessly gliding into air, except she met self-induced sonic turbulence halfway through. But she navigated her voice expertly amidst the deliberate gruffness she evoked to stress the storm she was singing about. When she phrased "tempest" as she did, she was skillfully performing what might be termed vernacular onomatopoeia. Her volcanic melisma dissolved peacefully into "raging"—an irony, to be sure, as she contrasted, even opposed, the stormy condition she described by drawing her voice back, at least for the present, into a serenely reassuring soprano. I was intrigued. After singing about the billows tossing high in a steady voice, she got guttural and let loose a minor vocal eruption as she raced up the scale in quaking glissando, telling us the sky was "oh-oh-h-h-h-vershadow-w-w-w-ed with blackness," with "black-ness" crisply and succinctly articulated.

On and on it went, as the singer unleashed growling,
groaning, lacerating syllables in wild succession, occasionally
stopping on a dime to accentuate the inherent drama of her
subject with an equally theatrical delivery. Okay, I thought,
maybe she has some Aretha-like ways, but I wasn't yet convinced she could hang with the Queen. That is, until the middle of the song. She gave voice to a series of otherworldly
ejaculations that in their sheer force seemed to bend back the
cast-iron sleeves on Pippin's radiator. She built slowly to a pat-
tern of repeating, swelling crescendos that only intermittently
resolved in sweetly whispered affirmations of God's peace in
the midst of the storm. She rained down such ferocious assur-
ances of divine intervention, that the storm from which she
promised God's protection seemed my only refuge.

There was no room in Pippin's house to hide from her
voice, no spot untouched by her vibrations, no plane unaffect-
ed by her seismic emissions, no space uninhabited by her
shaking, shouting, shivering, shearing sound. She unleashed an
eviscerating orchestration of notes to proclaim Jesus as "the
Master, I'm talkin' 'bout the Mas-*turhhh*"—and mind you,
she's wailing at the tip-top of her surging soprano—"of er-
her-herrrrrth and sky." She wasn't finished. "You see"—and in
the background, the choir in staccato affirmation picks up her
cue and chants "the oh-cean," before she picks back up and
finishes the thought—"ohhhhhhhhohhhhhohhh so sweet-lay,
obey, they gonna obey, thy we-ee-ill." I was all but done. She
had led me to the highest point of her shattering articulation
and suddenly, precipitously dropped me off a cliff of cascading

sound into an ocean of humming tranquility. I could only
slump in my seat and let her soothing, hushing, calming bene-
diction roll over me as she and her choir called antiphonally
for "pee-e-e-eee-e-e-eee-e-e-e-uh-yeece." For the next thirty or so minutes, I was thrilled and thrashed by the merciless
wave of sounds that alternately tiptoed and tore from Pippin's
speakers. In that time, I met Aretha's sonic daughter, her
gospel twin. It wasn't that their voices were necessarily the
same in construction—although they shared similarities of
tone, pitch and style at points. But they were identical in
effect, since both possessed a mesmerizing, tantalizing,
enthralling gift that demanded notice.

I had no idea as I sat in Pippin's house, transfixed by a
voice that I didn't believe could exist—and perhaps, didn't
believe *should* exist—that six years later I would meet its
owner as we journeyed together to London with Jesse
Jackson. Like me, Jackson had heard that voice and was
immediately smitten. He invited me into his office one day
early in 1990—I was working with him on his autobiography—and he enthusiastically located a track on a gospel
compact disc he had just received.

"Listen to this, Reverend, and tell me she ain't awesome,"
Jackson elatedly beseeched me. As soon as I heard her voice—
that voice—I smiled.

"Yeah, she's incredible, amazing, Rev," I replied. "I've played
all three of her albums to death."

I didn't tell him the story of how we'd met, that voice and

me, years earlier in Pippin's house. But I told her when we enjoyed downtime in England. We'd gone there with Jackson—me as his shadow amanuensis, she as his soloist, as he talked and preached his way around London—to help celebrate Mandela's release from prison, and to join in his campaign to keep the pressure on South Africa to end apartheid through sanctions from the world community. Toward that end, Jackson would meet with the Mandelas at the London home of deposed African National Congress leader Oliver Tambo, attend the Wembley Stadium concert for the recently released hero, and, well, just be Jesse Jackson. And that meant that Jackson would give sermons and speeches to galvanize international support for South African freedom and black self-determination.

When Jackson preached, she sang, and amazed the folk. She belted out gospel ballads and gospel blues, reveling in contemporary and traditional, soulful and jazzy, and even hipper, up-to-date songs dipped in the aesthetic fashions of black pop music. She even wowed the rapturously raucous black crowd in Brixton, so much so that Winnie Mandela grabbed her backstage and lifted her clean off the ground, no mean feat in light of the singer's compact, substantial frame. And I remember thinking that as much as I admired Mrs. Mandela, she wasn't a woman I'd ever want to tangle with.

Back at our hotel, I regaled the singer with the story of how I'd first heard her, and how utterly powerful and riveting an occasion it had been. A wide, beautiful smile broke across her attractive brown-doll face, set off by intense button eyes, apple-red cheeks, and framed by lush, layered, reddish brown hair. She was cute as pie and twice as sweet.

I reached into my garment bag and retrieved a copy of her first album, *Peace Be Still*, the one that Pippin had snagged me with, which she happily signed for me, ending with a common valedictory that still touched me deeply, "Love, Vanessa Bell Armstrong."

III. Showing a Brother Some Love

7

Nothing but Love

I had lectured at Harvard over the last decade on quite a few occasions, but this unseasonably warm April night was special. The Association of Black Harvard Women (ABHW) had chosen me to receive its 2002 Vanguard Award, given annually, as the association states, to recognize "black men who have been leaders within and outside the black community." I had been surprised, and deeply moved, when I received notification of my selection from the group's Social Chair, Kiratiana Freelon. My honor was to be conferred in a ceremony that also acknowledged the accomplishments of black male students at Harvard, which I thought was an especially supportive gesture. As it turned out, Kiratiana was a graduating senior who hailed from Chicago, where I was teaching at the time.

I arrived at the event in Cambridge nearly forty minutes late. I had to travel the short distance from Boston, where I'd spoken earlier that day at a town-hall meeting, sponsored by the charismatic, courageous. and gorgeously chocolate State Senator Dianne Wilkerson. My delightful driver, a young black man whose main job was acting, couldn't seem to fake a sense of direction. After countless twists, turns, and tracing over territory that we had already covered, my driver deposited me at the Kennedy School of Government's Starr Auditorium. As I bolted up the stairs, afraid I had insulted my hosts and tested the patience of the audience, I was greeted by a striking young lady, tall and golden, who reassured me that her sisters were not miffed at all. She delicately guided me in her high-high heels, deliberately descending the stairs of the bowl-like room that was neatly arranged in graduated tiers and uninterrupted aisles that traced across the space's semi-circular design. The mood was festive. The students and their guests chattered away in joyful abandon, oblivious, for the most part, to my tardy entry.

I spotted on the first row my dear friends of more than a decade, Dr. Hugh Morgan Hill, internationally known as Brother Blue, and his wonderful wife, Ruth, a research librarian at Radcliffe. Brother Blue, who has degrees from Harvard and Yale, spends most of his time in prisons, festivals, and on street corners plying his craft as one of the world's most gifted storytellers. In fact, he is the official storyteller of Cambridge, Boston, and the United Nations Habitat Forum. He is also an imaginative seer. Brother Blue's prophetic words have often inspired me and those fortunate enough to witness his performances and his oracular interventions, one of which he spontaneously and graciously directed my way that night after I had given my brief remarks. I also caught a glimpse of Michellana Jester, a friend studying at Harvard's Business School. I had met her in North Carolina when she and her fiancé, Sean, invited me to perform their inventive and unorthodox wedding—even more so since we lived on the buckle of the Bible Belt—combining Christian and Buddhist liturgy. After I greeted my friends and a few students, the program began. The young ladies of ABWH circulated through the room, bestowing a rose on each man who was present. It was sweet and endearing, and a nice reversal of gendered behavior.

ABWH's president, junior government major Kimberly Levy, opened the evening with a heartfelt welcome that was as analytical as it was passionate. "African-American males constitute one of the most misunderstood groups in the United States," Levy stated. "Paradoxically, society has thrust upon them the burden of being simultaneously invisible and overly visible. They are made overly visible by a media that seldom hesitates to shed a light on the number of African-American males who are incarcerated, on drugs, unemployed, or in gangs." Levy's remarks were greeted by nodding heads, and a string of "um-humh's" and "that's rights," always a delicious sign to speakers who thrive on give-and-take with a hyperactive audience. "Yet, these statistics conveniently neglect the fact that a great number of African-American males are responsible and faithful role models and leaders, men who make an honest living, support their families, and champion the interests of our people. Sadly, these are the black men that lie in the shadows of the national spotlight and who are largely invisible in American society."

My chest heaved with pride at the thought that this young lady and, by extension, her black female colleagues at Harvard, had been able to sift through the morass of images that malign black men to see our true worth. As inspiring as it was, I wasn't at all confident that an equal number of brothers were capable of returning the favor. Many of the stars of the hip-hop generation had made much hay, and even more cash, in creating twisted and demeaning portrayals of black women. Not only didn't these black men show love; they often trafficked in anger and contempt, even hatred, toward their sisters. But amazingly, and perhaps undeservedly, black women, including these sisters at Harvard, persist in loving black men.

"Brothers, we of the Association feel that you all deserve much more. No black woman should allow her brother to be reduced to a distorted stereotype. The *Tribute to Black Men* was designed expressly for the purpose of shedding a well-deserved spotlight on the many positive aspects of the black man that are obscured in American society." Levy softened my skepticism about black men being able to embrace and admire their women when she uttered her next sentence. "It was designed in response to the *Celebration of Black Women* which the Black Men's Forum started seven years ago." There is hope after all, I thought. Perhaps conscientious men in this generation might love our women without indulging the testosterone tantrums

against sisters that suffocate a truly courageous black masculinity. "Through spoken word, song, and dance, tonight
we recognize those phenomenal black men who are essentially worthy of much more recognition than we are capable
of giving in the span of one night."

It wasn't hard to imagine that Harvard black men were
eager to feel the waves of honor and recognition wash over
them. It was certainly an ego boost to have smart and beautiful black women of every shade, shape, and shore, show you
love. Levy was a prime example. Adorned in a cream, silk-
wool V-neck fitted sweater top, and a three-quarters length
khaki skirt, trimmed by a khaki and silver belt, the shapely,
medium-brown, five-foot-three-inch beauty with long, dark-
brown hair draping her pretty face, strode gracefully to the
podium in nude, leather ankle-strap high heels and proved
that high intelligence and glowing attractiveness are not irrec-
oncilable. And to the delight of the brothers who had gathered, Levy was in glorious company. The sisters who feted us
that night sounded great and looked good, forming a battalion
of brains and a rainbow of African extracted elegance.

Mipe Okunseinde, a short, slim, chocolate sophomore with
long braids, wore a beautiful turquoise dress as she glided to
the podium to recite a poem penned by a black male student
at North Carolina State University. The poem was meaningful
to the ABHW because it had been read at their first tribute
years before.

Then, Jetta Grace Martin, a slender freshman of medium
height and medium-brown complexion, who wore her hair in

short, natural braids and was smartly dressed in a brown tank top and black pants, gracefully performed a lyrical jazz dance.

Following Jetta, the crowd was utterly captivated as Akuorkor Ablorh, a senior music major, dramatically performed a poem she had written. The short, attractive, deep-chocolate spoken-word artist, who had big glasses and short, thick, permed hair, wore a red top and black pants as she enchanted us with her fiercely eloquent paean to black men, *Stranger: A Tribute to Black Men.*

Ablorh spoke about her fascination with the "human mystery" of manhood, of

> *Men with lingering boyhoods*
> *Boys on the brink of manhood*
> *The ones with skin that glows*
> *with generous drops of honey*
> *The ones with skin so rich*
> *they must be blessed with sun rays*
> *shining beneath their skin*
> *The ones shaded so deep*
> *blue shimmers across the surface*
> *of their midnight brown skin*
> *Beautiful*
> *You are beautiful*
> *In body and in mind*
> *You have the power*
> *to drive your struggles into exile*

You have the strength
to leave trouble by the wayside
the wisdom
to navigate your battles
and come out stronger each time.

She enchanted us as she spoke of the wonders of young men, and of old men, too.

Grace defines your wrinkles
Grace surrounds your scars.

Ablorh praised black men for knowing

what our color means
In this world
In this country,

acknowledging that black men

stand with a brand of bravery
I can't even begin to trace
You rise up in adversity
And somehow
make it tame
You huddle in corners
But find the courage to stand again.

Ablorh chanted her praise poem's depths when she conceded that

You face struggles
I don't understand
You meet challenges
as I struggle to comprehend
You accept consequences
as I challenge with blame
You exude patience
and I stand amazed
I am proud of you, brother
Even when I don't show it.

Ablorh confessed,

There will be times I'm deaf to troubles
And times you don't see them take hold,

but that black men and women should

not be strangers
Life is better lived in community
Brother
Father
Lover
Friend
You are beautiful

Inside and out
I adore you
I admire you
I appreciate you
Beautiful
Masculine mystery.

The house came down in riotous applause and appreciation for Ablorh's direct, simple, poetic love.

After Ablorh's verbal magic, Kiratiana Freelon—who, according to one observer, possessed the natural beauty of actress Thandie Newton—seized the microphone with her high energy and refreshing humor. The medium-height, long-braided, olive-complexioned economics major wore a denim skirt and jacket set, and boots, and introduced me in fine fashion. She closed by observing, "he's even appeared as himself on the popular show, *Soul Food*. Are you trying to become an actor now? You got some explaining to do on that one." Noting that I had attempted to "daily balance family, spirituality, and career," Freelon drew a conclusion I have not often sided with: "From the looks of it, he's doing a damn good job." And with that, she invited me to the podium to accept my award and to give a few remarks. I was profoundly touched and grateful for my award, and said so.

But it was the awarding of the class honors that was perhaps most affecting. Yadani Beyene, a short, light-skinned, Latina-looking sister with long, straight black hair, enthusiastically presented an award to her fellow freshman, Brandon

Terry, a brother cut from cliché: he was tall, dark, and hand-some. Terry had made outstanding contributions to the Black Men's Forum, the university's black male group, and had been outspoken in campus racial politics.

Alliah Agostini, a short, light-skinned sophomore with thick eyebrows and shoulder-length, permed hair, warmly feted Charles Moore, a short, dark, distinguished brother with glasses. Moore served as the Forum's vice-president—in fact, he was cited as a major force behind its recent revival—and was honored for his activism and for his election as the Black Student Association's next president.

The juniors chose computer science major Margaret Anadu, a short, attractive, dark sister with short, permed hair and a red dress, to memorably salute Brandon Gayle, who couldn't attend. Everyone seemed to agree, in body language and applause, that Gayle was quite a fellow. He was the president of the Black Students Association, a sometime liaison between the Harvard black community and the university president, an organizer of a meeting between the black students and a controversial white Harvard professor, and an all-around leader.

Finally, Kiratiana Freelon reemerged to bestow the senior award. "Now it is time for the last, and greatest, class award of the night, the one for the Class of 2002," she boasted, to hisses, jeers, and some supportive handclaps. "The awardee and I were in a class together in our first semester at Harvard: Economics 10. When I first saw him, I asked myself: 'Who is this guy with plaid slacks—and the nice and tight white tee shirt?'" The audience cracked up, and obviously they had an inkling of who the honoree might be. But Freelon persisted in her teasing, humorous mystery. "Of course, I did not say that out loud. Unfortunately, even though I noticed him three times a week in our section, we never talked during the entire first semester. But fate brought us into contact again. As freshmen, we both received notices that Eliot (a college dorm) would be our home for the next three years. It was there that I got to know Eddie Bruce."

In the midst of the applause, it became apparent where Bruce was sitting. I realized that I had caught a glimpse of him earlier, and he was a tall, slim, medium-complexioned brother who sported stylish glasses, and true enough, a tight shirt and pants. "We bonded over dinner conversations in which we discussed Afro-Germans, spoken word, social issues and politics," Freelon continued. "It seemed to me that Eddie Bruce did, and continues to do, everything. I found out that he worked more than twenty hours a week to pay his term bill. I learned of his dedication to public service and social justice, which he demonstrated through the prison education program, Harvard Students for Prisoner Reform, Peace and Justice Corps, Harvard AIDS Gift, and the First Year Urban Program." Freelon concluded her remarks by calling Bruce "an intellectual," and "thoughtful, artistic, caring, motivated, dedicated, and energetic. There is not one person in this room that can say a mean word about Eddie Bruce, not because they are scared of him, but because he treats everyone kindly."

Jennifer Sunami, a short, fair-skinned, black Japanese senior, presented the night's final ward, an achievement scholarship to Camal Adam, a Somalian refugee and student at Cambridge-Ridge and Latin High School. Adam moved many of us to tears in recounting his valiant struggle for survival after the death of both his parents, and in expressing his deep and genuine gratitude for the monetary aid to realize his educational ambitions.

As we contemplated Adam's words, a medium-height, medium-complexioned young lady, with thick, short permed hair, approached the podium. Jennifer Hawkins, a sophomore economics major, capped the evening with a Powerpoint digitized slide show of Harvard's black men, as Angie Stone's anthem of black male love, "Brotha," slithered in serpentine rhythms across the room. I couldn't help but hear Stone's lyrics in a new fashion. "He's misunderstood, some say that he's up to no good, around the neighborhood/ Well, for your information, a lot of my brothas got education." As the wonderful example of these Harvard sisters proves, it is often bright and beautiful black women who tell the world about the greatness of black men.

8

Beyond the Veil

"My goodness, do you think I sounded too angry?" Myrlie Evers-Williams nervously quizzed me as we ate our dinner.

"Oh, no, Ma'am," I quickly reassured her. "In fact, the righteous anger you showed puts you in league with the hip-hop generation in a way that many of your peers can't claim."

Evers-Williams and I, along with Mamie Till-Mobley, had appeared earlier in the day on *Oprah*, in 1992, to discuss unsolved hate crimes. The cords of racial terror bound Evers-Williams and Till-Mobley into a gruesome camaraderie: each had a loved one who had violently perished at the hands of white murderers in Mississippi. Evers-Williams had heard the fatal shots fired in her carport in 1963 that brutally ended the life of Medgar Evers, her husband of twelve years and the courageous field secretary for the Mississippi NAACP. Till-Mobley's fourteen-year-old son, Emmett, was ruthlessly abducted from his uncle's house, brutally beaten, shot in the head and tossed into the Tallahatchie River with a 200-pound cotton gin motor around his neck, all because he had allegedly made a "wolf whistle" at a white woman. His murderers eluded justice.

On *Oprah*, Evers-Williams directed her eloquent fury at white supremacy, and at the white supremacist—Byron De La Beckwith—who had escaped conviction in two trials for Medgar's murder, despite bragging about it in some quarters. In 1973, the police stopped Beckwith in his car outside of New Orleans, and discovered a time bomb, firearms, white supremacist propaganda, and a map to the home of a prominent Jewish activist. When questioned by the authorities, Beckwith cavalierly replied that he had shot Medgar Evers. He was more explicit at a Klan rally when he boasted, "killing that nigger gave me no more inner discomfort than our wives endure when they give birth to our children. . . . We ask them to do that for us. We should do just as much."

Over the years, Beckwith relentlessly disparaged Medgar's legacy. When he was arrested for shooting Evers in the back with an assault rifle, Beckwith defiantly declared, "I didn't kill the nigra, but he's gone and he ain't coming back." Beckwith was finally convicted for Evers's murder in 1994, after the martyred leader's valiant widow had asked Assistant District Attorney Bobby DeLaughter to reopen the case. Evers-Williams's quest, as well as DeLaughter's conflicted, reluctant pursuit, at least initially, is captured in the Rob Reiner film, *Ghosts of Mississippi*, starring Whoopi Goldberg as Evers-Williams and Alec Baldwin as DeLaughter—a well-intentioned but deeply flawed film that followed the trend of movies such as *Mississippi Burning* and *Amistad* by locating its center of moral gravity in the "good" whites who aid blacks in their struggle against "bad" whites.

Predictably, *Ghosts* downplays Evers-Williams's gargantuan and heroic persistence in bringing Beckwith to justice, while enlarging DeLaughter's diligence and courage. In fact, it was Evers-Williams's edifying vigilance that forged justice for her slain husband more than thirty years after his death. When Beckwith died in prison in 2001 at the age of 80, Evers-Williams said that he "now faces the ultimate judge," and that he "was the epitome of evil, who forever embraced racism and hatred, and who caused so much pain and suffering of so many people."

When I met her in 1992, Evers-Williams still ached in the unfulfilled hope to destroy the bigotry that had marred her family's life and the lives of millions of others. She fairly shook with rage at her martyred husband's killer, who was free to spread his venomous beliefs. Evers-Williams was an open wound of memory. She poured out stories of the fight for justice in what was arguably the most racially menacing state in the nation. I found it refreshing that her passions were palpable, and that her commitment to justice was steady and determined. Her pain was raw. Myrlie's discourse was hot with the blood of remembrance splashed across its sharp edges—it was as if Medgar had been murdered yesterday. I admired her spunk, her fire, her war against amnesia, an amnesia that had led too many of us to forget that, despite our undeniable progress, we had not yet made it to the Promised Land. Her birth certificate might have made her old school, but her birthright as a daughter of suffering gave her an instant passport into the geography of hurt that was occupied by millions of poor black youth.

That evening after *Oprah*, I delighted in assuring Evers-Williams that her redemptive anger was keenly relevant to today's generation. My wife and I broke bread with the fiery crusader for justice, and with the man who gave her a hyphen and a renewed sense of hope—her second husband, Walter Williams. A tall, handsome, mocha-colored man with deep waves of salt-and-pepper hair, Williams' robust frame and commanding physical presence heralded the rigors of his years as a longshoreman. His dashing appearance was a nice match for Myrlie's chocolate beauty. At dinner, she was adorned in a two-piece, knee-length, navy blue suit. Her hair was fashioned in a blunt cut Chinese bob that fell neatly along her jaw, and her beautiful face was set off by voluptuous lips—lips that Medgar taught her not to bite in shame, but to be proud of. Williams' gentle manner and supportive ways were striking, perhaps even unusual. He didn't at all mind his wife's intense devotion to racial justice, which meant thinking and talking constantly about Medgar.

"You see, I admired Medgar as well," Williams softly told me. "I'm in no way bothered by Myrlie's work. I support her one hundred percent." Myrlie drew from that support the determination to pursue and win election as chair of the national board of the NAACP, only the second woman to hold that position in the organization's storied history. Evers-Williams is widely credited with reviving the civil rights group's flagging fortunes during a tumultuous period in its tenure, restoring it to the prominence and esteem it presently enjoys. She boosted the organization's sagging finances and focused the group's attention on hot-button issues like affirmative action and fair housing and lending rules. And perhaps most important, Evers-Williams convinced Baltimore congressman Kweisi Mfume to become the NAACP's president and CEO, a move that has galvanized the group.

Of course, the fact that Myrlie Evers-Williams had remarried had distinguished her—and perhaps, in a fundamental way, had even divided her—from Coretta Scott King and Betty Shabazz, the two women with whom she shared a fellowship of agony that identified the trio by the nomenclature of their loss: "the widows." To a large degree, each woman was at once catapulted and circumscribed by her martyred husband's mystique and memory. If these women's lives were not their own after they married, it was even more the case that they were, in the aftermath of their husband's deaths, bound to men whose legends kept them alive in the public imagination, but unavailable to hold their widows at night. Thus, "the widows" faced a punishing irony: as long as they identified with—and were faithful to—the men to whom they had been married, they could secure a living for their families while furthering the cause for which their husbands died.

But it was a risk—to their images, and possibly to the images of their fallen mates—for the widows to have intimate relationships. It was if their very existence had no meaning beyond their functions as extensions of, perhaps substitutes for, their husbands. They were perennial proxies. The business of professional widowhood seemed to take on a life of its own. Even if the widows quietly exercised other options in their private lives, the implicit terms of the contract of their cultural support seemed to be rigidly cast: you may love who you will, but remain loyal to our beloved leaders in public view. The widows did not have the option to openly date, or at least it was not one that they could easily choose without stern consequences.

Of the trio, Myrlie has most deliberately cast off the expectations and encumbrances of her widowhood. First, she remarried, and for eighteen years was Williams' wife until he died in 1995 from prostate cancer. Then, she wrote candidly about her marriage to Medgar in her 1999 memoir, *Watch Me Fly*, detailing the pressures that can mount in the wake of being married in, and to, the movement. But Coretta Scott King and Betty Shabazz, before her tragic death, courageously weathered their share of storms and built substantial lives.

Coretta has had, perhaps, the toughest time occupying public space, since her husband cast the biggest shadow. The Moneta Sleet photo of Coretta consoling her youngest daughter, Bernice, at her husband's funeral, not only snagged a Pulitzer Prize, but it tugged at the nation's heart. I remember tracing my nine-year-old hand along the photo of her pretty face tilted by grief, sheathed beneath the black netting on her pillbox hat. What dignity, what calm, what courage.

I met Coretta Scott King in person, for the first time, more than a quarter-century later when I lectured at Ebenezer Baptist Church, the congregation her husband had co-pastored with his father until his assassination in 1968. On a later visit to preach at Ebenezer, I had, from the pulpit King made internationally famous, imagined out loud what might have happened if he had listened to Malcolm X the night before he delivered his world-famous "I Have a Dream" speech. (King had once confessed that he couldn't listen to Malcolm for too long, since the militant orator had the same effect on King as he often had on millions of other blacks: he made you angry, very angry, at unjust elements in white society.)

"I *had* a dream," I stated as I affected King's sweet Southern drawl. "But I'm *mad* now. We gon' have to whip some heads up in here today." The congregation readily caught my humor and rewarded me with hearty laughter. Since more than a few of them had heard King preach, I felt secure in the belief that I hadn't breached the trust of the church or irreverently abused King's memory. But I momentarily froze as I remembered that Coretta was in attendance. I fretted until after service, when Christine King Farris, a Spelman College professor and King's sister, warmly greeted me and remarked favorably on my impersonation of her brother. When I shook Mrs. King's hand, and posed with her for a photo, my humorous comments never came up in our brief exchange. If she was upset, she spared me the embarrassment of calling me out on the spot. As usual, she remained beautiful under her myriad burdens and responsibilities.

A few years later I met Coretta Scott King again when Oprah journeyed to Atlanta to promote her film, *Beloved*, at a packed Hillside Chapel & Truth Center, pastored by Barbara King, whom I happened to be visiting. Before Oprah's presentation, I sat in Hillside's ministerial office, which served as a makeshift green room, talking to Coretta and Bernice, now a distinguished preacher in her own right. Bernice told me how her father's death had impacted her, had kept her in an emotional shell, unable to trust folk for fear they would use her to exploit a relationship with her famous family name. I told her that I thought her apprehension was reasonable, even as it caused me to keep my distance, for fear that she might conclude I was just such a person in light of the book I had just begun to write on her father's radical legacy.

Sitting with Coretta and Bernice enhanced my appreciation for the magnitude of suffering endured by the King family in the loss of their father and husband. Without Coretta Scott King's tireless efforts, her husband's legacy might not have as quickly garnered national, indeed, global acceptance. And without her relentless advocacy, his birthday surely would not have become a national holiday, the first for a person of African descent in our country's history.

If Evers-Williams and King have fought for the future of their husband's pasts, then Betty Shabazz waged an equally important war to rescue her husband's reputation from naysayers who claimed he was a divisive symbol of violence and hatred. Betty Shabazz worked indefatigably, as did her two colleagues in pain, to rear her six children and to make certain that Malcolm's true legacy was honored. Medgar Evers and Martin Luther King, Jr., were clear candidates for American heroism beyond the color line they courageously resisted. Because Malcolm insisted on blacks loving and learning from themselves before they invited the wider, whiter world into the fold, he was a less obvious choice to be feted by cultural forces beyond—and at times, within—his community. But Shabazz's efforts helped to underscore the ecumenical and international dimensions of Malcolm's surprisingly catholic racial politics.

I met Shabazz on a few occasions, gazing on her smooth, attractive, ebony face, shaking her hand, and receiving her compliments on the book I had written about her husband. It was my book that led Shabazz to invite me to deliver the keynote address at what would turn out to be the last celebration of her husband's legacy that she organized before she tragically died in a fire deliberately set by her grandson. The celebration was held on the thirty-second anniversary of Malcolm's death in February of 1997, at Harlem's historic Abyssinian Baptist Church. The event featured inspiring performances by the poets Amiri and Amina Baraka.

I spoke that night of Malcolm's brilliant thinking, his contagious charisma, his propulsive rhetoric, and his edifying humanity. I also touched on his unfortunate gender politics and his long apprenticeship under the Honorable Elijah Muhammad, from whose beliefs he partially divorced himself when he split from the Nation of Islam less than a year before his brutal death. Although she publicly scolded me for, as she put it, "leaving my husband in the Nation"—by which she meant that, in her estimation, I had spoken too much about his twelve years under Muhammad and too little about his short but fateful year outside its ranks—Shabazz graciously thanked me for my speech.

When I learned that Shabazz had perished at the hands of her troubled grandson Malcolm, it underscored the trauma that had episodically intervened in her life as wife, widow, and way-maker for her daughters. But it was as well a haunting metaphor of the tragic generational tensions that flare in lethal fury in black life. Shabazz's life was marked by violence and pain. Her husband was assassinated before her very eyes, and in the presence of their four daughters. (The twins were born after Malcolm's death.) Their daughter Qubilah confessed that she conspired to murder Louis Farrakhan, the man her family held responsible for her father's death. Largely in response to her daughter's troubles, Shabazz ended her bitter feud with Farrakhan in a public gesture of rapprochement in Harlem in 1994.

With Shabazz's help, Qubilah struck a deal with the government: she would serve two years probation while seeking therapy to address her festering rage. Qubilah's life was stained by the sad legacy of violence that shaped her developing worldview. After all, she, too, had seen her father cut down by a hail of bullets. Although she grew up in middle-class comfort and attended Princeton University, Qubilah seemed unable to make the complex, jagged pieces of her life fit together.

Qubilah became a nomad. During her wanderings abroad, she met an Algerian man in Paris with whom she had a child. After the birth of little Malcolm, the Algerian disappeared, leaving Qubilah with greater reason to settle down and make a better life for her baby. But her inability, or disinclination, to seek the security of steady work or a stable home only upped the stakes of her emotional shakiness. It also exacerbated young Malcolm's behavioral difficulties. After complaining that his mother was abusive, the state temporarily removed Malcolm from his mother's custody. However, they shortly returned him to her care after declaring Qubilah innocent of the charge.

In this light, it was all the more ironic that young Malcolm should resent being sent to live with his grandmother in Yonkers, while his mother wrestled with her demons in Texas. His raw anger at being displaced, and enduring shuttling, uprooting, and expulsion once again—along with the psychic and social forces that bombarded him—kept him from responding reasonably to his predicament. Even now, we cannot be certain about the mix of motives that led young Malcolm to torch his grandmother's apartment. But we know that his disturbing behavior carried symbolic meaning far beyond Malcolm's unintended act of murder.

Malcolm focused his despair and rage on Betty Shabazz, whose proud body had borne his mother Qubilah. Her troubled body had, in turn, borne Malcolm. When Malcolm burned Betty Shabazz, he singed his most vital connection to a past he perhaps only dimly knew. He also silenced the person most capable of making his future more promising. In the eyes of many sympathetic onlookers, Malcolm's fatal act drew from the racial amnesia and moral disintegration that characterize younger blacks. By starting the fire that killed his grandmother, Malcolm fueled a fierce debate about how the younger generation, through crime, disrespect, and a pop culture laced with lewdness, is often literally destroying its ancestors.

If generational tensions tear at the fabric of our unity, they also shred the bonds that connect younger blacks to the heroic deeds of their female forebears. We must not forget that Myrlie Evers-Williams, Coretta Scott King, and Betty Shabazz, in their distinct fashions, maneuvered within, and occasionally beyond, the conventions of gender. They shaped careers in public service out of the ashes of their personal tragedies. By loving men who loved humanity, these women nurtured millions beyond the circle of their own kin. And by honoring their men even after their flesh had returned to earth, these women have given new life to their legacies, and resurrected in countless hearts the hope that love could vanquish death.

9

Womentor

"Excuse me, Miss, hold on a minute," I shouted across the university parking lot to the attractive, mocha-colored woman with the big eyes, wide smile, and shapely legs. "Who are you? I haven't seen too many sisters around here."

"My name is Ruth," she chuckled, amused no doubt by my chutzpah in nearly accosting her out of desperation to meet black people in Princeton. "And who are you?"

I told her my name and that I was a newly arrived graduate student in the religion department at the university. Although she never told me what she did, I didn't think Ruth was a professor or administrator at the university. I got the sense that she was a "townie," a local resident who lived in the borough of Princeton, but who had no high standing at the Ivy League school that dominated the city. That didn't bother me in the least. I was simply interested in getting to know black folk who could provide me extended kinship. I was feeling a bit isolated after spending the summer working, and studying German in a lily-white environment at the beginning of my Ph.D. studies. During our conversation, Ruth seemed warm and down to earth, with an almost shy demeanor, and disarmingly humble. I thought she might have been a departmental secretary; she had that air of quiet authority that derives from knowing you're in control even if you're not in charge. We promised to keep in touch, even though we failed to exchange numbers. I figured that the relatively small number of blacks in Princeton assured me that I would see Ruth again.

Three weeks later, I was invited to an informal soiree to mark the beginning of the academic year at the home of Al Raboteau, a distinguished religious historian and my new professor. As I mingled among the guests, amiably chatting with accomplished and apprentice scholars above the din of competing conversations, I ran into Ruth. She was there with her son, Khari, who was twelve years old, and her eight-year-old daughter, Maya.

"Michael, let me introduce you to Ruth Simmons," Raboteau enthusiastically stated.

"Oh, yes, we met a few weeks ago," Ruth gently interrupted, her bright smile beaming through her lips.

"Then you know that Ruth is the Director of Studies for Butler College," Raboteau posed as he turned to me, before excusing himself to greet another guest who had just arrived.

Princeton had recently decided to divide the freshmen and sophomores of its undergraduate population among five residential colleges. Each college had a "master," a faculty member who presided over more than five hundred students, in addition to a director of studies, who guided the academic careers of their charges. The masters also drew from the graduate student body two "assistant masters" to aid in governing each residential college. It was a position I happily took up a year later, in small part because I relished turning the linguistic, if not historic, tables and being thought of by the predominantly white student body as even half a master.

"You didn't tell me you were a big-time administrator at Princeton," I playfully scolded Ruth.

"I never told you *anything* about what I did," Ruth heartily laughed, defending her coy, even elusive, approach that day. "That was an assumption you made, now wasn't it?"

As I was to quickly discover, this was vintage Ruth Simmons. Long before she became the first black president of a seven sisters college when she took the helm at Smith College in 1995—and many years in advance of becoming the first black, and first female, president of Brown University in 2001—Ruth had been spoiling expectations, and challenging narrow assumptions, of what a black woman could do.

If I was in search of kindred hearts and community at Princeton, Ruth proved to be a large part of that, and so much more. Our bond had to do with an unspoken identification forged among those who have overcome economic hardship to attain academic success. My struggles had taken place up North, on urban terrain. Ruth's roots were in the South, where she was born, the youngest of twelve, into rural poverty. Her parents, Isaac and Fannie Stubblefield, were sharecroppers in the woods of Diley, Texas, a farming community approximately halfway between Houston and Dallas. For the first few years of her life, Ruth lived with her family in a dark, tin-roofed shack with three rooms: one for her parents, one for her seven brothers, and the other for the five girls. The Stubblefields lived in the country with dirt roads, no electricity, and with the nearest neighbors half a mile away. When she was seven, Ruth's parents moved the family to Houston. In her touching 1998 essay, "My Mother's Daughter," Ruth discusses how crucial that move was to her success in life.

"The sharecropper's life was, of course, a hard one for adults, but it was especially hard for children. Like the adults, children were subject to the whims of the seasons; whole families had to participate in the harvesting of the crops, particularly cotton and peanuts, and children had to miss a great deal of school as a result." Ruth wrote that school was "infrequent at best," and that most children did not finish their education. "It was critical, then, that I came to elementary school age at the time this system was changing." For Ruth, moving to Houston made a big difference in "the continuity of my education. Imagine this country family moving and going to the city of Houston! It was a difficult experience, initially, for us. Children laughed at us because of the way we spoke, the way we dressed, coming from a country town into the city. We were really poor then, but our family remained together and was a primary source of support in this transition."

Throughout her school years, Ruth had teachers who inspired her to excel. Her kindergarten teacher, Ida Mae Henderson, gave Ruth a sense of possibility beyond the rigid segregation she endured. Her high school drama teacher, Vernell A. Lillie, encouraged Ruth to leave Texas for the first time and to attend the historically black Dillard University in New Orleans. After she finished her career at Dillard—during which she spent a crucial junior year at Wellesley College, opening her eyes to the class divisions and gender opportunities of the wider world—Ruth studied at the University of Lyon in France for a year as a Fulbright scholar. In 1968, she married Norbert Simmons and did postgraduate work at George Washington University. Ruth headed to Harvard to collect a Ph.D. in Romance Languages and Literatures in 1973, while her husband finished law school at Boston University. Ruth began her academic career as an assistant professor of French at the University of New Orleans, and two years later she became an assistant dean in the college of liberal arts. Ruth moved to California, and served as an administrator and professor of Pan-African Studies at California State University, Northridge, and subsequently as a dean at Los Angeles's University of Southern California graduate school. After separating from her husband, Ruth headed to Princeton in 1983.

If our common economic struggles quickly forged a bond between us, Ruth's easy laughter made our friendship click. And it didn't hurt that she found much of my humor uproarious, even when her beloved Houston was the butt of my jokes.

"Sure, go ahead and dog Detroit if you want to," I would say to Ruth, defending my hometown's musical roots against the mock disparagement she had lobbed my way. "We all know the sterling musical tradition of Houston, Texas."

Ruth's snickering would trickle out, because she knew where I was heading.

"Yes, ladies and gentlemen, come with me through a tour of Houston's musical landscape," I'd announce, feigning a documentary tone as I narrated the city's meager musical offerings. "And what is the highlight of our tour? Ah, yes, a perfect specimen of Houston's high and noble art, Archie Bell and the Drells."

Ruth's snickering had built to guffaws by now, as I prepared to lower the boom on her hometown musical heroes.

"And what does our hero Archie Bell say at the beginning of this classic example of linguistic profundity?" I begged as Ruth was virtually keeling over. "'Hi everybody, I'm Archie Bell and the Drells from Houston, Texas,'" I drolly imitated Bell, affecting his high-pitched, Southern drawl.

"And here's the kicker," I insisted, as Ruth could only utter faint protests between the tornado of cackles in which she was engulfed. "He lays down some serious insight through his use of the language. Listen to him now: 'We don't only sing,' and I hope you all note that wonderful usage, 'but we dance just as good as we walk.'"

Ruth was gone, doubled over in delirium.

To her credit, Ruth could just as easily laugh at herself. When she invited me to give a lecture at Smith College, Ruth sent her driver to fetch me from New York, where I was then living and teaching, at Columbia University. During my introductory remarks, I acknowledged our friendship before launching a light-hearted volley.

"As we made our way from New York to North Hampton, I asked Ruth's driver to stop at her favorite haunts," I devilishly dead-panned. "So after our third liquor store..."

There was a room full of laughter, but none louder than Ruth's full-bodied gaiety.

If Ruth's humor was buoyant, her disappointment could be direct and forceful. When Khari was thirteen, he desperately wanted to attend a concert to be given by the pop artist Terrence Trent Darby in Philadelphia, a forty-five-minute ride by car, and only a little longer on the train. Khari is today a tall, chocolate, and strikingly handsome man with a mane of ambitious dreads, and a topflight musician—he often tours and plays bass with the recording artist India.Arie. He is an even more extraordinary human being, full of soulfulness, magic, and grace, possessed of maturity far beyond his years. Even as a teen, he exhibited remarkable poise and a compelling love for music, elements that sparked between us a strong kinship that endures to this day. On the phone one evening in Princeton, Khari poured out his heart's desire to me.

"Mike, man, I really want to attend this concert," Khari confessed. "You know what a genius Terrence is, and it would be *so* great to see him. But Mom won't let me go by myself, because she says I'm too young. And you know she's not going."

"That's no problem, brother," I immediately offered. "I'll be glad to take you."

"No way, that would be so cool," Khari enthused. Alas, our enthusiasm was short-lived. After Khari retired from our phone call, overjoyed that he had found an adult companion to the concert—or as it turned out, it was more like accomplice—Ruth rang me back. She was furious.

"Michael, are you trying to interfere with my parenting?" Ruth thundered through the phone.

"Oh, no, Ruth, I would never do that," I insisted. "I was just trying to make sure that Khari had a way to the concert. I wasn't at all trying to stick my nose in your family affairs."

"I've already told him that he can't go," Ruth calmly but firmly explained. "And when you tell him that you can accompany him, it upsets the instructions I've given to him."

"I didn't mean to do that, Ruth. I'm so sorry."

But she took even that angry occasion to teach, as she often did in our conversations that cast me as the little brother, and Ruth as the discerning and wise big sister.

"You see, Michael, you're treating Khari as if he is a poor child lacking resources," Ruth gently scolded me. "He is a solidly middle-class child, and there are many things he can do that other children can't. You mustn't confuse his situation with that of a kid who doesn't have privilege."

Ruth never once mentioned our own poor backgrounds, and I implicitly understood her lesson: I shouldn't allow my own earlier deprivation to cloud my judgment in forming attachments to anyone, even her own child. And neither

should I permit guilt over escaping want distort my perception of the world and the human relations on which it thrives.
And of course, that as well intentioned as my meddling had
been, it was still meddling.

Ruth never stayed mad long, and as soon as she vented her
ire, we reclaimed our pleasant rapport. She had a genius for
making others feel important. In fact, she built my sense of
confidence as a keen observer of the world by confiding in
me her feelings about one matter or another, testing and
sharpening my analysis of human behavior. This habit continued far beyond my Princeton years, as we discussed my problems and opportunities, as well as her predictably rapid rise
through the ranks of academic administration. When Ruth
asked me my opinion about a school she was considering
going to, or that was looking at her, I knew she valued what I
had to say, and took it to heart. That was an extraordinary
boost to my esteem, as well as a reminder that those friend-
ships thrive best that feature the give and take of honest communion. And Ruth wanted it straight, no chaser, just like she
gave it. When she swore me to secrecy as she pondered a
move, I honored the pledge, not only because she was my dear
friend and mentor, but also because I believed that a great deal
of our people's educational progress against stereotypes rested
in her accomplishments.

Of course I wasn't alone in that conviction. That was made
blissfully obvious when, at a Bard College conference celebrating the great Nigerian author Chinua Achebe's seventieth
birthday, Ruth matter-of-factly informed me, my wife, the

writer Marcia Dyson, Nobel laureate Toni Morrison, and noted Southern historian Nell Painter, that, pending official election, she had been tapped as the next president of Brown, as we sauntered across campus to the student center to eat our lunch. Ruth made us promise not to reveal her news before the official announcement, but we had more important business to attend to. Marcia, Toni, Nell, and I formed an impromptu coronation committee as we gleefully declared our pride in Ruth's achievement, realizing that it meant so much to her, to the nation, but especially to *the race*. Ruth was characteristically modest in revealing her new status and in accepting our joyful adoration.

A few days later, Brown University trumpeted her historic feat. Brown's chancellor, Stephen Robert, captured the day's meaning as he welcomed reporters and other witnesses and well wishers to the campus.

"This is a historic occasion, not only for Brown, but also for the entire Ivy League," Roberts said. "Today we announce the eighteenth president of Brown University and the first African-American to be named president of any Ivy League institution, Dr. Ruth Simmons." After Roberts praised Ruth for her leadership in higher education, and declared his expectation that "she will be a star at Brown," Roberts presented Ruth.

"It's very hard for me to explain what's going through my mind and through my heart right now," Ruth stated. "It would be impossible for you to understand because you don't know my personal circumstances yet. But when I was told I had been elected this afternoon as president of Brown, I said my ancestors are smiling. It's a wonderful moment for me. It's a wonderful moment for my family." When reporters were invited to ask questions, Ruth proved that her sense of humor would not fail at Brown.

"I'm Patrick Moos from the *Brown Daily Herald*," the young journalist stated.

"Yes, you're not the one who broke the story are you?" Ruth knowingly asked as laughter showered the room.

"Well, we're a team," Moos sheepishly replied.

"Okay, now you don't want to take responsibility," Ruth said, laughing.

Ruth showed her wisdom on issues of racial and gender representation when she responded to a question by *Boston Globe* reporter Patrick Healy about why she took the Brown presidency. After praising her students and her situation at Smith, and claiming that she had to be mightily persuaded to leave the women's college, she addressed what was perhaps an underlying assumption that had not yet come up that day.

"I always get the race question," Ruth said. "And I know none of you would do that. On one level, one doesn't want to feel, ever, that one is chosen because of one's race or gender. But on the other hand, let me tell you what happened to me this morning when I left the hotel and I was being driven to campus. A taxicab pulled alongside the car with a driver who I could see out of the corner of my eye was trying to get my attention. And I thought it was odd. He was waving, and I looked over and he held up the newspaper and he pointed to my picture and he said, 'Yessss!'" Ruth stuck her thumb in the air to mimic the cab driver's gesture of approval. "The point is, if that means something to a taxi driver in Providence, if it means something to a five-year-old in Fifth Ward in Houston, Texas, it's worth giving it a shot. So I'm here because I think my doing this means something for other people, and I think it will certainly mean something for me. And I owe it to all the people who helped me along the way, to contribute something, and that's what I'm trying to do."

In responding to a question from Jeniene Phillips of the *New England Cable News* about the "personal circumstances" about which she spoke, Ruth expressed the premise of her educational philosophy, one that rested on her early struggles.

"You probably don't know Houston well enough to know what Fifth Ward is, but it is a very impoverished area of Houston, just in the shadow of the downtown skyscrapers," Ruth pointed out, while acknowledging, in an aside, the presence of her older sister, Marie Raymond. "Our parents eked out a living in that area, and so we didn't have much. We went to segregated schools. We went to schools where we had wonderful teachers, to be sure, but they were different from the schools that other children went to at the time. But we were afforded education. Because we had the opportunity—I particularly had the opportunity for scholarships—I just feel so strongly that every child in this country, irrespective of their circumstances, should be entitled to a good education. *Every* child."

Ruth reiterated her commitment to every child during her

glorious inaugural speech. I had missed her 1995 Smith College inaugural address, "Vivat Academia," but now my chest swelled with pride as I watched Ruth electrify her audience in a soft drizzle on an overcast October Sunday afternoon. I was especially struck by her unswerving devotion to underprivileged students.

"Research universities should also honor the place of community colleges and all institutions providing access to the widest array of populations," Ruth asserted in a remarkable passage. "We should acknowledge the role that these colleges play in carrying out their excellent and distinctive teaching role and reward that excellence by admitting students from community colleges. Every university no matter what its mission should admit community college students who excel in their work because doing so encourages meritorious work, the awakening of learning at every moment of life, and a continuing openness to educational excellence." After the ceremony, I huddled with Nell Painter, and noted English professors Thadious Davis, of Vanderbilt University, and Nellie McKay, of the University of Wisconsin, as we remarked on Ruth's extraordinary overture to the disenfranchised.

I had seen Ruth live out this credo at Princeton, and at Spelman and Smith, too. I also saw her earn the affectionate monikers of "Doctor Ruth" and "Mama Ruth"—she often sat counseling students in their toughest hours away from school, while other difficult times were spent with their families in the hour of grief. I was touched by Ruth's quiet, dignified presence at the Houston funeral of our friend Stephen

Bolivar, a brilliant former Princeton student who perished tragically while pursuing a Ph.D. in sociology at the University of Chicago. Like Ruth, Steve had grown up in Houston's Fifth Ward, and had formed an attachment to Ruth based as much on pride in their common roots as on her academic acumen. I knew firsthand the comfort her presence could bring; when I was sent for several days to the infirmary at Princeton, Ruth was the only person I wanted to see. I called her on the phone to tell her.

"Hey, you haven't come over to see me yet," I whispered through the receiver, on the second day I was confined. "I thought you loved me."

"I haven't come to see you?" Ruth gently repeated my words as she added a flicker of humor. "And you've been there *so* long. I'll see you in a little while."

She came and spent an hour cheering me to health.

It is this side of Ruth, I suppose, that is most endearing to me, and that has, beyond her pathbreaking achievements, meant most to me as a man. Ruth has not only been a pioneer in opening doors for women, but she has tenderly, sensitively opened doors of insight for me into the vast, complex realms of black masculinity. As a graduate student at Princeton, I caught a glimpse of her silent encouragement when my wife and I joined Ruth and Khari at a concert performed by the jazz trumpeter Wynton Marsalis. Ruth bought the tickets; without her generosity, my wife and I couldn't have enjoyed such an elegant evening. When we approached the entrance to Trenton's War Memorial, the site of the Marsalis concert,

Ruth discreetly passed me all four tickets to hand to the ush-
ers standing sentinel at the doors. It was a small gesture that
had big results: it made me feel, in that moment, so much
taller as a man, and it opened a window onto Ruth's edifying
compassion. Nothing that Ruth has done since has undercut
the spirit of that moment, or more clearly symbolized her
profound humanity.

10

Class Workers

Every Friday, the diminutive, dark-skinned woman with the gorgeous face came to clean our leased apartment above a Philadelphia hotel. She was unfailingly cheerful, and her sweet spirit brightened our living quarters as much as any cleanser she brought. Deborah Bethea was a thirty-nine-year-old Philadelphia native who had been reared in North Philly, now one of the city's most notorious ghettoes. She had two sons from a previous relationship, one of whom had gotten into trouble with the law. Debbie was happily married to a man who was now retired, and she worked as a beautician to supplement her income. That much I knew from our brief interactions.

Debbie's work situation was familiar to me, and I became more and more curious about what kept her on an even keel in a job that was undervalued by most, and one that certainly didn't pay workers their worth. My experience as a house-cleaner in a Detroit hotel in the late seventies saw me chang-ing linen, making beds, vacuuming floors, and emptying trash—all talents my wife swears I lost when I left the city in 1979. I hardly got any tips, and the people I served were large-ly indifferent to me as a human being. They could care less that I existed, what my needs were, who I was, or what I thought. Their dictum was simple: clean the room and move along. And for God's sake, be gone when we return. The less they knew about us and interacted with us, the better chance their beliefs about how things worked—which ignored how most of the housekeepers were black, while most guests were white—would not be punctured.

I got used to this wall of racial difference, but I never accepted it. I go out of my way to tip those folk who bring me food, or make my bed, or render crucial service in a serv-ice economy that rewards the high-tech but frowns on the lowly laborer.

I suppose I was taken by Debbie because her hard work ethic and her beauty reminded me of my mother, Addie Mae, and my dear friend Barbara, both of whom worked hard to escape poverty. Mama was born in Hissop, Alabama, a pretty yellow girl who became a beautiful yellow woman. Her natu-ral beauty was so appealing that my father, Everett, an almost blue-black, thickly muscled laborer twenty years her senior, nicknamed her Ivory. She had high, apple cheekbones, full lips, thick eyebrows, a beautiful broad nose, and penetrating, dark eyes, honey-smooth skin, short, thick eyelashes, a thick mane of hair, and a svelte figure.

Mama worked tirelessly, endlessly, to keep her house, and her five boys, in line, long before she went to work as a para-professional with the Detroit Public Schools. When I heard "For My People," the ten-verse Margaret Walker poem that Mrs. James taught us in fifth grade, I always thought of Mama. In the second verse, Walker's decision not to punctuate brilliantly underscored the run-on sentence of labor to which many black women are consigned: "For my people...washing ironing cooking scrubbing sewing mending hoeing plowing digging planting pruning patching."

The poem not only captured Mama's domestic duties up North, but it neatly summarized her labor on the land down South. She grew up on an Alabama farm, working the soil with her siblings. "Growing up in the country on a farm was not very bad," Mama admitted. "The work was hard, the day was long, but that was the way of life back then." Mama absorbed her work ethic almost by osmosis, since every able body—and that was *every* body—pitched in to help. "I had to help with the work in the house and in the field," she said. "At the age of eight, my sister and I would get up at 4:00 A.M. She would cook breakfast, and I would churn the milk. Then we went to school at 7:00 A.M. We returned home at 3:30, and it was off to the fields to pick cotton at 4:30 for an hour, then back home to milk the cows, eat dinner and do homework." Addie Mae—her sister was Lila Mae; so many black women of their generation were identified by this unofficial middle name that Sharony Andrews Green wrote a beautiful little book entitled *Cuttin' the Rug Under the Moonlit Sky: Stories and Drawings About a Bunch of Women Named Mae*—was putting in sixteen-hour days before she was ten!

Her work didn't stop there. Mama chopped cotton, planted corn, spread fertilizer and peeled and cut fruit into small pieces to be canned. She shelled corn that was taken to the mill to be ground into cornmeal. Mama also gathered beans, peas, and other vegetables from the garden. Of course, there was the proverbial black culinary mascot—the pig. "My father would kill hogs in the winter, after it would get cold, and I would help my mother put away different cuts of meat," Mama explained. "I would help her clean the chitterlings. We would also make the best country sausage that you said was ever made!" On my visits to the farm as a child, I surely pigged out on homemade sausage.

"During the downtime, when there was no work in the field," Mama recalled, "I would read, play, and sometimes go visit friends that lived about three quarters of a mile away." When I look at her now, near retirement, with my father dead for twenty years, I can only fantasize about hitting the lottery to buy her a bigger house in a lovely part of Detroit so that she can enjoy her golden years. She is still vital, still active, still hardworking—when she lived with me for a couple of years in Chicago, she got to her bank job nearly an hour before she was due at work—and still a woman of extraordinary character and beauty. Despite the occasional difficulties we've had along the way, difficulties that mark the relationship of two hardheaded, strong-willed, verbally inclined people, she remains a source of undying inspiration to me.

If Debbie's hard work brought my mother to mind, her chocolate glow and chutzpah also conjured Barbara Perkins, my wife's best friend and an amazing woman. At forty-four, Barbara is a mother, wife, entrepreneur, teacher, civic leader, political activist, mentor, globe-trotter, and a courageous advocate for women and girls in Los Angeles. She is a stunning beauty, a coffee-colored charmer with an ideal African visage: her prominent cheeks frame her stately nose with two perfectly cupped nostrils, and her gapped-teeth smile is adorned by unobtrusive, gold braces, while her oval jawline sweeps up on either side into two lovely, long ears that often sport the most dashing earrings. Her daintily arched eyebrows trace their gentle trajectory over her radiant and dancing dark eyes, at once devilish and full of the delight of living. And like her best friend, she rests on a magnificent cushion of flesh that undulates gently in her smart attire.

What has struck me most about Barbara is her tireless, constant work—and that of her husband Stan, one of the first black captains in the Los Angeles fire department. Stan is a handsome, brown-skinned, fifty-five-year-old high-school graduate who embodies the best of black manhood in his Renaissance genius. He is a gourmet cook, firefighter, entrepreneur, father, a connoisseur of fine clothing, an aficionado of great music, and a dancer of remarkable skill. In short, he's the kind of dapper brother who is totally at home in his skin and unafraid of the universe, and fiercely determined to succeed on his own terms. He was handed nothing in life but he has created a world of opportunity for his family, including his two children, the beautiful and brilliant Kelsey, a fifteen-year-old carbon copy of Mom, and Cody, a gifted, good-looking, and buoyant thirteen-year-old chip off the masculine block.

When we first met Stan and Barbara, I was compelled to blurt out after viewing their frenetic itinerary—besides everything else, they run a cooking and catering service—"Y'all must be Jamaican."

"Close, darlin'," Barbara sweetly intoned. "I'm from the Bahamas."

Barbara had a tough time in climbing out of deprivation, but she cherished her difficult days as the prelude to prosperity. Barbara was born in Miami, and lived there in her grandfather's house with her mother, Barbara Jane, and her aunt, Sally Mae, and her four siblings and two cousins. "Granddaddy was my mother and Aunt Sally Mae's rock," Barbara stated. "He purchased his home with the GI Bill, and moved his two adult daughters in with him so that they could all help each other. Granddaddy lost his leg to diabetes, and he needed help. Since my mother and aunt were both single mothers, the situation worked out well for everyone. They needed help as well."

When she was six, her grandfather died, and Barbara's mother received an offer she couldn't refuse: to let her youngest daughter go live in the Bahamas. "My Aunt Kathleen's gift of love to Barbara Jane was to offer to take custody of her youngest daughter, Barbara Ann," Barbara continues. (I've got a cousin named Barbara Ann, and I know a lot more women with that middle name, so I suppose a generation of black Maes created a second generation of black Anns, long before Sheniquas and Tamikas rose to prominence. Perhaps these insistently individual names—and we might throw in comedian Martin Lawrence's mythic alter ego, Shenaynay—are a form of linguistic rebellion against Southern nomenclature.)

"All the other children living in the house were actually a little jealous," Barbara says of her move to the island. "None of us really knew what life was like in Nassau, Bahamas. But we had heard so many wonderful stories from our grandfather who had just died. In fact, that's why Aunt Kathleen was visiting, to attend Granddaddy's funeral." In a difficult and emotional decision, Barbara was allowed to go. Funds were low, and the burden of feeding and clothing another child in the family would be removed from her mother's shoulders. To Barbara, living in the Bahamas was like living in paradise. "It was the most physically beautiful place, with hibiscus and birds-of-paradise flowers growing wild across the island," Barbara fondly recounts. "The sea was a part of daily life. We depended on it. I spent so much time at the Market Place, next to the dock, and I spent almost every weekend on the beach. It was the only outing my family approved of, except church, of course, which we attended at least twice during the week, and almost all day long on Sunday." But if Barbara was in paradise, it surely wasn't the Garden of Eden. The island's gorgeous geography was mercifully juxtaposed to its dreary economy, which was brought home by the hardship it imposed on many of its citizens.

"I grew up without running water or electricity for many years, at least until I was fourteen," Barbara admits. "That's when I began to earn seventeen dollars a week, and I took my tithe from that. I also contributed to the household. I helped to put in a toilet and a sink. We never did get a bathtub, but I was fond of my oversized round tin tub. We had all the basics, and we weren't doing so bad compared to others. There were many families that had more than we had, but there were many who wished they had the little we had."

Barbara learned to work hard because there was no other way to survive, a lesson she glimpsed in her aunt's diligent efforts. "Aunt Kathleen was a proud woman who worked in some of the finest homes as a domestic. She always worked for foreigners who would pass her on to the next family once they moved on. She had a reputation for being reliable and good at what she did. I worked all my life to be like her. She strived for excellence in everything she did, and she expected no less from me." Barbara's aunt was demanding, perhaps even exacting, but Barbara bears no resentment for the stern manner.

"She loved me with all that she had to give," Barbara gently recalls. "Her love was tough, but it was constant, and it was sincere. Even when I was hurt, or overwhelmed by her expectations of me, I never doubted her love for me. I never doubted her commitment to my well-being. It was only after I became an adult that I realized that she had given me far more than what she got when she was a girl." In her maturity,

Barbara realizes that even as she wanted more from her aunt—more nurturing, more emotional support, more affirmation—she was incapable of giving it. "What we both didn't understand, for very different reasons, is that *we* were the greatest gifts we could have given each other. That's a lesson I think about a lot now that I'm a mother of two children." But Barbara keeps mementos from those days to remind her of her pilgrimage from humble roots. "We were dirt poor, so to speak, but we were clean, proud, and dignified. We had a strong sense of self-worth. I thank my Aunt Kathleen every day for that gift. The two-room house I grew up in remains on the island, just as I left it. It belongs to me now, and I visit it each year. I keep a kerosene lamp, a washboard, and a slop jar in my home in Los Angeles to remind me of those days in my life."

Although Barbara, like Mama, faced tremendous odds, she transformed her deprivation into a determination to succeed in life. Mama and Barbara were foremost in my mind when I cornered Debbie one day and asked her to sit down and tell me her story.

"Okay, I'll talk to you after I clean up," she said.

"No, no, that's all right, you don't have to clean up today," I responded. "Please, have a seat and let's chat." I had seen my wife do something similar while we vacationed in the Caribbean. I'd often find her cleaning our room, while she ordered for the housekeepers an exquisite lunch from room service—food the servants were often not allowed to eat. One might rightly think of it as a small act, or more harshly, as the guilty gesture of the black middle class, but for that half-hour, it brightened the day of the desperately poor black workers. I harbored no such fantasy about Debbie's brief respite from work, but at least she wouldn't have to worry about one room on her itinerary, and hopefully, she'd have fun talking about her life.

"I still live in North Philly," Debbie said as she sat on our couch in her black and white housekeeper uniform, her jet-black hair crisply feathered and newly done. "They call it a ghetto, but it really wasn't rough when I grew up there. It was quiet. You didn't have to worry about barring up your house. You could sit outside, and the kids went to bed early. Everything was smooth sailing. But now they call it Beirut. It's a heavy drug area. We have cops on every corner now."

Debbie was one of nine children, including eight girls and one boy. Her mother was a homemaker and her father parked cars at a local hotel, earning enough money to support his brood by working hard and winning good tips. Debbie's parents met and married early: her mother was fourteen, her father sixteen. Debbie's mother was pregnant with their first child, and both she and Debbie's father won the approval of their parents to wed. Debbie's parents remained together for twenty-one years before divorcing.

Debbie got her first job one summer while attending junior high school, helping to monitor children at a daycare. Later, in the tenth grade, she found a job working at McDonald's as a cashier after school. She was at school by 7:00 A.M., and at work by 1:30, where she remained until

9:00. Debbie gained a good deal of insight into human nature from her job. "Working at McDonald's was a good experience, because it let me know that I had a good personality for working with the public and dealing with other people," Debbie said. "I was a head cashier, which is also known as a certified cashier. I also cleaned the lobby, and wiped the tables down. I also wiped the bathroom down, because everything had to stay clean. I also cleaned the cooking areas. My job wasn't just focused on staying on the register. At McDonald's, they train you to do every job." Despite the hard work, the pay wasn't great. Debbie made $4.25 an hour, but she never let that deter her from doing her job well.

"It was a rough place to work," Debbie conceded. "Because you had to deal with so many different personalities. People come in, you take their order, and they expect immediate service. If they don't get it, they'll say, 'You're not fast enough.' Or they'll come back and claim that you didn't give them the correct change, even though the cash register tells you exactly how much change to give them. Or they'll complain, 'you didn't give me this,' or 'you didn't give me that.'" Debbie recalled some difficult situations at her low-waged work. "It is stressful. Because some people come in, and they throw hot coffee at you, or they throw their milk shake at you. It's rough."

"Wow, that actually happened?" I interrupted her.

"Oh yes," Debbie replied, with a hint of laughter in her voice. "People have thrown the whole plate of food at me." But that wasn't the worst of it. Debbie shared a sad, poignant story of another experience she had.

"I had just clocked in," Debbie began. "A long line was backed up in the dining area. I saw this lady, who said she had just had a baby, and had walked right out of Temple University Hospital. She was absolutely naked, just like the day she came into the world."

"Was she mentally disturbed?" I asked.

"She must have been," Debbie replied. "Because it was cold outside, and she walked into the restaurant, sat down, and said she wanted something to eat. She was a big, heavy, black woman. She wasn't tiny. And she didn't look like she had just had a baby—there was no swelling around the stomach whatsoever. She looked like she had just stepped out of a mental hospital. The manager came out and put his coat around her, and he called the emergency vehicle and had the officers come get her."

Debbie continued to work at McDonald's until she graduated from high school. During the summer following her sophomore year, she took an additional job that foreshadowed her present line of work. "I got a housekeeping job at State Road Hospital," Debbie said, referring to a Pennsylvania institution for the psychologically challenged. "I always liked to clean, from the time I was a little girl. I always used to help my mom clean around the house. And so I decided then that if I didn't do hair, I would clean. And now I do both."

When she graduated from high school, Debbie got a job at another fast-food establishment. "I was a certified cashier, so I went to work at Roy Rogers," she said. "We used to wear the cowgirl hat and the cowgirl boots, and the little jean dress with the apron across the front." She stayed for six months, working from 6 P.M. to 2 A.M.. Debbie was laid off after half a year's work. While she was unemployed, she met the father of her two sons, a Philadelphia bus driver. "I was going to the eye doctor once, and he was my bus driver, although they call them bus operators," Debbie recalled. "And everywhere I would go on the bus, he would be the driver. So one day, I said, 'I'm going to say something to this man,'" she continued, laughing at the memory. "And, not knowing that he was really noticing me all along, I did the flirting. Once, when I was heading home, I waited for his bus at the bus stop, and since he was the fifth bus going up the route, I figured that he would be the fifth bus returning. I got on the bus, and I didn't realize that he actually knew the stop where I was getting off." After the driver called her stop, Debbie headed to the front of the bus, where the driver handed her a transfer. She wanted to say something to him, but she was too shy to speak. She simply smiled and got off the bus. "I wondered why he had given me the transfer, since I wasn't catching another bus. I finally flipped the transfer over, and there was his name and phone number on it, asking me to call him after he got off of work. That's how we got together."

Soon, Debbie got pregnant, moved in with her boyfriend, and had another son two years later before they broke up. Debbie then got a job as a certified cashier at a thrift shop. "I was a floor girl, and I was responsible for organizing clothes on the racks. I worked there for a couple of years, before I met my present husband." They met in 1987, and married seven years later. He is twenty-two years older than Debbie, with five grown children. He has been a steadying influence on her two boys, even though her older son had a brush with the law, leading Debbie to send him to an out-of-state disciplinary institution where he recently completed his G.E.D. A year after her marriage, Debbie took her present job as a house-keeper for the leasing units in the temporary apartments above a Center City hotel.

"When a tenant moves in, I have to make sure everything is thoroughly done," Debbie stated. "The baseboards, the walls, the kitchen, including every cabinet and the oven, the floors, the bedrooms, the bathrooms, everything has to be flawless and clean." When I asked her about her workload, Debbie replied, "Monday through Friday, my board is filled with all leasing units. And if we are really busy, they'll add hotel units as well. I could have thirteen leasing rooms on a Friday, plus a new tenant, which means I have to do all of my rooms, plus that new 'move-in.'" Tips are pretty sporadic, sometimes good, but more often, lousy. "Sometimes a leasing unit tenant will leave you a dollar on the pillow." Given that she makes less than nine dollars an hour, her tenants' lack of generosity, even gratitude, is all the more hurtful. Unsurprisingly, most of the tenants are white, most of the housekeepers are black. But that's not where the racial dynamics end. "We have some white women here, but they won't stay," Debbie told me. "I've been here for seven-and-a-half years, longer than a lot of the other housekeepers, and I have seen maybe four or five white girls since I've been here.

No Chinese. A couple of Spanish girls, but that's it. They don't stay. And not many black girls stay either. There is not one girl here from when I started. The white women don't feel like they make enough money to clean these large suites."

As we were about to part, I couldn't resist asking Debbie if she thought people look down on her because of her job. Her answer was surprising. "No, not people who are professionals," she answered. "But there are quite a few people who check out what I do, people who don't have jobs, who don't work, and they say, 'I would never do that. I would rather go without before I do what you do.' I feel like that's looking down on me." Debbie said that professional women adorned in suits usually envy her work. "When I was catching the subway, I would wear my uniform beneath my coat, and when it was cold, you really couldn't tell that I was a housekeeper. And I would see females dressed in a nice suit and carrying a brief-case. And we'd sit together, and they'd ask, 'What do you do?' When I told them, they'd say that I had a good job and that they wished they were doing what I do. They'd say, 'I'm in front of a computer all day, with my eyes hurting me.' I'd say to them, 'You don't want to do what I do.' But they'd say, 'As long as it's an honest dollar, I'd be more than happy to do it.'"

Of course, Debbie didn't for a moment believe that such folk would genuinely be more happy doing her job, especially if they viewed it as a relief from hard work. "I'd say, 'All right, give me your briefcase and you take my uniform, and go to my job. I guarantee you will be calling me before lunchtime.' This is very hard work. When I first started, after I got home and stretched out on the bed, I wouldn't even hear my husband coming in from work. My whole body would ache."

Debbie is determined to keep up her disciplined regimen at work as an example for her sons. "I've got to survive for my children," she said with calm resolve. "I have to be a role model for them, because if I'm not a role model for my boys, I believe they will just wander off and say to themselves, 'My mom wasn't nothing, why should I be anything?' You know, some kids have that in their minds."

As she left, I gave Debbie a hug, and slipped her a "love offering," as they say in church, for her precious insight and generous time. As my door closed, I thought of Debbie's tremendous character, her steely determination, her hard work, her great beauty, and her quiet embodiment of the splendid virtues of black womanhood—virtues shared by my mother and Barbara. All three of these black women are fiercely proud role models for their children, and for many more people than they might ever imagine.

Part 2

Halls and Hills

IV. Pens and Pages

11

Revolutionaries

"Professor Davis, I must confess that you are the reason so many brothers of my generation joined the revolutionary struggle," I said to Angela Davis upon meeting her for the first time in 1994 at a conference at Princeton. "And I can't lie—it was because you were so fine that we got hooked, then we started digging the politics." I wasn't necessarily proud that this was how things happened, but it was true nonetheless.

Davis was to shortly publish "Afro Images: Politics, Fashion and Nostalgia," her essay about the complications and frustrations of having her identity to a younger generation focus on her famed Afro. "Such responses I find are hardly exceptional," Davis would write, "and it is both humiliating and humbling to discover that a single generation after the events that constructed me as a public personality, I am remembered as a hairdo." I was especially glad the essay was written before she encountered me, or else I might have ended up as one of its cautionary anecdotes. Thank God I had enough sense and revolutionary etiquette not to have reduced Davis to a hairstyle.

I registered my appreciation for her role as social prophet a couple of years later in a long sentence from my essay on black public intellectuals. "A long time ago—when gangsta rappers had the bourgeois blues in their diapers while she was stepping to the revolution; when most celebrated intellectuals were eating their Wheaties, going to Jack and Jill, and courting in the front parlor while she was applying Marcuse to social misery; when more-radical-than-thou critics were enjoying the creature comforts that stoke their dizzy nostalgia for marginality while she was taking three squares in a cramped cell; and when most post-feminists were getting pedicures to put their best foot forward at the debutante while she wore jungle boots at the front line of class warfare—Angela Davis lived what we mean by black public intellectual." But perhaps the roots of the revelation of her revolutionary appeal to me peeked through when I ended my paean by writing in the vernacular: "And she still fine!"

Of course, I had found Davis's Afro appealing, but not simply because it made a fashion statement. Davis's hairstyle in the '70s was a crucial political symbol to a people who had been taught to hate our bodies and appearances. Her Afro was a symbolic salvo in the war to liberate our identities from the worship of the white world, a liberation that was embodied in the "Black Is Beautiful" slogan that many blacks adopted.

When I got my Afro in the late sixties, my mother told me that such a move would forever alter my curly locks.

"You won't be able to get your hair back the way it is now," she warned.

Hair was, and remains, a huge signifier of status in black America. Yellow Negroes like me with soft, curly hair—with "good hair" in that hurtful, implicit comparison to black hair that is kinky, or, in the terms of that devilishly delicious British archaism, "contourtuplicated"—were viewed as higher in the beauty hierarchy than dark-skinned blacks with coarser, matted hair. Thus, to surrender membership in the aesthetic aristocracy betokened in curls was a gesture of political dissent. I had already adorned my neck with the granite, African-headed "tiki." The move to the Afro was the next logical step in my pilgrimage to pride.

When Angela Davis's Afro'd image mushroomed across the global mediascape, it did more than highlight the extraordinary attractiveness of a political renegade. Her presence underscored the legitimacy of black attempts to wrest the dignity of our images from the vicious machinery of self-denigration and the imitation of European ideals of beauty. Moreover, her willingness to sacrifice her elevated cultural status, and to fight for black freedom in the most dangerous fashion possible, made an important statement about how social privilege breeds moral responsibility. Angela Davis's beauty didn't merely reside in her physical stature; it was bone-deep, rooted in the love of black flesh, 'fros, and freedom. When ubiquitous posters of her flooded the ghetto of

Detroit, demanding her freedom from political imprisonment in the early '70s, I pointed to them with a profound sense of identification that I didn't fully understand until years later, when my critical instincts caught up with my "natural" impulses.

My engagement with the politics of Davis's images was heightened when I encountered the photos on her 1974 book, *Angela Davis: An Autobiography*. The book's hardbound back cover featured four black-and-white photographs. The first photo captures Davis as an adorable fifteen-month-old infant in a white pinafore, a watch on her wrist, Mary Jane shoes on her tiny feet, with soft, cottony curls, a gapped-tooth smile, cute pug nose, and an angelic smile. The second photo pictures Davis at seven, her hair in two braids held by berets, a midriff top with a ruffled flounce, short baggy pants that stop four inches beneath the knee, bobby socks, and strapped, toe-out sandals.

The third photo features an eight-year-old Angela, adorned in a short Sunday dress with ruffled, capped sleeves, double-layered ruffles at the hem, anklet socks with lace trim at the top, and a medium-brimmed hat placed near the back of her head in a three-quarter tilt, revealing short bangs and a cascade of pressed curls flowing from the back of her head and falling to her shoulders. The final back cover picture presents the revolutionary in the making in her junior year at Brandeis University, featuring Davis in a feathery, cropped bouffant framing her face, her ears barely peeking out and revealing only the small of her forehead, highlighted by a pensive smile as she rests her chin gently upon her cupped hands.

By contrast, on the full-color front cover, Davis is featured in a full, face-framing Afro whose tightly curled, expansive halo falls right above her super-arched eyebrows. Davis contemplatively peers forward on an angle. Large, thin, silver hoops in her ears set off her softly beautiful face, perfectly elliptical light-brown eyes, and pursed lips. She wears a simple black sweater, delicately cut to reveal a smooth neckline.

For me, the images of Davis on the front and back covers of her autobiography were a visual tour through class, aesthetic history, cultural privilege, racial pride, and revolutionary power. Of course I didn't possess the language to express such conceptual rigor at the time. Neither did I possess the theory to interpret the convergence and clash of images in cultural and historical terms. Nevertheless, I knew there was signifying going on, whether it was intended or not, and that it was related to Davis's remarkable journey.

Davis was born in Birmingham, Alabama, in 1944. She lived with her parents in the projects until she was four, when her family joined the Negro middle class, or, as she points out in her autobiography, "the not-so-poor." Her parents were college-educated teachers, but her father bought a service station in the black section in downtown Birmingham. Davis grew up, for the most part, in segregation. As her neighborhood began to accommodate more blacks—hers was the first black family to integrate the area—it became known as Dynamite Hill because whites bombed the homes of blacks to discourage "mass invasion," a tactic that didn't work.

Davis went to the Elizabeth Irwin School in New York at

fifteen, and in 1961, she entered Brandeis University, where she graduated with honors. Davis' journey led her to Germany to study philosophy, after which she returned to the States in 1967, to pursue her doctorate under Herbert Marcuse, her undergraduate adviser, at the University of California at San Diego. Davis became more politically active, working with SNCC and the Black Panthers to confront her country's deepening racial crisis. In 1968, she joined the Communist Party. She taught philosophy at UCLA a year later, but was fired by Governor Ronald Reagan and the board of regents because of her Communist ties. A court ruling overturned her dismissal, but the regents refused to renew her contract in 1970.

Then her life took a fateful turn. Davis had been an outspoken advocate for black political prisoners, including the prisoners who came to be known as the Soledad Brothers. After prison guards at Soledad prison killed inmate George Jackson, his younger brother Jonathan tried to free another prisoner from a Marin County courthouse by taking hostages. A shootout ensued, and four people were killed. The guns Jackson used belonged to Davis, and while she was nowhere near the courthouse at the time of the fracas, she was charged with kidnapping, conspiracy, and murder. Davis immediately went into hiding and was placed on the FBI's ten-most-wanted list, until she was captured in a New York motel. That's when the "Free Angela" rallies and posters sprang up around the world. Davis served sixteen months in jail before she was released on bail in 1972, and eventually acquitted of all charges. I had learned this story in bits and pieces from local radicals, and of course, from reading Davis's finely honed narrative.

To be sure, the photos on her autobiography were not explicitly political, but her photos were certainly racially significant. They symbolized an evolution from colored girl to Negro young lady to black woman. Thus, not only the style of politics was being referenced, but also, the politics of style. Davis's book cover testified to the cauldron of color caste, class privilege, educational hierarchy and occasionally, class suicide, which seethes in black America. As her hair changed, so did her political identity and consciousness. Of course, there is no strict correlation between racial authenticity and follicle correctness. As Davis suggested, there is no right way to appear as a revolutionary. It is, perhaps, one of the negative consequences of her global fame that it froze in the minds of millions of people the definitive image of the righteous revolutionary. Still, it is noteworthy that Davis literally left her straightened mane behind—and on the back cover of her book—and emerged in life, and on the front of her autobiography, as a mature woman in quest of freedom for the world's oppressed peoples.

But Davis has leapt from her book cover, and from the republic of the image that has fixed her, into the arguments and activism that extend her restless pursuit of liberation. And she has continued to play with, and through, her hair, continued to style her politics of resistance to acceptable aesthetic norms with moral grace and beauty. At the Princeton conference where we both lectured, Davis had her hair in dreads, and she has since switched between that and twists, and a crinkled, curly coif.

Of course it would be dreadful for Davis's political and intellectual brilliance to be reduced to a hairstyle, especially a hairstyle shorn of its political meaning. As she said on Australian television a few years back, "It's not that I mind it, but it's just that I think it would be much more productive if there were a little more substance to that historical memory, because as a matter of fact, the Afro—even though it became a hairstyle—has a political history, since the police were known in certain parts of the country to single out people who had Afros, because of the political significance of that hairstyle. The fact that the hairstyle has become disembodied, so to speak, and is what survives of the era, is a little disheartening."

At the same time, as Davis's remarks suggest, it is important to grapple with the politics of style and aesthetics, including hair, because it has huge significance in our culture, and because young people, especially in hip-hop, speak so vibrantly through their bodies. If we could, through a discussion of Davis's styles, encourage black youth to confront the varied and conflicting meanings of their styles, it would surely advance the political consciousness Davis has spent her heroic life creating.

When I finally got the chance to meet Davis, and to make my big confession, she graciously locked arms with me and sat me down for a delightful tête-à-tête. I was reminded all over again why I love and admire her, and discovered new reasons to embrace her radical thinking. I felt a great affinity for Davis because she bravely instigated critical debates about the nation's malevolent obsession with prisons, the subject of her Princeton talk. At the time of Davis's speech, my brother Everett had been in prison for half a decade; he has now been locked away for fourteen years. Her brilliant discussion of the prison-industrial complex was rightly disturbing, warning of the unchecked force of the state to contain and punish citizens. But it was also oddly reassuring, even comforting. I knew that many people of color, including my brother, were wrongly imprisoned, or imprisoned for offenses that got white men or women a slap on the hand from the justice system. It was heartening to know that a woman of her stature was willing to lay her intellectual and cultural capital on the line to defend men and women who were often voiceless and faceless in the country's scheme of justice.

Davis's example rang in my mind as I traveled with a group of black intellectuals and activists to Cuba in 1997, and met another brave black revolutionary who had risked her life in defense of her people's freedom: Assata Shakur. Although she has been recently lionized in the haunting and eloquent lyrics of the rapper Common's "A Song for Assata," Shakur has not, for the most part, been engaged by younger generations in black communities. Undeniably, that has a great deal to do with the fact that since 1979, Shakur has lived either underground or outside the United States, surfacing in 1986 in Cuba. Her story is not nearly as well known as Davis's. Although born in Jamaica, New York, Shakur—christened as

JoAnne Deborah Byron, and known later by marriage as JoAnne Chesimard—was, like Davis, reared in the South, in Wilmington, North Carolina, where she was taken in by her grandparents when she was three. She became a political activist, participating in student protests, the antiwar movement, and in the black freedom struggle.

Shakur joined the Black Panther Party, and as a result, was subject to COINTELPRO, the program initiated by the FBI to harass and stamp out political groups and figures deemed troublesome because they challenged the racist and antidemocratic policies of the American government. In 1973, Shakur and two other members of the Black Panther Party were pulled over on the New Jersey Turnpike, the site most recently of infamous racial profiling cases that sparked a national debate on the subject. A violent confrontation ensued, and Shakur was shot, she described, with both arms in the air, and then shot once more in the back while she lay on the ground. In the gun battle, state trooper Werner Foster was killed, and one of Shakur's compatriots, Zayd Malik Shakur, also lay dead. The third Panther who was present, Sundiati Acoli, is still serving a life sentence for Foster's death.

The near-fatally injured Shakur was eventually taken to a hospital, where she said she was threatened, beaten, and tortured. In 1977, Shakur was charged and convicted of murder by an all-white jury, and sent to prison for life, with an additional thirty years and thirty days added to her sentence. Shakur spent six years in prison, two of them in solitary confinement inside a men's prison. In 1979, Shakur was able to escape, to paraphrase the Beatles, with a little help from her friends, and was granted political asylum by the Cuban government.

A year after our trip to Cuba, Shakur was targeted by New Jersey Governor Christine Todd Whitman, now Administrator of the U.S. Environmental Protection Agency, who mounted an effort to have the race rebel returned to the United States. Whitman argued that the United States should refuse to normalize relations with Cuba as long as Shakur remained free on Cuban soil. The state of New Jersey placed a $50,000 bounty on her head for the successful return of Shakur to the United States. The New Jersey state police even asked Pope John Paul II to help them return Shakur to the States when he visited Cuba in January of 1998. Upon hearing that news, Assata penned a letter to the Pope, writing that "I have advocated and I still advocate revolutionary changes in the structure and in the principles that govern the U.S. I advocate an end to capitalist exploitation, the abolition of racist policies, the eradication of sexism and the elimination of political repression. If that is a crime, then I am totally guilty."

When we journeyed to Havana, in Shakur's fiftieth year, she was in fine form. Like Davis, she had become an international symbol of the struggle for racial equality and social justice. And similar to Davis, Shakur's 1987 volume, *Assata: An Autobiography*, features the revolutionary on the cover of her book. Shakur's tilted head, with a regal nose, looks over her left shoulder in a mushroomed, medium-sized Afro. She has thick eyebrows and full, luscious lips, through which peek, ever so faintly, front gapped teeth, as her big, beautiful, dove eyes peer directly into the reader's face. By the time I encountered her, Shakur was wearing flowing dreads, and was still remarkably fit, voluptuous in fact, and sexy, too, with a smooth, pretty face etched with fine lines of suffering and suspicion.

I got a whiff of her self-protective manner when a few of us drank with her at a bar, and a member of our party requested that she move her seat, which would have placed her in a vulnerable position. "Oh, no," she politely demurred. "But I don't sit with my back to the door. I never know when someone might be approaching who will snatch me and attempt to return me to the United States."

Later that evening, as the tape recorder ran, Shakur settled her lithe frame onto the floor of a hotel room and regaled our party with a virtuosic display of revolutionary rhetoric. Shakur spoke first about race and racism in Cuba. "When I came to Cuba, at first people were very reluctant to deal or to talk about race, to talk about racism," she said. "You could talk to anybody; they would say, 'Well, there is no such thing. It's been eliminated.' And what I think they meant was that all laws that upheld segregation in terms of housing and neighborhoods had been virtually eliminated." Shakur explained to us that historic patterns of segregation existed in the nation, especially in the geographical isolation of the black people. "In other words, old Havana had a huge number of African people and all of them have not moved to other areas. In areas that were historically black, there are still a lot of black people living there. But I think that the nature of neighborhoods has changed completely and areas that were completely white before are now very mixed."

In the aftermath of the revolution, Cubans believed that racism would fade away as a result of the equality and justice that prevailed. Cubans prided themselves on not having a totally European or African ancestry, but one that was racially mixed. But there were still problems. "Of course, Cuba inherited a racist mentality of white supremacy that existed for hundreds of years," Shakur added. "This was one of the last places where slavery was abolished, in 1886. All the racist ideas that upheld slavery, that justified slavery, were present here. There was a systematic whitening process that was institutionalized in the Spanish form of colonialism. Those attitudes did not disappear after the revolution. In fact, I think that many people felt that the revolution gave them more of a possibility." She argued that Castro and other leaders at the Third Congress of the Cuban Communist Party, however, "talked about race, they talked about gender, and they talked about young people. And there were changes made." Shakur said that such a movement was not long-lasting because after socialism collapsed in Europe, "the revolution was looking at basic, bare survival." As a result, issues of race were marginalized.

Shakur also talked to us about tourism and the global economy, gender, class, the family, social and political alienation, multiculturalism, her optimism about the future, and violence and youth culture, and the amnesia that feeds it. "One of the problems I have with young people, they do not understand what we mean when we say we were fighting for freedom," Shakur offered. "A lot of times, we cannot articulate what our vision of freedom is, so how can we expect them to continue something that we can't express? They're talking about the youth culture, the violence, and some people say that, 'Well, rap creates violence.' I think our consciousness creates what comes out of our mouths and what comes out of our mouths reflects our consciousness." Shakur indicted corporate capitalism's role in the exploitation of vulnerable young blacks, which often leads to self-destructive habits and criminal activity. "Big business uses what comes out of young African people's mouths to pollute other young African people with ideas that are very capitalist. Most [rappers] are saying, 'We want the shit, we want the sneakers, we want the gold, we want everything. You told us we can't have shit, so we're going to be gangsters.' [They're] illegitimate capitalists; that is the only difference."

Shakur also criticized the images of racial authenticity, and the idolization of thug culture, that lead to a social dead end for black youth. "You look at all the videos and you see models making fifty dollars a day, shaking their butts around a swimming pool in a big old house, somebody with their pants hanging down and drawers sticking out, and people think that's 'keeping it real.' That is selling the capitalist dream to people who cannot even sniff at it. They're going to jail and can't even make commissary money. I spent big time in jail and I know what's in there. There ain't no Rockefellers or gangsters up there. But there is a dream that's being sold just like *The Godfather*." Shakur lamented that "the violence of the society is big business," and how, as a result, the question facing Cuba and all just societies is: "How do you build new values? How do you build new human relationships?"

Shakur spoke poignantly about images of black women in the tormented visions of black youth culture, musing on the effect they might have on the family. "They talk about black women being with the families and stuff like that. And all I can think of is: If every guy walked off a video, if one day all these guys came talking, 'Bitch, come get the money; ho, hood rat,' etc., if all these guys walked off the videos and tried to marry somebody, can you imagine that this is some way for human beings to live in, and raise a family?...If we consider political change in more than a structural way, in more than a power way, I don't see how we're going to get social justice, 'cause who is going to live in the society of Snoop Doggy Dogg?"

Shakur was quite moving, as well, as she discussed the need for revolutionaries to pay attention to the intimate matters of human existence. "I had millions of powerful images of what being active in a movement for social change meant. Now I'm in another place in my life—and maybe this is a touch-feely stage that I'm going through—but I like the idea of people relating politically and relating personally, of communion, coming together, having picnics, of people talking about themselves as human beings and not just about social change in the abstract."

Shakur ended our evening eloquently, speaking about the personal and political lens through which she views citizenship, social transformation, and the black diaspora. "I'm one of those people who had to piece my life together with Band-Aids. And I mean that physically, mentally, and every other way. So I don't look at the U.S. as being my country…I'm one of those people that has been alienated. I am a victim. I feel like Malcolm…But I understand that this is a process, and what's going on with us has to become connected with what's going on in Africa, with what's going on in the Caribbean. Because I do see us winning, not by ourselves and not just looking at the United States as this isolated place, but looking at our African ancestors—and whether they are in Cuba, whether they are here—and our spiritual ancestors, whoever they may be."

Angela Davis and Assata Shakur are among the most brilliant, gifted, and beautiful women our race has produced. Their zeal for revolution has not abated. Instead, their vision of social change has been sharpened, and in some cases, redefined, as they remain alert to the movements for freedom that abound. They are the lungs through which justice for our people breathes. Their lives trace the anatomy of greatness black women can achieve when they are willing to sacrifice life and limb to right what is wrong.

12

Taylor Made

"Hi, I waited around to introduce myself," the lithe, strikingly beautiful brown-skinned woman with one of the most recognizable faces in all of black America, said to me. The year was 1998, and I had just gotten off a plane in New York City. "I am such an admirer of your work, and I wanted you to know that."

When Susan Taylor uttered those words, it was as if all of black America was speaking to me. In her fiercely articulate and melodic tone, Taylor captures the rhythms of the black heartland. Her words are often read as the most pristine expression of black spiritual yearning in our nation. Her "In the Spirit" column, which appears monthly in *Essence,* the magazine she has been identified with for more than thirty years, is the watchword of moral beauty in black America and the strong, sure pulse by which millions measure their emotional health. As proof, her books that feature similar essays, including *In the Spirit* and *Lessons in Living*—and a third book, *Confirmation*, co-authored with her husband, the brilliant critic Khephra Burns—have sold hundreds of thousands of copies. Susan Taylor is black America's Queen of Inspiration, the perfect embodiment of racial pride and sisterly solidarity in an age when either virtue has been diminished by self-hatred or cultural attack.

"Thank you so much for *your* wonderful work," I replied to Susan. "What you mean to us is incalculable, beyond words. Please keep spreading your magic."

Since then, I have come to cherish Susan as a dear friend and wise counselor. Her words have often melted confusion in my head and sent me searching for the elusive self-love that she has taught a nation of blacks to pursue with remarkable resolve. If Susan has trumpeted the gospel of loving oneself, it is not because she learned its stirring accents in her own home. In a number of columns, Susan has openly discussed the lack of tenderness she experienced during a difficult upbringing. She remarked on "the picky criticism that so characterized my mother's attitude toward me." Earlier, Susan wrote about the time she "responded unemotionally to my mother's insults and harshness. I didn't storm out the door; there were no tears, no attitude. Something in me had shifted...She'd been hurting my feelings all my life. I was neither the bad girl she had perceived me to be, nor the irresponsible woman of her invention." Susan reiterated in a later column that her "mother found me difficult, and her harshness toward me hurt my heart."

Fortunately, Susan's grandmother nestled her warmly in a womb of love. Susan recalled the "feeling of confidence and comfort" she received during the summers before her tenth birthday, a feeling she has since worked to reclaim. "Come summer, my grandmother [called Mother] would take my brother, Larry, and me from our cramped Harlem apartment to her rambling home in Englewood, New Jersey." Susan conjured the reverie of crossing the Hudson River in "Mother's big black Buick," which was like "entering a new world where I felt cherished. Mother would give me lots of kisses. She'd do magical things with my fine, kinky hair and 'grease' my skinny brown legs so they'd glow." Susan greatly enjoyed the freedom of roaming the land, catching fireflies, dancing in the rain, and jumping the ocean waves at the shore. "I could ride my bike all day, and believed that if I dared lift my wings, I could rise and soar like an eagle. When I was with Mother, I was the sky and the surf and the rain."

When summer was over, Susan went back home to face the strains of affectionless parents. "I'm a lovebug, but Babs and Lawrence, my parents, never seemed to touch or talk to each other much. Likewise, touching and tenderness were absent in any communication between them and me." Her childhood experiences made Susan more determined to luxuriate in love as an adult. Still, she learned crucial lessons growing up in the storied capital of black America.

"I was born and raised in Harlem, a safe Harlem, in the 1940s and '50s," Susan, who was born in 1946, recalled of the neighborhood in which her Caribbean immigrant parents owned a clothing store. "By the end of the '50s, it became a little dangerous, as drugs began to come into the community and run roughshod over it. I was there at the end of the glory days." The vibrant memory of Harlem has undoubtedly fueled Taylor's determination to rescue black America from material deprivation and moral decay. Susan draws upon her family's example to project the possibility of strong entrepreneurship as one answer to eroded black self-determination. "My grandmother, Rhoda Weekes, who came to the United States from Trinidad in 1916, had a little tailor shop and went on and really built a major business in Harlem," Susan said. "And even her mother, who I am named after but never had the honor of meeting, had a hot pepper sauce business and a soda business in Trinidad in the late 1800s. So I come from a long line of black women entrepreneurs."

It was not only her foremothers' sturdy sojourn in their nation's business mainstream that inspired Susan to succeed. She also derived strength from the collective efforts of black women whose backs were against the wall, but whose faces looked upward and beyond the misery of their immediate limitations to confidently claim a victory they trusted would fully come through their children. "I think when we look at the history of black women who made a way out of no way, who, without the resources that women of other cultures in this nation had to support them, our women just used those internal strengths and the kind of strength that we draw from each other," Susan said. "And they raised families, built schools, and churches, and took care of white families, and went back across town and took care of their own families and their parents and their husbands' parents. So I feel like I come from a mighty race of women."

Susan was a bright child, and her inquisitive intellect was fed at Catholic schools, where she was an excellent student. That didn't stop her teachers from withholding affirmation. Susan wrote, "The Irish nuns who taught me didn't hide their disdain for the Black-skinned children in their charge." After she graduated from high school, Susan eventually married William Bowles, who owned a thriving hairdressing salon. When she became pregnant, her husband began having affairs, leading Susan to divorce him soon after their daughter was born. Financially strapped, Susan faced the difficult task of rearing a daughter and paying a $400 monthly rent from the $500 she earned each month as a beautician. She began to suffer symptoms of enormous stress in the grip of her negative circumstances. One afternoon, after leaving the office of her physician—who admonished her to reduce the pressures in her life—Susan had a life-changing encounter. She happened into a church service where a clergyman preached that one could control one's life through one's mind, and that God lived within. Susan internalized his message, and found new energy and focus, and a determination to rescue herself from impending emotional disaster.

Susan's entrepreneurial instincts flourished, and in 1970, she started Nequai Cosmetics, taking her company's title from her daughter's middle name. Susan's company fit a need black women had to find cosmetic shades to match their skin colors. She created a successful line of beauty products for black women, marketing them out of a salon in the Bronx, and also taking them to the Caribbean, establishing a very solid business. When Susan heard that a fledgling magazine named *Essence*—started by four black businessmen, including Edward Lewis and Clarence Smith—was looking for a beauty editor, she tapped into her newfound self-confidence and applied for the job.

"I had nothing beyond a high school diploma," Susan said—she later earned a B.A. from Fordham University—"but I was a licensed cosmetologist. I presented myself to Ida Lewis, and she believed in me, because I believed in me, and she gave me an opportunity to create a beauty story for *Essence*. That was well received and she gave me a second opportunity. That was well received again. Then there was a real shake-up at *Essence*, and Ida left, and Marcia Gillespie became editor-in-chief. At that point, Marcia brought me in not only as beauty editor, but also added fashion to my job. That was in 1971. I started in both those capacities, responsible for the covers—and fashion and beauty—until 1981, when Ed Lewis promoted me to the editor-in-chief's position."

Since she ascended to that post, Susan has become the face and defining spirit of *Essence*. She is the most vibrant and powerful symbol of a magazine that, to Susan and its founders, is much more than a distinctive brand in the marketplace. "We are really on a mission," Susan declared. "And the mission is to put the tools of empowerment in the hands of our people." Of all the empowerment struggles she has waged in the last thirty years, Susan has perhaps most visibly been involved in image warfare for black women. When *Essence* was launched in 1970, there were, besides *Ebony* and *Jet*, precious few media outlets for black women to reflect their critical intelligence and their surpassing beauty. "There are so few places where black women can be affirmed in this society," Susan argued. "In fact, what we're conscious of is our absence—the absence of our images. So in *Essence*, yes, black women's beauty, intelligence and power is affirmed on every page." Although *Essence* began as a fashion magazine, its readers soon demanded a more rigorous engagement with the social forces that shaped their lives. *Essence* responded by broadening its intellectual horizon and deepening its political content. "The editors have really stayed very close to the issues that concern black women," Susan said. "We've not bitten our editorial tongue and we've really reported honestly on black women's lives and their concerns."

Under Susan, *Essence* has been an especially crucial vehicle to rebut the vicious stereotypes that plague black women. Through her visible bully pulpit, Susan has done battle with the negative images that persist in the culture, images that can have devastating consequences on the psyches of black women. Susan has relentlessly urged teen girls "who might not have strong role models within their homes" to seek them beyond their families. She has encouraged teen girls to "read widely," perusing the "work of strong women writers, like Toni Morrison and Alice Walker." She has also urged her young charges to read "about the queens in history, and women who led countries and municipalities and states. And there's a long and rich history of women who forged this country; it wasn't all done by men. And I think, 'To the victor belongs the spoils.' Whoever gets to write the story gets to tell it." Susan said that because "there are people who are racists and sexists," we must "build coalitions and change people's minds." Susan has been vigilant in fighting the harmful images that cloud the minds of black girls because she has painful memories of youthful struggles with her self-image and identity.

In fact, one of the most poignant memories I have of Susan is her confession on national television that she was beset by doubts about her beauty as a growing child. "When I was growing up, I was looked at as very thin and unappealing," Susan said in 1999 on ABC's *20/20*. "My legs are very, very thin. And I thought about getting silicone implants." In a split second, she reflected on her frank admission but trooped on, recognizing, it seems, that her words might bring comfort to other girls who were similarly plagued. "I can't believe I'm saying this on television. This insecurity about my legs really happened as a young woman walking through the streets of Harlem. And you know, when men would call out things to you, or boys would call out things, if you didn't acknowledge them, they called you a skinny so-and-so."

Susan also stated that she tries in the pages of *Essence* to combat the rigid views of beauty that prevail in our society—views tied to body type and pigment—but that a narrow standard is still dominant. "You should be five-seven, at least," Susan summed up this punishing ideal. "Five-nine is even bet-

ter today. A woman should have high cheekbones. You should
be curvaceous, but very thin, a very thin waist, roundish hips,
high, round behind, but not too round, not too high. If you're
blonde and fair and blue-eyed, then you're perfect. If a woman
doesn't look like that, it often causes her great anxiety." As an
example, she pointed to a dispiriting trend among Asian
women. "It's interesting and very sad to see how [that ideal]
oppresses women," Susan lamented. "We have Asian women
who are opting for eye surgery to make their eyes appear
more European, missing what is so uniquely beautiful about
Asian people."

Susan concluded that minorities and others had to pressure
the nation's image managers to produce more realistic and
healthy representations of women of color. "I think we need
to say to image makers in Hollywood, and on Madison
Avenue, and those of us in magazines, that, 'You've got to
show us a more real representation of who we are as people,
because it's damaging our children,'" Susan argued. "'It's
already damaged us, and those of you who are in those positions have a responsibility as image makers to at least make
people feel comfortable in their skin.'" Although it seemed a
lesson that should have been learned decades before, the
nation stood in need of schooling, and for that night on television, at least, Susan was their teacher.

Of course, the role of teacher is one that Susan has vigor-
ously pursued, both within the magazine and beyond its
bounds. She regularly travels to university and community
venues. I am invariably lecturing at a school where she has

been, or preceding her in the path of enlightenment. As she has spoken to college students about her personal and professional struggles, Susan has encouraged youth to call on their spiritual and moral gifts, as well as their intellectual and racial resources, to create meaningful lives. Her advice has been particularly helpful to black students who come from religious homes, but who are not well equipped to balance critical inquiry and spiritual introspection. It is not uncommon for students to tell me that Susan's powerful words and her reassuring demeanor have changed their lives. Her messages have been direct and transforming: as you change the world, you must change yourself. Self-love is critical to the process of social revolution. Positive images have an edifying effect in forging psychological health. And the Spirit dwells in each of us, awaiting our cooperation to expand its world-shaping, world-changing presence.

At Princeton University in 1996, Susan argued that blacks should advance personally and professionally, while promoting positive images to spark the advancement of blacks around the globe. Susan also said that many blacks lacked the critical thinking and pride in traditional values that were prominent in earlier times and that enabled black progress. "You need to remember what your ancestors lived through in order for you to be here," Susan said. She also urged the Ivy Leaguers to realize their economic power by becoming conscious consumers. Finally, she stressed that the key to the empowerment of the masses is self-empowerment. "You have to give yourself to yourself before you give yourself away," Susan stated. She ended her speech with a pledge of renewal: "I can do this. This I can do. Because I am human and divine, because God is alive in me."

Susan reinforced and expanded her message to students at Iowa's Drake University in 1997 during a Black History Month address. In the university's Bulldog Theater, Susan reflected on some "Lessons in Learning." She encouraged the students to love themselves by spending time alone and by becoming vocal about matters that concerned them. She also urged the students to become more self-critical, and critical of the world they live in. "If we were thinking critically, the problems wouldn't have reached here." As a result of inaction and disinterest, problems multiply. "There is no mobilization of effort, no outcry," she said. "The continuing pain through-out this country is dependent on our inertia. There really is a large task at hand." Susan argued that fundamental social change depends not on the government but on ordinary citizens. "What we have to do is figure out how we can hold this nation—our nation—to a higher moral standard." She also suggested that imagination and creativity could help over-come the nation's problems. Spurning easy answers, Susan implored the students to accept the challenges that offered them the opportunity to grow. "Life is not easy; it's simple, but it's not easy," she said. "Challenges are a natural and important part of life. If not for our challenges, we'd never come to know our strength."

Susan argued that spiritual reflection and meditation are important avenues to personal growth. "Quiet time is the

most important time that any of us can take," she said. "We're
losing ground because we're biting our nails to the quick,
running around in circles, trying to do more and more, putting more and more on our agenda and not taking anything
off." But self-love is the most important thing one can learn, a
virtue that comes in spending time by oneself. She suggested
that the loved self is the precious vehicle through which God's
power and presence flow. "God doesn't work *for* you, but
through you," Susan said. "When you're loving you, everything
in your life begins to work. The only love you really need is
your love. That's the only love you can count on." Arguing
that black history is a triumph, and not a tragedy, Susan ended
by suggesting that contemporary blacks should be grateful for
the sacrifices of our ancestors, a memory that might tame our
cynicism and shortsightedness, and focus our attention on the
uplifting features of our condition. "The wonder is not how
many of us have perished, but how many of us have survived."

The survival of black people against overwhelming odds has
also been a constant theme of Susan's public advocacy. More
than a decade before I met Susan, I recalled that one of her
most animated public debates on television centered on the
effect of drugs on black youth. During an April 1986 appearance on *The MacNeil/Lehrer News Hour*, Susan tangled with
American University scholar Arnold Trebach over the lethal
effect of drugs on black communities. Initially, Susan participated in a one-on-one interview with pioneering journalist
Charlayne Hunter-Gault. Susan told Hunter-Gault that drugs
are "big business" that generates "a lot of money" and that

social gatherings could hardly be held without their destructive, ubiquitous presence. When asked by Hunter-Gault why so
many people resorted to drugs, Susan posited that people "who
are proud and feeling good about their lives" don't habitually
do drugs. She cited societal pressures as a cause, and then linked
drug usage to the kind of labor people perform. "We know that
also in this nation a lot of people are doing rote work, menial
work, work that they're not pleased with. In order to break the
boredom, people reach out for a drink, a sniff of cocaine, a couple of tokes on the freebase pipe."

Susan told Hunter-Gault that drug usage among the
nation's youth was especially intense because the country had
"the first generation of American children who are worried
that their future will not be intact for them," and the first generation "coming along, graduating from schools, I mean, totally
prepared, without a marketplace that's prepared to receive
them." Susan argued that adults were sending youth mixed
messages about drug usage through a contradictory pop culture. She contended that youth can't detect the destructive
consequences of drug usage through the haze of glamorization
that surrounds it. "Somehow it's been seen as hip to be high,"
Susan said, "and I think we have to make it unpopular to get
high. We have to first begin to explain this to children, and
they have to interact with people who have been drug abusers.
They need to hear firsthand how drugs ruin lives. Yes, we don't
have to ask ourselves why people take drugs. People take drugs
because it makes them feel better for a moment. And then it
fries your brain and then it kills you. That's the truth."

When Arnold Trebach argued for the decriminalization of some drugs, and suggested that we tell youth that "many people use all of these drugs without getting hurt," Susan sharply rebuked him. "I don't know anyone who can dibble and dabble in drugs over a period of time and not get hurt," she said. "That's a dangerous statement. That might make youngsters feel, 'Well, you know, I'm going to be in that percentile, that group that doesn't get hurt.' That's how most people approach drugs. They see their friends dying from drug abuse." When host Jim Lehrer turned to Trebach for a response, he was piqued. "I am a scholar, first of all," he replied. "I spend my time reading all the information," and what he read, he claimed, suggested that only some folk got addicted to drugs, and he wasn't interested in telling youth "prophylactic lies" to protect them. Susan jumped right in.

"Well, Mr. Trebach, what about freebasing?" Susan retorted. "What about this thing called crack rock? It's the most addictive drug known to humankind. There are people who will try it one time and not be able to resist it ever again. What do you say to children, 'You might be able to do that once in a while and not get hooked'?" Trebach said he "knew nothing about crack. I've just been reading some stuff on it, and I haven't spoken to anybody who's used it." Susan shot back immediately, "Well, if you're a scholar, Mr. Trebach, you've got to know about crack." When Trebach suggested that he wasn't going to "pick up the hysteria which we generally deal with on these drugs and throw them at our kids," Susan retorted that "we all need to get hysterical about crack. It's time to get hysterical, and I think that hysteria is going to lead to some kind of change." When one considers that the "political economy of crack" was only beginning to flourish, and that the crack epidemic was at its brutal beginning, Susan was prescient in her call to prevent a scourge that claimed thousands of lives in poor, urban black America. Tragically, her foresight proved to be prophetic.

Susan's keen insight was rewarded in 2000 when she was inducted into the Hall of Fame for "literary geniuses" as part of the tenth Annual Gwendolyn Brooks Writers Conference on Black Literature and Creative Writing. During her keynote address at the conference's closing session, Susan argued the necessity of black cultural literacy. "What we do as writers has an impact on our people," she said as the crowd enthusiastically applauded. "We must be literate about our culture and history and know what shapes us. It is about knowing who you are, knowing your history, not only during Black History Month. We must be conscious of the struggle of black people. Our people are in crisis everywhere, from Ivory Coast to America. This is our watch. We must reaffirm our commitment to our people. We must use our skills to empower our people and tell the people the truth."

I have witnessed Susan telling the truth from a distance for twenty-five years. And for the last five years, I have seen her up close—in a spiritual retreat in Brazil, in empowerment seminars in New Orleans at the annual *Essence Musical Festival*, in private conversations in New York—empowering our people by telling them the truth. Susan Taylor—a woman of entrancing speech who possesses the regal bearing of our queenliest sisters; a woman whose trademark braids bespeak a profound connection to the continent that birthed her; a woman whose voluptuous lips suggest our sensuous inheritance from lovely foremothers; a woman whose flawless chocolate skin shines with the incandescent glow of African beauty; a woman whose piercing eyes flash the brilliance of wise ancestors full of majestic intelligence and ennobling warmth; and a woman with a radiant smile that delivers light to poor souls captured by the painful night of self-ignorance—has not only *told* the truth. She has *been* the truth, for me, and for millions more.

V. The Politics
of Representation

13

Waters on Fire

"To your mind, is there even any approximate heir to his legacy in our world today?" Bryant Gumbel asked me in 2000 on CBS's *Early Show* about a successor to Martin Luther King, Jr.

"Well, I think there are many people," I responded. "I look at Maxine Waters, who is an incredibly intelligent, highly gifted, rhetorical master, as well as a politician."

I repeated my praise for Waters the next day in an interview with correspondent Ray Suarez on PBS's *Newshour with Jim Lehrer*.

The high regard in which I hold Waters draws from her bold, courageous, and relentless pursuit of justice, not only for her immediate constituents as a California congresswoman, but as a national leader of the poor, besieged, and voiceless. Whether addressing the inequities in applying the death penalty, the ongoing need for equal pay for women, or the collusion of the CIA in Contra drug trafficking in the ghetto, Waters has been unafraid to speak her mind and tell the truth.

I first caught a glimpse of her alluringly handsome, rich-cocoa face, her gorgeously voluptuous lips, her petite and shapely frame, and her formidable intelligence in 1990, in a meeting for an initiative for Jesse Jackson. Waters had been a vocal member of Jackson's two presidential campaigns, in 1984 and 1988, and now she was consolidating national support as she prepared to take her place in Congress. She had already served for fourteen years in the California State Assembly, sponsoring legislation to divest the state pension funds from South Africa, to buttress affirmative action, to prevent child abuse through training, and to prohibit police strip searches for nonviolent misdemeanors.

Over the next decade, I got an even better chance to personally witness Waters's political magic up close, even as I often followed in the wake of her linguistic whirlwind. I met Waters again in 1994 when we both testified in the United States Senate before a Juvenile Justice subcommittee chaired by Illinois Senator Carol Moseley-Braun. Entitled "Shaping Our Responses to Violent and Demeaning Imagery in Popular Music," the hearing aimed to get at the roots of social pathology caused, or encouraged, by contemporary music. Moseley-Braun declared at the outset to the standing-room-only crowd of over three hundred that rappers were not singled out, but of course, they were, especially Snoop Doggy Dogg. The proceedings turned out to be a referendum on gangsta rap, the subgenre of hip-hop that was then the rage, or scourge, of the nation, depending on where you stood.

In the high-stakes political battle to associate a unique moral decadence with performers who hailed largely from her district, Waters, due to her principled advocacy of artistic freedom, had little choice but to defend the lives and lyrics of these black outcasts. Although she has never been uncritical or undiscerning in her support for rappers, Waters has consistently been at the forefront of protecting their right to unrestrained speech.

On a brisk February morning in 1994, Waters took her seat, alone, at the Senate panel table, to tell her side of the story of gangsta rap. Waters argued that rap emerges from its environment of production, a suffering and brutal context of poverty, rage, and despair. She quoted a lengthy passage from Snoop Doggy Dogg's "Murder Was the Case," in which a young man facing death asks: "Dear God, I wonder can you save me?/ My boo-boo is about to have a baby, and I think it is too late for praying." Waters conceded that epithets against women in the music are dispiriting, and that the relentless cursing is indeed offensive, but that as bad as it was, it wasn't the worst of what young blacks confronted. "But I have to tell you all," Waters pleaded to her congressional colleagues, "I am more truly bothered and grieved, however, by the painful landscapes these songs paint—story after story about young black men losing their way and losing their fight in this nation of ours." She concluded that Snoop, Ice Cube, Ice-T, Queen Latifah, Dr. Dre, and Yo-Yo, "are our artists and our poets. Let's not lose sight of what the real problem is. It is not the words being used. It is the reality they are rapping about."

Waters's empathy with the black despised has its roots in her own humble origins. She was born in 1938, the fifth of thirteen children reared by a single mother in a St. Louis housing project. Her mother, Valerie Moore Carr, worked a series of low-waged jobs to supplement the meager money she garnered on welfare for her large brood. Waters began working at the age of thirteen, laboring in factories and segregated restaurants. Her future brilliance flashed in her high school years; the yearbook predicted that she would one day become the Speaker of the House of Representatives. But the fulfillment of her promise was years off.

After she finished high school, Waters married and had two children. In 1960, she and her family moved to Los Angeles, where Waters worked in garment factories and at the telephone company. She eventually organized a Head Start program in Watts, after graduating from California State University at Los Angeles and being divorced from her husband and rearing her children alone. Her Head Start experience prompted her to become politically active, and soon Waters became the chief deputy to Los Angeles city councilman David Cunningham. She not only managed Cunningham's campaigns, but she became active in the campaigns of Senator Alan Cranston and Los Angeles mayor Tom Bradley, the first black to ascend to the city's helm. Her tireless work earned her a reputation as a legislative and organizational whiz, and a spot in the state legislature in 1976.

If Waters's early struggles have fueled her passion for the poor, her fiery and fearless stances on behalf of the oppressed—whether by racial, sexual, or economic forces—have galvanized progressive forces throughout the nation. Waters has spoken bravely to troubling social issues that few of her colleagues are inclined to engage. In the aftermath of the Los Angeles riots of 1992—a social conflagration to which she heroically responded, and which thrust her immediately onto the national scene—Waters introduced a bill to provide $10 billion to combat urban decay, arguing that America's urban centers deserved the same massive support tendered to Russia and Israel. The bill would also provide job training for black males between seventeen and thirty, promote an increase in black ownership of small businesses, and toughen antidiscrimination banking laws.

In 1996, the year she was elected to chair the Congressional Black Caucus (CBC), Waters called on the "House to pass legislation authorizing an Iran-Contra-type Select Committee to investigate the charges raised by reporter Gary Webb from the *San Jose Mercury News*, and others, regarding this government's knowledge of drug-related activities in the early 1980s—connected to the C.I.A.'s early efforts to fund the anti-Sandinista rebels in Nicaragua." Waters took a great deal of heat from the political establishment and the media over her stand; some painted her as a political kook lost to conspiracy mongers on the left-wing fringe. She soldiered on, and although the House did not pursue the matter to the liking of community activists, Waters managed to spark a crucial national debate about the role of crack cocaine, underground economies, and the willing, or inadvertent, complicity of the government in the social suffering of poor blacks. Waters remained consistent in her attempts to force the government to confront the destructive consequences of the vaunted war on drugs, which, in the words of Tupac Shakur and Lani Guinier, is a war on poor black and brown people.

She was especially vocal on the racial disparities in sentencing recommendations—predictably, poor blacks and Latinos were mostly caught with crack cocaine, and wealthier whites were arrested for abusing powder cocaine. In 1998, President Bill Clinton directed the Justice Department to bring before Congress new sentencing recommendations that called for a five-year mandatory minimum threshold for crack, at 25 grams, and a corresponding threshold for powder at 250 grams, a 10-to-1 ratio. As patently unjust as these sentencing guidelines were, they were actually an improvement—the former recommendations reflected an atrocious 100–to–1 ratio. To twist a Clinton phrase applied to affirmative action, it mended, but didn't end, the racial disparity. It still took ten times more powder cocaine than crack cocaine to warrant the same sentence.

Waters was courageous enough to oppose a political ally when the White House claimed it had consulted with the Congressional Black Caucus in generating its new sentencing recommendations on crack and powder cocaine. "We have fought very hard to make people understand the disproportionate impact of these disparities on African-American and

Hispanic communities," Waters wrote President Bill Clinton in a letter on behalf of the CBC. "These impacts have been cited by the U.S. Sentencing Commission, General McCaffrey"—who was the nation's drug czar—"and even the President. Yet, these new recommendations call for continuing disparities, rather than eliminating them as they should be." Playing no favorites, even with friends, Waters added the damning blow. "While the recommendations are an improvement, they are far from fair. If the White House had consulted with us, as they claim, considered our views and then rejected them, that would be one thing. We wouldn't be happy with their conclusions, but we could live with that. But to claim consultation when there was none, is unacceptable."

A year earlier, Waters stood in the halls of Congress to decry the gender wage gap on the Thirty-fourth Anniversary of the Equal Pay Act. "Thirty-four years later—and women still don't have pay equity," Waters thunderously declared. "Thirty-four years later—and women still face a glass ceiling. Thirty-four years later—and we still have a long way to go." Waters said she was proud to stand with her female colleagues in Congress to mark the anniversary, but that the Act had not remedied the undervaluing, and underpaying, of women's work. "White women still face a pay check that is only seventy-one percent of what men earn. Women of color face even more severe inequities: Black women earn only sixty-four cents; Hispanic women only fifty-three cents for every dollar earned by a white man. That racial disparity is our next hurdle." Waters argued that when women are paid lower wages, the entire family suffers, since the ideal of the nuclear family was long since debunked, and women worked alongside their men to provide for their families.

Moreover, black and Latino women anticipated current trends of work among white women, largely out of economic necessity. "Women of color—families of color—have rarely had the luxury of a woman staying home as a full-time mother." Waters also assailed the wage gap as "the opportunity gap. Women are segregated into jobs that are traditionally low paying—clerical support or service oriented. Less than thirty percent are in the higher paying managerial positions. Until that glass ceiling is lifted, equal pay will still mean lower wages because the opportunities for advance will be fewer." Waters ended by suggesting that the approaching millennium should reward the efforts of women and all working people. "We are moving toward a new century. That new era should mark full equality for all American workers, no matter what their gender, no matter what their race."

If Waters has been vigilant on the drug war, she has been equally insistent that her congressional colleagues address the racial disparity in the death penalty. Of course, Jesse Jackson has been a vocal opponent of the death penalty for years, on the grounds that it severely discriminates against blacks and Latinos. And Supreme Court Justice Thurgood Marshall, in *Furman v. Georgia*, had concluded that capital punishment "is imposed discriminatorily against certain identifiable classes of people." In 1998, the Death Penalty Information Center issued a report, "The Death Penalty in Black and White: Who

Lives, Who Dies, Who Decides." The report proved that the race of the defendant is the greatest determining factor in administering the death penalty. Black defendants are four times more likely to receive the death penalty than whites and nonblacks who commit the same crimes. The report also showed that in the thirty-eight states that impose the death penalty, ninety-eight percent of the prosecutors who decide to seek the death penalty are white, while blacks and Latinos constitute one percent of prosecutors who decide the death penalty.

Further, in ninety-three percent of the states where race and the death penalty have been examined, the death penalty was much more likely to be imposed for the murder of a white victim. Waters argued in a press conference that the report was "troubling, but not surprising. This report clearly demonstrates that racism in the application of the death penalty is pervasive. I know that some of my colleagues want this issue to go away, but it will not." Waters called on the General Administration Office (GAO) to "study how District Attorneys are elected or appointed. The study will also look at the term of office, the role of prosecutors in the implementation of the death penalty, abuse of discretionary power, and the criteria considered for outreach and diversity. We will also ask the GAO to outline steps that can be taken to eliminate racial disparities in the imposition of the death penalty."

Waters's strong beliefs and uncompromising commitment to airing her views have led to assaults, especially from right-wing commentators like Los Angeles's Jesse Peterson, founder of B.O.N.D., an acronym for the ill-named Brotherhood Organization of a New Destiny. I debated Peterson on the 2001 King Holiday on the Fox News show *Hannity & Colmes*. Peterson has made a career of attacking black leaders like Maxine Waters and Jesse Jackson, for whom he holds an annual national day of repudiation on King's birthday celebration.

"Jesse Jackson and Maxine Waters and others, for the last forty years, have managed to brainwash and demoralize black Americans," Peterson stammered. "Most black Americans are suffering not due to racism but to lack of character."

"I think that in response to B.O.N.D., which seems to be Bitterness Organized for No Destiny," I shot back, "the reality is this: that Jesse Jackson and Maxine Waters have been some of the most powerful, prophetic leaders over the last thirty-five years. They both exhibit extraordinary leadership. It's one thing to be critical. I think all of us are subject to criticism. But on the other hand, to heap this kind of bitter calumny and rhetorical vituperation on their heads without justifying it by appealing to facts is ridiculous."

I ran into Waters again when we both served as panelists at a town hall meeting sponsored by Tavis Smiley at the University of Southern California, immediately before the 2000 National Democratic Convention. After our confab, Waters invited me to hang with her during the Democratic convention.

"Why don't we get together Tuesday morning and go over to the Democratic National Committee Black Caucus meeting, where Joe Lieberman is going to appear," Waters urged.

"I'd love to do that, especially since I want to see the fall-out from his place on the ticket," I replied in accepting her invitation.

Ever since Al Gore had announced Connecticut Senator Joseph Lieberman as his vice-presidential running mate, there had been wide concern in liberal and progressive black camps. Lieberman's past flirtations with attempts to end affirmative action made him an especially vulnerable candidate among black voters. The prospects of supporting the first Jewish candidate to be selected for such an honor was heartening to blacks who had forged powerful, though troubled, coalitions with Jews in the past. To be sure, those alliances had been weakened over strong black support for Palestinian rights, and by vocal Jewish opposition to affirmative action. Gore was sending an unmistakable sign that the conservative politics of Bill Clinton would have a prominent place in his potential administration, a sign that was surely troubling to liberal and progressive blacks. After all, Clinton supported the death penalty, enacted welfare reform, and transformed the Democrats into a fiscally conservative party that took more pride in balancing the budget than mending the safety net for black and brown mothers.

At the Los Angeles hotel where the black caucus of the Democratic Party huddled, Waters fled to the front to look Lieberman squarely in the face. It was sweetly strategic, since, as Newhouse News Service reporter Jonathan Tilove observed, "With the notable exception of U.S. Rep. Maxine Waters of Los Angeles, who has raised questions about the

Lieberman choice, the rest of the black establishment has lined up behind him." Lieberman did a predictable song-and-dance about his historic support for blacks, and attempted to explain away his support in 1995 of Proposition 209—the California ballot initiative that scrapped racial and gender considerations in the Californian public sector—as "naïve." Lieberman's saving grace was that he had consistently voted in the Senate to defend weakened versions of affirmative action.

During his appearance before the caucus, Lieberman publicly recognized Waters, telling the crowd it was her birthday, and leading the singing of "Happy Birthday."

Afterward, Waters, who had been noticeably absent from the dais that included many other members of the Congressional Black Caucus, joined Lieberman on stage, as they briefly held hands. Lieberman had not yet convinced Waters to relent in her demand that he reassure black voters of his principled commitment to issues of racial justice. And he could be certain that if and when she did support him—and she did, eventually—it would be based on an independent assessment of his value to blacks, in the Party and the nation, and not as a result of groupthink.

After the event, Waters grabbed me again.

"Come and go with me over to the Shadow Convention," Waters signaled me. "I've got to give a speech on national drug policy, and I think they definitely need to hear from you as well." Arianna Huffington, the columnist, activist, and self-described "recovering Republican," had helped to organize gatherings at both the Democratic and Republican

Conventions of 2000, to "shadow" these ornately orchestrated events with more to-the-ground thinking about social issues, especially the war on drugs, along a continuum of political thought.

I was more than a little surprised by Waters's offer. I had been in the company of black leaders of all sorts, at every level, for years, and many of them were uncomfortable with, even put off by, intellectuals and critics, especially those who had notoriety and an independent base of cultural appeal. Many of these leaders didn't mind you operating behind the scenes to supply them critical thinking; neither did they mind throwing you a bone or two when it made them look good, when it added to their prestige of having a big brain around to render praise or give analysis of their projects. But rarely did I encounter a secure leader who was neither intimidated, nor inclined to be crassly utilitarian, in his relation to the black intellectual. Waters proved to be a refreshing exception.

As we took the short drive over to the Shadow Convention, Waters and I chatted about our perceptions of the caucus meeting, and our ideas about the troubling direction of the national Party, with its conservative, neoliberal politics. When we arrived a few minutes later, Waters and I went to the green room, before tracing our way along the crowded wall of the convention hall to the holding area backstage. There we met Huffington, and *Politically Incorrect* host Bill Maher, whose show I was to appear on shortly, as well as Susan Sarandon and Tim Robbins, the politically progressive acting couple, and Jesse Jackson, who was slated to speak after

Waters. We all greeted each other warmly, and then Waters was whisked on stage to speak.

"Thank you, thank you so very, very, much," Waters gleefully responded to the thunderous applause that greeted her introduction. Then she got right down to business. "There is no war on drugs going on in America today, and Barry McCaffrey needs to resign right now." She was interrupted by applause. "He needs to stop pushing policies that send our tax dollars to Columbia, supporting these right-wing dictator types!" More applause welled up from the audience. "And move out of the way and allow us to develop some good policies that are going to stop incarcerating the victims of this so-called drug war." Waters then gave a critical context to her efforts to call the government to account for its policies. "I want you to know that you are seated in this building right on the edge of the community that the CIA allowed to be over-run with drugs. They turned a blind eye to the dumping of tons of cocaine into this community, all the way back down through South Central Los Angeles, that has destroyed lives, destroyed families, literally destroyed our communities. As a result of what they have done, they have left a lot of broken homes, a lot of young people were incarcerated." But Waters wasn't letting black folk off the hook. "One young man, who was stupid enough to go along with the okey-doke, found himself with a life sentence for cooking up the cocaine that was dumped into the community, the profits from which were used to fund the war down in Nicaragua, the Contras versus the Sandinistas."

Waters was fiercely eloquent as she waylaid the hubris and heartlessness of politicians whose policies hurt poor black and brown people. She argued that California should lead the way in a new drug policy.

"I'm going to tell you why, why we've got to lead the way for it in California, in my own state. California ranks number one in the incarceration of drug offenders. Nearly half of all drug offenders imprisoned in California last year, were imprisoned for simple possession of drugs. In New York, ninety-one percent of those imprisoned last year for drug offenses were locked up for possession of one of the state's three lowest level drug offenses." Waters lauded a community activist who was present for his efforts to "stop the madness" through a ballot initiative, Proposition 36, designed to decrease the number of citizens locked up for minor drug offenses. After praising these efforts, Waters sailed to her conclusion.

"I'm going to just wrap up by saying to you, with less than five percent of the world's population, the United States has one-quarter of the world's prisoners. The rapid expansion of the U.S. prison industrial complex has been fueled by the so-called war on drugs. On June 8, 2000, the Human Rights Watch released a report which found that African-American men are imprisoned for drug crimes [at a rate greater than] thirteen times that of other citizens. I have said over and over again, America has a problem with drug addiction and we cannot continue to incarcerate our way out of this health crisis. I have introduced HR 1681, the Major Drug Trafficking

Prosecution Act, to correct the misguided policy of mandatory minimum sentencing."

As she gestured toward me backstage, Waters gave her concluding remarks.

"I want to bring on a friend of mine, but I just want to close by saying that this 'lock 'em up and throw the key away' mentality has got to stop. We have got to understand we cannot continue to spend more money on prisoners than we are spending on education." Speaking of politicians who reaped financial benefit from campaign contributors who "have a stake in us keeping people in prison," Waters drove home her theme. "They want the prisons to grow so that they can make money in this privatization of the prisons. You have to understand there is a direct connection between the growth in this industry and the campaign contributions and the public policy. We're smarter than that. We're not going to continue to let them do it."

As she was interrupted by waves of applause, Waters embraced the crowd.

"God bless you! Thank you! Thank you! I want to introduce my friend. I want to introduce you to a man that you need to know, Michael Eric Dyson, Professor of Religion at DePaul University. You think I've got some thoughts about this imprisonment of young people; that I've got some thoughts about this lack of a real war on drugs; that I've got some thoughts about the prison industrial complex—you ain't heard nothing yet. Michael Eric Dyson, come on out here."

As I stepped onto the stage, I hugged Maxine tightly, not only for her generous gesture of having me to speak, but for her life of dedicated service to speak for those who can't speak for themselves, a life driven, like mine, by the palpable memory of deprivation, and the recall of gentle souls who didn't deserve the predicament in which they were trapped. Maxine Waters is a giant of a woman, a prophet in political dress who continues to fire our social imaginations about the wondrous possibility of helping those who can't help themselves, and thus fulfilling our highest obligation as citizens and human beings.

14

Lee Way

As I strode to the pulpit to preach at the 7,000 member strong Union Temple Baptist Church, nestled in the heart of Anacostia, one of Washington, D.C.'s poorest black neighborhoods, I fixed on the warm, open, attractive face of Barbara Lee, an instant American hero. After offering greetings to Union's distinguished pastor, Dr. Willie Wilson, I turned my attention to the subject that consumed the nation. This was September 16, 2001, the first Sunday since the horrible events of 9/11.

"I leaned over to Dr. Wilson and asked, 'Is Congresswoman Barbara Lee really *the* only person in the United States Congress to stand up against the machinery of war and vote 'No'?" I shared with the congregation my rhetorical question to Wilson. "And at a time, be reminded, when our sentiments and passions have been shaped by the media to make us believe that the only alternative is to stick our colossal military foot on the necks of people throughout the world without trying to negotiate—which is why we left Durban and couldn't even talk at the table at the World Conference on Racism."

I had just written about the United States' unfortunate withdrawal from the United Nations sponsored "World Conference against Racism, Racial Discrimination, Xenophobia and Related Intolerance," in my weekly column for the *Chicago Sun-Times*, which appeared, coincidentally, on 9/11. It was a topic I could depend on my black audience being familiar with, and judging by their response, I was right.

"That means this is the same government that refuses to acknowledge our pain and the domestic terrorism that we confront on a daily basis in Watts, Oakland, Harlem, and Detroit. The same government refuses to stop racial profiling and police brutality—that's terrorism, too. And now we, as people of color, are being seduced into believing that the only alternative is to do to 'them' what has been done to us, to bomb them as they have bombed us."

As the congregation's enthusiastic endorsement subsided, I spoke directly to the woman who had succeeded Ronald Dellums, one of the nation's most progressive and fearless politicians over the last quarter of the twentieth century.

"So I want to thank you, Congresswoman Barbara Lee, for your bravery, and for your courage. God bless you."

My prefatory remarks were my public declaration of sentiments I had already shared with Lee when we chatted in the pastor's study before the morning service began. On this

Sunday morning, I gave Lee a big hug, not only for me, but for all people who loved justice, and who applauded her singular moral strength in standing up to President Bush, and more important, in voting against war.

I had been reading and watching the appalling discourtesy that blanketed Lee in the press—and the demeaning assaults on her reputation as well—all because she chose, in good conscience, to withhold her vote of support for a joint resolution of Congress authorizing the president to "use all necessary and appropriate force against those nations, organizations, or persons he determines planned, authorized, committed, or aided the terrorist attacks on September 11, 2001."

Lee represents California's ninth district, a well-documented hotbed of progressive politics. Before climbing to Congress, she served as chief of staff for Dellums, a pacifist who regularly spoke out against U.S. military action. Lee told me that when she rose that day in Congress, she knew she was making a monumental choice.

"But I had consulted with pastor, and I had a clear conscience," Lee told me. "I knew everything was going to be all right."

The pastor to whom she referred is Dr. J. Alfred Smith, the senior minister of Oakland's Allen Temple Baptist Church, a vital church where Lee belonged and where I had had the opportunity to preach. Smith is an accomplished preacher, and the former head of the Progressive National Baptist Convention. He is also renowned for his gritty social activism: he took on local drug dealers, and at one time had to have bodyguards because of the death threats brought on by his courageous stance. Now it was Lee's turn to bear the cross of scornful criticism, to be protected by a bodyguard because of the death threats she received in the wake of her stand.

That morning as I preached, I easily spotted the government agent assigned to squire Lee through her official duties. The sight of a United States congresswoman having to be defended from Americans who were angry at her for exercising the right to free speech and dissent that made the country great—and which, ostensibly, was a right that any act of American aggression would protect—would have been laughable were it not tragically ironic.

Lee had come to her spiritual home to seek solace and sanctuary from the insane deluge of acrimony that rained down from her fellow citizens. And while it is an overworked metaphor to suggest that a brave person stands alone, Lee was by herself. In the pastor's study that morning, I discovered to what degree.

"No religious organization, women's group, or any other institution came to my defense," Lee responded when I quizzed her about the help she might have been offered from these usually reliable sources of support.

"In fact," she added, without a trace of bitterness, "many of my colleagues in Congress called me to say that they respected my views, but that I shouldn't use this occasion to express my conscience. They argued that I should voice my opinion, but that I shouldn't dissent from a unanimous vote. I couldn't follow their advice."

While Lee listened to her conscience, others, even in her own Party, found it difficult to heed her wise words. Still, her convictions governed her vote—a gesture that defied unregulated political power and defended principled pacifism. The words she uttered that historic day are haunting in their simple eloquence.

"I rise today with a heavy heart," Lee confessed, "one that is filled with sorrow for the families and loved ones who were killed and injured this week. Only the most foolish or the most callous would not understand the grief that has gripped our people and millions across the world. This unspeakable attack on the United States has forced me to rely on my moral compass, my conscience, and my God for direction. September 11 changed the world. Our deepest fears now haunt us. Yet I am convinced that military action will not prevent further acts of international terrorism against the United States."

Her last line suggests a critical truth that the nation must confront in the aftermath of 9/11: we are dealing with a new kind of enemy, one that is neither dependent on nor discouraged by traditional measures of warfare, and one that is sustained by an international network of hatred for American empire. Lee's wisdom on this point has only become clearer as we have fought to subdue a shadow opponent who moves by stealth and conspiracy, forces that are largely unimpeded by conventional measures of attack.

"This resolution will pass although we all know that the President can wage a war even without it," Lee continued, nodding to the temptation of most recent presidents to override the balance of powers and make war without consulting Congress. "However difficult this vote may be, some of us must urge the use of restraint. Our country is in a state of mourning. Some of us must say, 'let's step back for a moment and think through the implications of our action today so that it does not spiral out of control.'"

One need not have been a therapist to grasp Lee's insight that we should refrain from making fateful decisions in the grip of grief. As an analyst of the American psyche, Lee performed an important, if thankless, task: urging us to confront our fears instead of venting our anger in acts of aggression that might bring catharsis, but no end to our troubles.

"I have agonized over this vote. But I came to grips with opposing this resolution during the painful memorial service today. As a member of the clergy so eloquently said, 'As we act, let us not become the evil we deplore.'"

Lee's courage was, to me at least, contagious, and I drew from her ennobling example when I appeared later that month, on *Politically Incorrect*. I suggested on that show that black Americans had little reason to romanticize Osama bin Laden, especially since the recent acts of terror had begun on African soil with the bombing in 1998 of the American Embassies in Nairobi, Kenya, and Dar es Salaam, Tanzania. But with the hatred that the country faced on 9/11, I suggested "America is now a black nation." I also noted that American domestic terrorism, and right-wing ideology, provided a powerful lens through which the nation might look to better understand our predicament.

"In this country, when we talk about some of the ideas put forth by a Tim McVeigh, or people who are engaging in the murder of doctors at abortion clinics," I argued, "the problem is not whether you are Christian or Muslim or Jewish. The problem is: are you a fascist or fundamentalist? And do you believe that your viewpoint is the only one to be taken as legitimate, and is the only one that has moral resonance?"

But taking a page from Lee's book of political courage, I also connected the experience of terror to the rhetoric of acidly conservative forces in our nation.

"The arguments that bin Laden is making against the West, I've heard Bill Bennett make," I said. "I've heard right-wing Rush Limbaugh make them: 'American Multiculturalism and Western popular culture are crazy, stupid, and ridiculous.' And they've made the most ridiculous arguments, in terms of race, and in terms of class and gender and culture in this nation. And I say, 'That's the same stuff.' I don't see the difference between Bennett and Limbaugh and [these anti-American] arguments, in terms of the moral context."

Lee's willingness to take heat for unpopular views inspires me to link black vulnerability and national insecurity in the wake of 9/11: I sought to illumine the unacknowledged history of terror directed toward black life on American soil, while underscoring how the nation had been baptized into the black experience.

"The reality, however, is that African-American people in particular, but others as well, understand that low-grade terrorism is what we confront in this nation every day," I insisted.

"You tell me about arbitrary violence? What happens if my son, who lives in Atlanta, goes out today, and, in reaching for his wallet, some policeman 'mistakes' it for a gun, and then murders him? I tell you, that's terrorizing to me. Now, it's low-grade terror; it's not on the spectacular scale about which we've spoken, but it is an insidious, everyday factor that robs us of a sense of security in this nation. And that's what I think we all feel. That's why I say we're all black now. Everyone understands what it means to be black right now in America."

I also had Lee in mind when I defended the indispensable role of dissent in sustaining democracy.

"When we look at the flag waving, it's not that [blacks] are not American," I argued. "We love America, but we make a distinction between patriotism and nationalism. Patriotism is the critical support of your country in light of its best virtues, and trying to correct it when it's wrong. Nationalism is the uncritical support of America, right or wrong."

When Barbara Lee voted her conscience, she was vilified, but she may be vindicated in the not-too-distant future, like many prophets before her. In the glow of his ascension to heroic status, for example, it is easy to forget that Martin Luther King, Jr., incurred the wrath of the nation when he spoke out against Vietnam in the late '60s, only to look like a sage within a few years. On September 23, 2001, in an opinion piece published in the *San Francisco Chronicle*, Lee explained her opposition to the congressional resolution granting Bush unlimited power to make war. "It was a blank check to the president to attack anyone involved in the

September 11 events—anywhere, in any country, without regard to our nation's long-term foreign policy, economic and national security interests, and without time limit. In granting these overly broad powers, the Congress has failed its responsibility to understand the dimensions of its declarations."

One needs look no further than the saber-rattling of the Bush administration in their lustful itch to attack Iraq—and Bush's early insistence that he didn't need Congress's approval for such aggression—to spot Lee's prescience. A *Washington Post*-ABC News poll suggested that in September of 2002, three-quarters of the American public believed that Bush should seek the approval of Congress before going to war with Iraq. But many of these same citizens were also angry with Lee, who, with her vote, opposed giving the president the very unilateral power he was given on September 14, 2001, by a Congress that believes it should be consulted before the nation's military personnel and resources are committed to war. Even at this early date, Lee looks like a prophet.

Lee's prophetic presence pervaded the sanctuary on that healing Sunday after 9/11. When I concluded my sermon, Lee embraced me with encouraging words.

"You blessed me today," she said as she gently squeezed my hand.

But the truth is that wise black women like Barbara Lee have for centuries blessed our race and nation with wisdom, compassion, and moral vision. But too often, we have punished them for their prophetic insight, and ignored their gifts to our peril.

15

More Than the Law Allows

"Would you mind staying on for a second segment to discuss Jeffrey Rosen's article on critical race theory?" Charlie Rose asked me before we began a taping of his popular show in November 1996.

"Not at all," I replied. "I'd be pleased to do so."

I had developed a friendship with the architect of critical race theory, Kimberle Williams Crenshaw, a brilliant legal theorist who has written intelligently and forcefully about race, racism, the law, black feminism, domestic violence, and civil rights. She is a formidable intellectual whose pioneering vision of relating the law to culture, society, and everyday life, led her to formulate what she termed "critical race theory." As media personality Tavis Smiley—for whom Crenshaw contributes regular commentary to his National Public Radio Show—summed up her dual professorship in colloquial terms, "Kim Crenshaw is so bad and brilliant that she teaches at not one, but two, leading law schools: UCLA and Columbia." Kim is also a warm and gorgeous woman, a honey brown-skinned beauty whose cherubic cheeks, expressive eyes, voluptuous form, and sandy-haired dreadlocks cut a remarkably striking figure.

I had also forged warm relations with Patricia Williams, another partisan of critical race theory. Williams is a Columbia University legal scholar — and later, a McArthur "genius" Fellowship winner — whose fusion of personal narrative and erudite legal reflection in her first book, 1991's *The Alchemy of Race and Rights: A Diary of a Law Professor*, pioneered a new genre of writing within the infamously sterile halls of legal academe. Williams is a tall, distinguished, beige woman, possessed of a regal air and unique attractiveness that radiates through her warm face, her shock of wiry, naturally expanding black hair, her shy smile, and her arresting eyes.

Kimberle and Patricia are sororals of a black female genius, and two of our nation's finest legal minds, whose intense intellectual ferment evokes celebration and controversy. I knew the latter was in the offing on the *Charlie Rose Show*. Therefore, I wanted to stick around to defend an intellectual movement that meant a great deal to ordinary black people, even though I knew most had never heard of it.

I was scheduled to appear on the show to discuss race in the aftermath of the O.J. Simpson criminal trial. The other guests included my dear friend and Smith College president Ruth Simmons, the legendary journalist Carl Rowan, and distinguished public intellectual and Columbia University historian Manning Marable. It happened that George Washington University legal scholar Jeffrey Rosen was also scheduled to talk about his recently published *New Republic* review essay, "The Bloods and the Crits: O.J. Simpson, Critical Race Theory, the Law, and the Triumph of Color in America." Rosen's essay had been praised by newspaper columnist Maureen Dowd, according to Rose, as a "brilliant piece that exposed and explored a lot of important ideas." Rose wanted to take advantage of our presence to help get at the meaning and controversies of critical race theory.

After we finished our segment, the affable and intelligent Rosen joined us. Right off the bat, Rose asked him to explain critical race theory. Saying he didn't want to be "too superficial," Rosen took a stab at breaking down the complex, academic theory for the general public.

"I think that the critical race theory movement was born out of frustration with the achievements of the civil rights revolution of the 1960s," Rosen declared. "The dismantling of formal segregation, critical race theorists believe, failed to improve the status of blacks, or to eradicate racism, or really to improve race relations." Rosen said that the critical race theorists also claim that "our perception of facts" is shaped by race, "and because the white majority can never transcend its racist perspectives, formally neutral laws will continue to fuel white domination."

Rosen was on a roll, and Rose had no interest in interrupting. In fact, Rosen appeared to be interviewing himself.

"So what is the solution to this bleak state of affairs?"
Rosen asked rhetorically, though it nicely served the show's
purposes.

"In the academy there are two solutions that are increasingly taught in the law schools," Rosen claimed. "One is a
movement that's been called storytelling," where critical race
theorists develop narratives "of black empowerment that
might help challenge dominant racial perspectives." Rosen
argued that these theorists have "celebrated things like racial
conspiracy theories that are widely accepted in the black
community, even though they're factually untrue."

I was itching to jump in and argue with Rosen. True, I
wasn't a law professor, but I had studied and taught critical
race theory. I thought Rosen's views were well stated, even as
they veered into the sort of intellectual panic that grips many
mainstream legal scholars when they encounter critical race
theory. But it wasn't quite the time for my rebuttal.

"And then the second prescription, which is known as
legal instrumentalism, is often actually a call to race war," he
continued, while praising Rowan for having deplored such a
prospect. "Some scholars actually embrace the possibility.
And particularly, the most radical scholars have called on
black jurors to acquit black defendants, even when they're
guilty, as a form of racial payback, when sending black men
to jail would not be in the instrumental goals of the black
community. So, in short, it is a very stark challenge to a liberal ideal of the rule of law." Rosen suggested that such a
tack prevented "transracial agreement." In parsing the in-

famous O. J. Simpson criminal trial, Rosen accused lead attorney Johnnie Cochran of "meticulously applying the academic premises that I've discussed with some rather distressing results."

I could hold my peace no longer. I believed that Rosen was presenting an accurate account of some elements of critical race theory, but distorting other features, and I said so. I contended that Rosen's argument about the relation of knowledge and race in critical race theory was misleading, and that critical race theorists maintain a strong link between politics, culture and legal theory to explain the influence of race and gender on the law. I also suggested that Johnnie Cochran was not creating racial division, but acknowledging the radical difference in racial perceptions that already existed between blacks and whites.

After Rosen and I had at it for a few more rounds, punctuated by insightful comments from Ruth and Manning, the host turned to me with a pointed question.

"Well do you support, and are you an adherer of critical race theory?"

"Oh, certainly," I immediately replied as I referred to the volume edited by Kimberle that had collected the major writings of the movement. But I also wanted to highlight the intellectual achievements of black women who don't often receive recognition for their work or, when they do, don't often get the chance to speak for themselves.

"Have Kimberle Crenshaw on the show, have Patricia Williams," I urged Rose. I realized that the debate I had just had with Rosen was only a proxy for the rich dialogue that both of these pioneers could inspire.

In the years since that show, I have learned so much more from Patricia and Kimberle about how they envision the law, how they think it works, and how they use critical race theory to combat injustice. I have also dug more deeply into their considerable work, and I have seen them cogently expound their views in a number of forums.

Williams has greatly expanded the reach of her thinking, especially her social and cultural critique, by writing a lucid, provocative column for *The Nation* magazine. She has taken on a raft of socially relevant issues. In "An American Litany," a column from 1998, Williams wrote about the presidential panel on race inaugurated by Bill Clinton. "After more than a year's worth of labor, the president's advisory panel on race has come back with what by all accounts is a series of 'modest' recommendations aimed at promoting 'harmony,' 'dialogue,' and 'reconciliation,'" Williams wrote. "What times, I think. It took fifteen months just to agree that we should speak nicely to one another."

In a column entitled "Bulworth Agonistes," Williams registers her ambivalence about Warren Beatty's racially charged and politically provocative film, *Bulworth*. "I've gone to see Warren Beatty's political farce *Bulworth* three times now, trying to figure out what I think about it," Williams confessed. "For a popular medium, it's pretty radical. Yet despite the range of *Bulworth's* controversial aspects, the most-discussed issue in the media has been not its take on health care or the insurance industry or campaign finance but the interracial relationship between sixtyish Bulworth and the balefully beautiful and very young flygirl played by Halle Berry." Williams suggests that *Bulworth* is a "wild dream of a movie, a West Side Story-ish allegory, a collage of symbols and telescoped meanings. Perhaps its limitation is that the image of social unity as miscegenation, while well and good as metaphor, is rendered a bit too literally for an American audience, and thus never escapes the paradigm of sexual politics parading as Realpolitik."

Williams had earlier helped to analyze the notion of interracial sex as a means to social change in the film when she commented to the *New York Times* that intermarriage "remains a solution posing as a political tool." That's because, she argued, most black people are already "racially intermingled. Redemptive sex won't do much, if it fails to grapple with the complex histories and causes of racial hatred and violence." Williams's words were not simply the result of scholarly reflection, but rooted, perhaps, in her heritage as the great-great-granddaughter of a slave and a white lawyer.

Years later, I heard Patricia allude to the same point, in a highly charged political context, as we shared a roundtable panel on ABC television's Sunday news program, *This Week*. The roundtable was hosted that morning by Cokie Roberts, and also featured conservative commentator George Will. We covered three subjects: homeland security, the peace plan of Hosni Mubarak, president of Egypt, and a California ballot proposal for racial privacy. Williams was brilliant on all three.

Roberts asked Patricia if President Bush's move to create a department of homeland security was a political or an administrative gesture.

"I think it was probably both," Patricia replied in her characteristically calm demeanor. "I think it's desperately needed as some sort of organizational move." Her next sentence revealed her progressive political interests. They were cast this Sunday in the form of worry about the nation's wretched history of abusing civil rights and civil liberties.

"My great concern is that the majority of what I think the public is concerned about has to do with the lapses in the FBI," she stated, "lapses within the CIA. The organization which falls under the new Homeland Security bureaucracy still doesn't directly address that particular form of lapse, which is exemplified by, for example, the investigation of Timothy McVeigh, or the young man who, I think, was drawing smiley faces with his bombs of mailboxes, but didn't fit the profile." Williams also expressed concern about "how things like the USA Patriot Act, which expands surveillance rights and powers with the CIA, and with the FBI," will "intersect with the investigative powers, the data analysis, that are attributed to this new bureaucracy."

I seconded Patricia's point. I also argued that many blacks were skeptical of the administration's wide-ranging effort to use surveillance of citizens in the war against terror, especially in light of the sordid history of COINTELPRO, the FBI's program to monitor, control and destroy domestic groups— including many civil rights and black freedom organizations—deemed a threat to national security. "I think that people who were then victimized have concerns right now."

I knew that this wasn't the kind of dialogue that *This Week* was used to hearing: a plainspoken, progressive perspective rooted in the historic injuries to minority populations that are usually overlooked in domestic and foreign policy debates. (How much this was true would be later revealed in the pages of the *National Review*, which commented that Williams and I "come at racial issues from a hard-left perspective." After that, accuracy gives way to half-truths, as the magazine calls me "a voluptuary of gangster rap" who argues that Tupac Shakur "emancipated blacks to display their pathologies without shame," while calling Patricia "an unapologetic feminist neo-Marxist.") Patricia brought her moral wisdom to bear on the peace proposal of Mubarak, and the insistence by Israeli Prime Minister Ariel Sharon, as she framed it, that "there can be no peace talks until there is peace. And there's a certain kind of circularity to that. And how one pushes past that intractable position, is, I think, the entire nutshell of what we're talking about."

When the discussion turned to race, Patricia was equally acute.

Cokie Roberts began, "I'd like to move to something that might be happening in this country coming up on the California ballot, a proposal to put on the ballot a racial privacy initiative, which would say that no agency can classify an individual by race, ethnicity, color or national origin," Roberts then turned to Patricia for a response. Williams quickly girded her loins and let loose.

"I'm terribly concerned that in calling it racial privacy, people think that, in fact, you're protecting the public from unethical use of data," Patricia gently but firmly declared. "In fact, this particular initiative would prevent state agencies of any sort from collecting any data on race, ethnicity, national origin—with the exception of law enforcement." That last phrase allowed Patricia to expose the race conscious assumption that lay beneath the supposedly race-neutral policy being touted. Then she pounced with a vengeance.

"In addition, it would not make any exception for surveying or overseeing what one traditionally thinks of as profiling, so that there could be no tracking—I think that is how the initiative describes it—of law enforcement gathering data or arrest records." But she wasn't just taking aim at law enforcement; she had bigger fish to fry, exposing the twisted logic behind the initiative's stated racial aims. "There can be no official data about how segregated schools or neighborhoods are. And I think that that's, in fact, quite the opposite of what one might think of when one hears the notion of racial privacy or some sort of color-blind ideal. In fact, this neutralizes, silences, makes blind—not just color blind—and, in fact, takes the teeth out of, many of the parts of the Civil Rights Act. There can be no enforcement mechanism."

And then, ever so subtly, but with skill and power, Williams alluded to her racial makeup, and the complexity, even arbitrariness, of racial identity, when she fired a rejoinder to George Will's insistence that the Census Bureau in 1990 "had five categories you could check for your race," and that in

2000, there were sixty-three, "because Americans are more and more like Tiger Woods."

"I am Tiger Woods, to some extent," Williams said, brilliantly playing off of the famous Nike ad featuring the famed golfer, while underscoring her larger point. "But the reality is that race is two things. One, race, we think of as culture. It may be something I identify with, in terms of how I was raised within a particular group. But it is also a social imputation that has significant consequences." In one fell swoop, Williams challenged the biological basis of race and schooled Will, and the nation, about how race is made not only in genes, but in society and history as well.

It is that same ability to "drop science" that has characterized Kimberle Crenshaw's lyrical, politically sophisticated public interventions, whether on television, on stage, or in the lecture hall. Crenshaw is well known for her argument in legal circles—put forth in groundbreaking articles like "Mapping the Margins: Intersectionality, Identity Politics, and Violence Against Women of Color"—that race, gender and class, among other features of social identity, intersect in complex fashions, most of which are rarely acknowledged. As a result, feminists often overlook race, while black communities often slight gender. Her complexity of analysis surges forth wherever she shares her intellectual gifts. Kim skillfully translates her understanding of critical race theory in a reasoned and passionate manner. As a professor of law every other year at UCLA (she spends the alternate years at Columbia), Crenshaw has played a critical role in galvanizing political support for affirmative action, the policy that has been broadly assaulted in California.

I caught Kimberle breaking down the politics behind the policy for the American public one night on CNBC's now defunct *Equal Time*, addressing a Houston ballot initiative that preserved affirmative action.

"Listen, one of the things going on here is that I think many Americans, and many of these voters, recognize that there's a difference between a policy that simply prefers people who are unqualified, versus a policy that's meant to bring people in who've been excluded," Kimberle explained. "At the school where I also teach—Columbia—there used to be a time that all the people who taught there were men. As a consequence, all the bathrooms were male bathrooms. Now when women came in, we had to change that policy. We had to make some of the bathrooms available to women, and no one sees that as a preference. They see it as correcting policies of exclusion."

The added virtue of that show is that Kimberle skewered right-wing diva of the moment Ann Coulter. When Coulter claimed that in Houston, the defeat of the ballot initiative to scrap affirmative action represented "a majority of people trampling on the rights of the minority," and that "it's a majority of the people discriminating against twenty percent of white men," Kim unleashed a pithy but pungent rebuke.

"You know, Ann is being apoplectic here," Kim asserted, before explaining the fear at work in conservative white circles. "The truth of the matter is, I think, conservatives are concerned that they finally have recognized that there really is a difference between affirmative action and preferential treatment, and when white people are aware of it, they are for affirmative action as well. The people leading this were white businessmen. And if that turns out to be a strategy that other people pick up, all of these initiatives are going to fail and that's what conservatives are worried about."

A year later, in July 1998, Kimberle defended affirmative action in *Essence* magazine, effectively summing up Martin Luther King, Jr.'s attitude to racial preferences in an apt analogy. "While today's critics of affirmative action equate this policy with racism," Kimberle argued, "Dr. King found a significant moral distinction between using race as a welcome mat and using it as a No Trespass sign." Kimberle proved that she could put her body where her principles are when she participated in a "walk-out" in support of affirmative action, at UCLA, in October of the same year. She gave a rousing speech at Los Angeles's Meyerhoff Park at the culmination of the protest.

"The argument that affirmative action is preferential treatment has been used against people of color for the last 125 years," she said. "In 1964, some people felt that even civil rights laws were preferential. We should not stand for it any longer." Kimberle urged her colleagues to renounce the stigma of affirmative action to take advantage of a policy that redresses discrimination.

"We should be proud to be beneficiaries of affirmative action," Kimberle proclaimed. "It doesn't mean we're any less qualified."

In a speech entitled "Clarence Thomas, the Law and the Color-Blind Hustle," delivered before the National Bar Association in 1998, Kimberle, who served as part of Anita Hill's legal team in her fight to block Thomas's elevation to the Supreme Court, delivered a scathing analysis of the hypocritical politics of race used by Clarence Thomas and his conservative supporters. Thomas had bitterly complained about the protests by leading black lights against his scheduled appearance before the group.

"Americans slip into bizarre contortions—a routinized dance—whenever Clarence Thomas is at issue," Kimberle argued. "Let's call it the color-blind hustle: a carefully choreographed way to both affirm and negate race in a post-civil rights world." Crenshaw argued that liberals "and conservatives alike depicted Thomas as one of a long line of unpopular dissenters who have traditionally relied on the First Amendment to protect them from the silencing power of the slate. But, of course, from a clear-eyed, right-side-up view, we know that Clarence Thomas *is* the state, or at least one of the most powerful actors within it." Kimberle said "Thomas' claim that his opinions (which, together with those of eight other individuals, are the most powerful opinions in the land) are suppressed by 'racist' black and liberal critics should earn him little more than hearty derision. But these postures continue to beguile and intoxicate us, because we are caught up in the color-blind hustle."

Kimberle observed that we have seen this hustle before when "the fierce opponents of affirmative action stood mute while President George Bush declared that race had nothing to do with Thomas' appointment." She says the color-blind hustle is "especially pronounced in this specious dichotomy between self-help and civil rights." Kimberle argued that the efforts of blacks to appeal to the courts to protect their interests are viewed negatively, and are seen as a demand for "a hand out rather than playing pluralist politics." But she proclaimed that nobody "ever says to corporations, environmental groups, women's groups, the Christian right or any other group that they are wrong to look to the law and the courts to further their interests."

Kimberle concluded that the "only way to avoid the hypnotic allure of this hustle is for...our various allies to recognize that African-Americans must have the same latitude to resist reactionary ideologies that liberals routinely exercise within their own political arenas."

Over the last five years, I have shared many panels with Kimberle. As a result, we have had the opportunity to strengthen our friendship and to discuss the issues about which we both care so deeply. Recently, Kimberle and I participated in a town hall meeting in Detroit, sponsored by the city's vibrant young mayor, Kwame Kilpatrick, and the local NAACP, which features the largest Freedom Fund fundraising dinner among the civil rights organization's branches throughout the country. The other panelists included Congressman John Conyers, Congresswoman Carolyn Cheeks Kilpatrick, Johnnie Cochran and Al Sharpton. Kimberle eloquently pressed her view of political responsibility.

"I think we really need as a community to develop an expectation that we will have a political scorecard," she suggested. "We will know exactly what our politicians, the people that we have supported, have done."

After the panel, Kimberle and I spent the evening discussing the origins of the movement she had founded. I had heard the story in bits and pieces, and I had read a couple of articles she had written explaining the events that led to the formation of critical race theory—including the introduction to her edited volume, *Critical Race Theory: The Key Writings That Formed the Movement*. But on this night, Kimberle sketched for me a concise and elegant summary of her movement's history.

"At the time that we began talking about an alternative to liberal approaches to race and law, it was obvious that the civil rights movement hadn't solved these issues," Kimberle told me as she sipped red wine. "The court certainly did not play the role of the liberating institution. In fact, it was as much a part of the reproduction of our racial oppression as it was an institution to provide some relief." Kimberle said that she and her cohort viewed law schools "not simply as sites of integration, but as sites that resisted some of the deeper implications of integration." For example, at Harvard Law School, where Kimberle took her J.D., the idea of racial progress ended with black student enrollment. Crenshaw says that the view that the curriculum and the faculty should reflect the values of integration and racial equality were not fully accepted by the administration or the faculty.

"So critical race theory actually began as a student movement in elite institutions such as Harvard," Kimberle said, "to
force these institutions to be more reflective, and to be more
responsive to our presence, and to various issues of racial
power that we were concerned with and wanted to study. We
were always challenged to explain what it was about race and
law that was so significant and distinct that it couldn't be captured in a course on constitutional law, or with a legal aide
placement." As a student leader in the effort to integrate
Harvard's law school, including a boycott, Kimberle took that
challenge very seriously. "It was somewhat of a catch-22,
because they were forcing us to articulate something that we
wanted to learn. Nonetheless I was really taken with the
challenge, and when I left Harvard, I decided to go to graduate school to study it and to take it on."

Before she invented critical race theory, Kimberle and her
fellow travelers were active in the movement known as critical
legal studies, a leftist movement among legal scholars that
championed class struggle and viewed the links between culture and law as critical to interpreting legal theory. "We were
obviously attracted to them," Kimberle says, "partly because
some of the controversial things they believed didn't seem
controversial to us at all." For instance, critical legal studies
contends that law is political and that it is indeterminate, ideas,
as Kim argued, that are central to the history of black struggle.
Not only weren't the ideas of critical legal studies off-putting
to Kimberle and her colleagues, but, as she phrases it, "their
ending position was our starting point. Unfortunately, they

really were more interested in crafting post-Marxist critiques, while we wanted to develop, on top of that—and intersecting with that—a race analysis." Predictably, the white leftists spurned the focus on race, spurring Kimberle to create a radical alternative to critical legal studies that incorporated its progressive politics while simultaneously shining a light on race.

"So, I wrote *Race, Reform and Retrenchment*"—critical race theory's manifesto, published in the *Harvard Law Review* in 1988—"as an interaction with critical legal studies and with traditional liberal race theory. And it really was an attempt to begin to piece together a leftist perspective of law that was race conscious." Other scholars were interested in the same effort. After Kimberle began to teach at UCLA, she felt a need to formalize the unique approach to law that she was pioneering. She sent out a call for others to join her in forming a new movement that drew on, but was distinct from, critical legal studies, and that was separate from the centrist tendencies of black scholars who frequented the Association of American Law Schools. With the help of a core of graduate students at the University of Wisconsin Law School, where Kimberle took up residence during a semester off from UCLA, she crafted a proposal to fund a conference. She issued invitations to scholars—including Derrick Bell and Charles Lawrence—who had been sympathetic to the boycott by Harvard Law students to demand greater concentration on race in the curriculum. Of the forty scholars invited to attend, thirty actually came. Many of the theorists read papers, while respondents were charged with providing an intellectual rationale for the evolving approach to law and society that the group expressed. As a result, critical race theory was born.

"I totally made up the name critical race theory," Kimberle told me. "It was a way of indicating that it was a leftist project." She called her approach critical to flag its intellectual and ideological outlook, while underscoring its explicitly theoretical orientation so that potential participants would not be misled about the movement's priorities. "I wanted to make it clear that this was a space where theory predominated, and that it wasn't simply the horse following the cart." Kimberle said that critical race theorists bonded together so that they could "tell an alternative story" to the one "being told about the success of the civil rights movement in the courts," namely, "that racial discrimination had effectively been eliminated and the law was an effective tool in that regard, and the courts were receptive." Critical race theorists fought the notion that the legal "decisions that were being made were simply apolitical decisions that were law-based," and not, as Kimberle and her cohort argued, "ideological contestations about the scope of racism." Kimberle and her fellow theorists "were dealing with attempts to legitimize a virtually unchanged structure of racial power in society, and law was as much a part of legitimating society as transforming it."

When I asked her why critical race theory is relevant to ordinary people, Kimberle provided a ready answer.

"Well, obviously, what is happening now is that the courts have gone forward with what they were doing before, which is drawing an end to active change," Kimberle said. "Moreover, they are insulating white racial power, like when you can't get affirmative action, or when you can get it, but the court strikes it down. They are essentially saying that the status quo can't be changed, not even by courts, and especially not by legislature." In her mind, too many blacks uncritically embrace the belief that the courts are the exclusive answer to black progress. As a result, blacks have a problem comprehending the courts' conflicted role in aiding and preventing racial liberation. "African-Americans have difficulty being politically savvy enough to know that the courts are just another institution, just like the legislature, just like the executive branch. You need to know how to work them, how to play them, but not be beholden to them in the way that I think we have been."

The law is central to shaping the destinies of black Americans. In our recent past, it has at crucial moments been used to press for social liberation. Throughout our history, the law has often been formed and manipulated to undermine our social standing and to roll back many of our hard-won achievements. It is in our best interest to understand how we can use the law to enhance our freedom. It is also crucial for us to know how the law works against our racial ideals and struggles. Kimberle Crenshaw and Patricia Williams are two of the sharpest legal thinkers we have. They have authored pathbreaking scholarship while relentlessly advocating the interests of our society's most vulnerable citizens. Above all, they are committed to changing society by changing how we view and employ the law. These bold and brilliant black women are critical figures in our ongoing struggle for justice.

Part 3

Hurts and Highs

VI. Fingering the Jagged Grain

16

Another Saturday Night, or, Have All the Brothers Gone to White Women?

"Look at me," the sister blurted in exasperation. "It's Saturday night, and I can't buy a date."

I was at a black-tie event for Chicago's 100 Black Men, an organization devoted to improving the lot of young black males. The event drew many of Chicago's black elite, including prominent clergy, physicians, entrepreneurs, and politicians. After the ceremonies were over, my frustrated female had spotted me across the cavernous room in the Hyatt Hotel. She was a tall, statuesque woman, voluptuous in the way that sends black men hankering after something to hold on to because they've been waylaid by breathtaking beauty. Her skin was brown and smooth—all sweet chocolate dipped into sensuous ebony hues—and her sparkling eyes set like flaming candles above her arching cheekbones. Her hair was a stylish black splash, with her limbs elegantly gesturing and her hands delicately pointing as her painted, manicured nails punctuated her message.

As we talked for half an hour, it was clear that she was not only drop-dead gorgeous, but also bright as all outdoors, down-to-earth but schooled, witty and urbane but a true homegirl, used to the corporate game she played as an executive but wearing her status loosely. Highly intelligent, educated, perceptive, in love with her people, down for the cause, a lover of black men—and she was alone, by herself, without a date in sight on a Saturday evening that brimmed with romantic promise.

"What am I supposed to do?" she asked me. "I'm not trying to get married tomorrow—I'm not pressuring black men that way. I just want somebody to spend some time with, someone with whom I can have a good discussion and a good meal, and somebody I can laugh with. I just want a date, for God's sake, not a husband!"

She had nothing against husbands, should a relationship develop in that direction. My lovely interlocutor simply sought to underscore her lack of desperation, a desperation that she had to defend herself against because of the frequent complaint by black men that they feel the noose of matrimony tightening around their necks on the second date. Besides, an equally stunning Afro-Cuban executive who was barely five feet accompanied her. She was highly articulate and scrumptiously attractive. Her very pretty, cocoa-brown face was lit by a radiant smile. And her petite but exquisitely crafted figure pressed warmly against the soft fabric of her evening gown as her charismatic glow haloed her curly, flowing locks.

"I'm extremely fortunate," my magnetic Afro-Cuban conversationalist enthused. "I found a wonderful man who recognized my worth. It's extremely important to be with someone who appreciates and respects you, someone who's comfortable with himself, and who'll therefore be comfortable with you, a man who's not threatened by a strong black woman." As if by cue, he approached, and true to his wife's word, he was a splendid symbol of black masculinity: tall, dark, and handsome, and like his wife, Ivy League trained, and from my hometown, to boot.

"Sister, I just don't understand it," I confessed. "'Cause you finer than the print at the bottom of a contract whipped up at midnight by a shady lawyer. You should have brothers beating down your door—or at least standing in line to take a number so they can catch five minutes of your time. I don't know what I can do in your case, but I've got to think about this problem because if I've heard it once, I've heard it thousands of times from incredible black women who simply want a little love." It was true. I had traveled across much of the nation for the last decade, and beautiful, bright black women from every walk of life repeated her story with frightening regularity.

I was frustrated by my failure to adequately explain the painful mystery of why perfectly wonderful black women are often by themselves. Perhaps they are punished for their success, reviled for their strength and independence, feared for their security, hated for their heart, loathed for their determination to survive, and yet still loyal to black men. I didn't have to romanticize black women to appreciate them—after all, I had married three black women with wildly differing results. But I knew the tough situation they confronted was not mostly of their own making, despite what social theorists or barbershop pundits had concluded.

The statistics seem to reinforce the gloomy outlook for black women. In essence, black women are less likely than other women to marry in the first place, more likely to divorce, and less likely to remarry. Only fifty percent of black women are expected to be married by the age of twenty-eight, compared to eighty percent of white women. Black women are less likely to remarry after a divorce than white women. Only thirty-two percent of black women remarry within five years of divorce, while fifty-four percent of white women, and forty-four percent of Latino women, get married again. As if to underscore how tight and complicated relationships are for black folk, even when marriages are broken, they don't necessarily lead to divorce. Many sisters experience a marital breakup without having their relationships legally terminated. Just sixty-seven percent of black women who were separated from their husbands were divorced three years later. Although this statistic might be interpreted as thirty-three percent of black women try to work out their relationships during separation, it is just as likely that the high percentage of sisters who don't terminate their relationships suggests an inclination—perhaps the desperation—to hold on as long as possible.

When the Centers for Disease Control issued a report in 2002 highlighting some of these numbers, a journalist friend—I'll call her Dorothy—shared with me her email exchange with a black male colleague—let's call him Henry—who had some interesting things to say about why black men over thirty-five find it tough to be in relationships with black women. Henry said that his college-educated, high-professional male friends in their late thirties and early forties are quite comfortable being single and feel no compulsion to marry. Henry and his friends are wary of women over thirty-five who've never been married. They figure that any reasonably attractive woman who is bright and not angry at men is likely to have lived with someone or been married by thirty-five, even if the relationship failed and she's in circulation again. When Henry's women friends describe their negative behavior and attitudes toward men, he lets them know, when pressed, that "no man is going to stick around for that."

Henry wrote that while we hear a great deal about men being the cause of women's failure to find a mate, there is little discussion of how women are responsible for their fates. Henry tried to avoid discussions with his never-married, over-thirty-five female friends because the truth is painful, and only when they are pushed will they admit they have issues that keep them single. Moreover, Henry believed that "too many women view themselves as perpetual victims; the stories they tell about their previous relationships usually involve them as the victims of male treachery and the narrative doesn't allow any possibility that maybe they had some personal qualities that would make a man not want to be in a long-term relationship with them." Besides the decreased prospect of fertility for women over thirty-five, Henry said that many women are overweight, and that trying to force black men to find plus-size women attractive "is like trying to convince a guy who is indifferent to spectator sports that a baseball strike matters."

In one of her responses, Dorothy, who is forty-something and married for the second time, told Henry that she could sympathize with many of his observations, though she was mystified by the double standard. "Perfectly acceptable looking sisters sit at home on Saturday nights because they don't look like Vanessa Williams (either of them!), Ananda Lewis, or Halle Berry—yet these same men who are insisting that they have to have fit and trim women have pot bellies, raggedy nails, and shoes that are run down at the heels. Maybe they think their Jaguars make up for it? Maybe they figure the numbers are so in their favor they don't have to, in Archie Bunker's words, 'run to catch the bus.' It's at the stop, doors open, motor running, waiting for them to hop aboard.'" Dorothy reminded Henry of the quote from journalist George Curry, who once told her "any brother could get over in DC 'long's he can read, write and don't have no running sores.'" Dorothy confessed that were she single, she'd have to throw in the towel. "All I know is I'd be home by myself with a book before I'd allow myself to wait on some of these brothers to lower their impossibly high standards and ask me out!"

There are many social scientists, armchair analysts, ghetto critics—and some black women themselves—who believe that is it black women who set impossibly high standards for potential partners. To be sure, there are many other reasons besides high standards that keep black women from marrying, including their educational achievements and socioeconomic standing, both of which are higher on average than black men's; the substantial mortality gap between men and women; the disproportionate incarceration of black men; the poor labor force participation of black men; black men's lower occupational status; the dramatically decreasing rate of black men seeking higher education; and the increasing rate of interracial marriage among black men.

The incarceration of black men is a huge problem, especially when it is a zero-sum game between brothers in prison or in school. In what seems an eon ago in hip-hop years, rapper turned actor/director Ice Cube proved hip-hop's prescience when he asked the question, "Why more niggas in the pen than in college?" It's taken more than a decade for social science to match the science Cube dropped when he was a bad-boy rebel, long before he became a mainstream media darling in comedies like *Friday* and *Barbershop*.

According to the Justice Policy Institute (JPI) report "Cellblocks or Classrooms? The Funding of Higher Education and Corrections and Its Impact on African American Men," hip-hop has been on the money. And cash is precisely what is at stake in the booming prison industry that lusts to house more blacks in local penitentiaries. The more black bodies are tossed in jail, the more cells are built, and the more money is made, especially in the rural white communities where many prisons thrive. In 1995 alone, 150 new prisons were constructed and filled, while 171 more were expanded.

But money is also at stake when it comes to making a crucial choice: to support blacks in the state university or the state penitentiary. As the report makes clear, we have chosen the latter. During the 1980s and 1990s, state spending for corrections grew at six times the rate of state spending on higher education. By the end of last century, there were nearly a third more black men in prison and jail than in colleges and universities. That means that the number of black men in jail or prison has increased fivefold in the last twenty years. In 1980, at the dawn of the prison construction boom, black men were three times more likely to be enrolled in college than incarcerated.

In 2000, there were 791,600 black men in jail or prison, while only 603,032 were enrolled in colleges or universities. In 1980, there were 143,000 black men in jail or prison and 463,700 matriculating in higher educational institutions. In effect, the cellblock or classroom choice boils down to a policy that, whether intended or not, is genocidal. We would permit no other population of American citizens to be locked away with such callous disregard for the educational opportunity that might help stem the tide of incarceration.

It is hardly a coincidence that, as blacks have become cogs in the machinery of the prison economy, their chances of being college educated have been drastically reduced. The engine of the prison-industrial complex is fueled by the containment of black upward mobility and the disenfranchisement of black citizenry. In many states, felons are ineligible to vote once they leave prison. First we deny these men a solid education, and then we deprive them of the right to help reshape the policies that have harmed them.

One of the tragedies of this state of affairs is that it undercuts the advances of black males in higher education over the last two decades. Between 1980 and 2000, three times as many black men were sent to prison as were enrolled in college or the university. In 2000, at least thirteen states had more black men in prison than in college, and from 1980 until 2000, thirty-eight states, along with the federal system, increased the prison population more than they swelled the ranks of higher education. If the planners of state budgets continue this destructive trend, they will compensate for a loss of revenue by cutting spending on education and social services, two critical means by which blacks escape poverty and the prison trap. If black men are in prison and not in college, they have two strikes against them in their bid to become viable partners to black women. Black male imprisonment has a double-whammy effect on black women finding mates among their male peers: it separates black men from society, and it severely erodes their prospects for higher education.

Even with these facts supporting the diminished choices faced by women, there is still the perception that they are just too picky. *Ebony* magazine has through the years addressed the issue, in articles such as "How Black Women Can Deal with the Black Male Shortage," "Black Women/ Black Men: Has Something Gone Wrong Between Them?" and "Do Black Women Set Their Standards for Marriage Too High?" The black male shortage article, from the May 1986 issue, cited Census Bureau statistics that there were at the time 6.4 million more females than males in the United States, and that there were 1.4 million more black females than males.

According to the article, Dr. Ann Ashmore Poussaint and other experts suggested that black women stop blaming black men and society for their dilemma. The experts argued that women should take a closer look at themselves, their attitude about men, and their approach to finding a mate. "There are many single women who complain about loneliness, but when they do meet interesting men, they project a negative attitude or seem to always get into debates over feminist issues. Others aren't shy about flaunting their professional and financial successes, giving men the impression that they either don't need or have time for a meaningful relationship."

These sentiments appear to be informed by the reluctance to embrace feminist principles as a viable alternative for black women, or by a presumption that female success is the catalyst for the downfall of black men. But Poussaint also argued that too many black women eliminated suitors for superficial reasons, including profession, skin color, height, weight, income, education, family background, and social graces or contacts. She said that if a woman felt she was lowering her standards by dating or marrying a particular kind of man, she should reconsider her priorities. Poussaint and others were not suggesting that black women lower their standards, the article said, but that they should broaden their outlooks, including, some experts said, dating men outside their culture, although other experts strongly opposed interracial relationships.

In the higher standards article, printed in January 1981, *Ebony* explored the black male complaint that black women are more interested in what black men do than who they are. It also grapples with the black male perception that black women are more concerned with professional stature, high income, college degrees, and good looks. They tested this perception—which was really a hypothesis about black female behavior put forth by black men—by engaging twenty-five young women at Spelman College in a group discussion. To the question, "Is a man's status really important to a Black woman thinking about marriage?" *Ebony* reports there "was a resounding 'Yes' from the group."

Some of the students claimed that they were attending college to better themselves, and thus, they seek mates who match their efforts and achievement. The gap between a black male bus driver and a black female attorney would be hard to surmount. Since the vast majority of black men in 1981 held blue-collar jobs—a statistic that remains unchanged to this day—and because black women's route to professional achievement was not as difficult as that of black men, the magazine contended, the tensions between the genders would only increase. Many of the young Spelman women recognized that they might have difficulty in finding mates with comparable achievements, and hence believed they could afford to wait. The article explores the class rift between high achieving, highly motivated black females, and black males hampered by persistent racism and differing socialization.

If the issue of black women having higher standards for relationships was a concern twenty years ago, it is even more prevalent now. According to some research, black women have been less willing than white women to marry men with lower status and undesirable traits—those who are younger, previously married, less educated, or unattractive. In short, black women prefer attractive men who are near their age and who have a stable career. For those black women who have never been married, they prefer mates with no previous wives or children. The younger the black woman, the greater her expectation that her man meet the criteria she deemed important. Further, black women who have higher status are more invested in building careers and less urgent about finding a mate. The economic independence of high-achieving black women, and the deteriorating economic conditions of black males, severely depletes the pool of potentially marriageable black men.

In our nation, people tend to marry folk who have similar educational backgrounds. That poses a huge problem for black men and women, since the ratio of highly educated black men to women has been said to be as small as sixty men available for every one hundred women. There are nearly 400,000 more black women than men enrolled in higher education. Black women are now earning more than sixty-three percent of all college degrees awarded to blacks. There are nearly four million black married couples in the United States, and among them, just under ten percent have marriages where both spouses have a college degree. Slightly more than one percent of them are marriages where both spouses had graduate degrees.

Moreover, black women with higher levels of education are disproportionately affected by the shortage of black men with similar levels of education. In the 1930s, only eleven percent of black women were expected not to marry; today, less than forty percent of black women are expected to marry. One might conclude in analyzing these statistics that there is no shortage of black men for black women to marry, but that black women choose to remain single rather than marry partners who do not meet their expectations. Further, educated professional black women seek to marry only those men they find acceptable by high standards; thus, lack of motivation, not availability, is the critical issue.

But that would be extremely shortsighted. While it is true that such numbers might translate to black women being "picky," the reality is that black women seek to meet and marry those men with whom they have the greatest degree of compatibility. Black male resentment of black female achievement, especially among black men who have not enjoyed the opportunity to succeed, may translate to unwarranted hostility toward black women. Many brothers feel that black women are the pawns of a white establishment that seeks to hold them down. As a result, black female movement through educational and professional ranks is to some black men a symptom of black women's complicity with a racist system. Rather than offer an astute analysis of our condition—that in a patriarchal culture, black men *do* represent a specific threat to white male power that black women don't, and hence, in some instances, white men prefer the presence of black women in professional settings—black men often confuse the consequences of racism with a desire of black females to undercut them.

Further, for a black man to reach beneath his class station to embrace a black woman reinforces the status quo: as breadwinner, he can provide for his family, and thus remain "head of the house." For a black woman to behave similarly upsets the status quo: if she makes more money and is better educated than her partner, the resentment of her man can become burdensome, sometimes abusive. I know a lot of brothers who felt they could take a woman making more money than them, but once the reality of her higher status set in, it usually took on social meanings beyond a paycheck. Issues of control inevitably arose, and the question of who was in charge followed in its wake. Since black men struggle with a society that sets up expectations for appropriate masculine behavior—take care of one's family, be gainfully employed, be a financial success—and then undermines their attainment, black women are often the psychological scapegoat of our anger. The rise in black male domestic violence is poignant testimony to such tensions in the black home.

It would be hard to blame black women for wanting to be "equally yoked," but that does not mean there aren't sisters who are dismissive of black men outside of their income or educational bracket. In my early twenties, a young lady I had grown quite fond of and with whom I had become intimate, bluntly told me, "I'm attracted to you physically, and I think you're very smart, but you're a minister, and you won't make a lot of money. I need a man who will be financially well-off, so I don't think we can have a relationship."

I was stunned and hurt, and from that day forward, robbed of any illusions about how poorly some sisters can behave. Still, the grim reality is that black men often despise women's success as the unfailing predictor of domestic trouble. I will never forget a black man who told me that his wife's education had hurt their relationship because she no longer understood her place. "She became a 'phenomenal woman,'" he declared with bitter irony, citing in his resentful put-down the famous Maya Angelou poem of the same name. I have heard similar comments repeated by brothers time and time again.

Despite all of this, many college-educated black women marry black men with significantly lower levels of education. In marriages where black women have a college degree, only 45.9 percent of their husbands also have a college degree. More than one quarter of black women who have a college degree are married to men who have never gone to college. And four percent of black women with a college degree are married to black men who didn't graduate from high school. By comparison, nearly seventy percent of white women with a college degree married men who also had a college degree, and only twelve percent of white women with a college degree married men who never went to college. While black women may prefer mates who are educationally compatible, they have often chosen mates whose lower achievement makes their marriages vulnerable to divorce and spousal abuse.

Other black men complain bitterly that many black women prefer the hard-core, thugged-out brother, the bad boy, the player. A brilliant young Vanderbilt University professor of mathematics, whom this thinking victimized, wrote an essay about his experience for *Essence* magazine. Jonathan Farley is a tall, slim, attractive brown-skinned young man, a summa cum laude graduate of Harvard who took a doctorate in mathematics from Oxford University and is an outspoken advocate for the Black Panthers. In his essay, he recalls a painful episode: a young lady with whom he fell in love only wanted to be his friend. But the worst of it is that she took him to dinner to heal his wounds by telling him why he struck out. "She outlined the difference between men like me and the men Black women preferred, between mere African-Americans and 'niggaz': African-Americans are safe, respectable, upwardly mobile and professional Black men. Niggaz are strong, streetwise, hard Black men."

Jonathan pointed out that his erstwhile love had a question posed to her by a friend: if she was walking down a dark street at night, who would she want by her side, an African-

American or a nigga? She told Jonathan that black women sought a strong protector. Jonathan writes that he "tried to explain that physical strength had ceased to be a survival trait back in the Stone Age." Further, he warned her that women who prefer niggaz to African-Americans were making a costly mistake since African-Americans, by virtue of their "higher social and economic status"—and wasn't this what black women wanted?—could better protect them and give them the security they desired. Since many young black women grow up without fathers in the home, even college-educated black women often settled for dropouts and drug dealers.

Because of his experience, Jonathan found himself "resisting my own impulses to open a door, start a conversation or even say hello to many young black women I meet, for fear of appearing too gentlemanly and hence unworthy of their attention." Jonathan argued that even black men who were "raised in the suburbs don the attire and attitude of street thugs so that they, too, will be chosen." He concluded his essay by admonishing sisters to "leave the players in the playground," and that "Knights in shining armor don't have to have gold teeth."

Many black women have admitted that this is far too frequent a flaw among their sisters. Many sisters claim to have outgrown such an inclination, chalking it up to their youth and their failure to know what kind of man would really be a good partner. Once they mature, many black women are attracted to brothers whose stability and substance are prized above the flashy danger of destructive black men.

If some black men chafe under the restrictive mythology of the ghetto tough, many more black women are passed over for an equally nefarious reason. Recently, when I lectured at a northeastern college, a young lady approached me after my lecture. As we chatted about a number of issues, we began to discuss the dating situation at her college for black women. That's when she dropped the bombshell on me.

"Professor Dyson, my boyfriend broke up with me earlier this year," the attractive chocolate sister told me.

"Why'd he do that?" I asked her, noticing that her heart was heavy, her eyes tearing up as she spoke.

"He said I was too dark," she said lowly.

"That can't be right," I protested on her behalf. "Did he actually tell you that?"

"Right to my face," she replied, as if still in shock.

Although many black men are rarely that blunt, their actions speak just as harshly. The preference for light-skinned women finds painful precedent in black culture. It dates back to slavery when the lightest blacks—whose skin color was often the result of rape by white slave masters—were favored over their darker kin because they were closer in color and appearance to dominant society. Unfortunately, despite the challenge to the mythology of inherently superior white standards of beauty, there persists in black life the belief that light is preferable to dark. Music videos have historically presented light-skinned black women as the most desirable women. Even as browner women have more recently won space in the culture of representation within our race—a few of them, like

Carla Campbell, Angela Basset, and Valerie Morris appear in videos, film, and on television news, respectively—there is an undeniable subordination of darker skinned black women to lighter sisters in everyday life.

A bright, beautiful, and brown friend of mine—I'll call her Renee—recently told me that she dated for a year a famous football star, a very dark brother, who told her that he almost didn't ask her out because *she* was so dark. One of his gridiron colleagues, an equally chocolate brother, said within her earshot that Renee was not the kind of girl he usually dated since his other women had been much fairer. Renee also reported to me that an all-star NBA player told her that in order to fit in, he had to have the same car, same house and same-looking woman as most of the other basketball players—meaning, women who are very light-skinned or of mixed heritage, since these women are "hot" now.

Renee shared with me a painful email missive from an intern who worked in her office that testifies to the persistence of virulent beliefs about skin color in black America. The young lady said that she and her friends felt that "as normal/average looking young Black women, we are no longer desirable." She has "many friends who are dark-skinned and have natural hair who complain that they can never get attention from Black men." She also commented on what she and her friends have termed "hybrid chicks," girls who are showcased and admired in music videos because they "are exotic looking, either half Black and Asian or half Hispanic."

What is remarkable is that such self-defeating prejudice persists despite the growing prominence in some circles of beautiful dark-skinned black women. There is Ingrid Saunders Jones, the enormously gifted corporate executive who, from her perch as a senior vice president of Coca Cola and head of its foundation, has funneled tens of millions of dollars into black America in aid of charitable, civic, and cultural causes. Ingrid is a glamorous woman with flawless, honey-dipped ebony skin, healthy, sculpted eyebrows, soulful and sexy eyes, cascading, jet-black hair that is often pulled back into a ponytail, a blinding smile, perfectly lined lips, and a fifties-style sensuality. There is Vanessa Bell Calloway, the intelligent and strikingly beautiful actress and co-host of BET's talk show, *Oh Drama*. Vanessa is a shapely, buff sister with a dewy, espresso-brown complexion, clear, bright eyes, perfect white teeth, and a glittering sexuality—and a laugh as strong as her personality. There is Darlene Clark Hine, a brilliant Michigan State University historian—and former president of the Organization of American Historians—who has written several path-breaking books on black women's life and history. Darlene is a deep, rich maple-colored beauty with entrancing features: big, expressive eyes, succulent cheeks, sexy, full lips, and milk-smooth skin, framed by a flow of layered, shining, silky, silvery hair. And among the younger generation, there is Aunjanue Ellis, a superbly talented actress with Ivy League credentials—she attended Brown University—and graduate training at New York University. Aunjanue is a smoky, sultry chocolate stunner whose megawatt smile, thick black tresses, chiseled cheeks, sweetly burnished flesh, alluring eyebrows, riveting dark eyes, luscious and life-affirming lips, svelte and taut physique, and comely legs make the gorgeous thespian a vision of soulful sensuality.

The continued preference for lighter sisters among blacks bears witness to psychic wounds that are not completely healed. The poisonous self-hatred that pours freely in the rejection of dark blackness is painful evidence of our unresolved racial anxieties about our true beauty and self-worth. Dark black women have often been cast aside and looked down upon because they embody the most visible connection to a fertile African heritage whose value remains suspect in our culture and nation.

As long as black men continue to spurn the root of our reality—summed up, perhaps, in the saying, "the darker the berry, the sweeter the juice"—the longer we will be separated from the source of our survival. While we are wise not to envision our blackness in literal terms—it is not simply about skin, but about sensibility, aesthetics, culture, style and the like—it would be foolish to deny that the debasing of blackness is often about the debasing of blacks in our skin, through our skin, *because* of our skin. While race is more cosmic than epidermis and flesh—encompassing politics, social structure, class, and region—our place in the world, and our reward and punishment too, are profoundly shaped by color.

As big a barrier to the flow of love between black men and women as the issues I've discussed are, perhaps none is more controversial, or as hurtful, as the rejection many black women experience when black men date and marry white women. As I lecture and preach across the country, black women of every station corner me, or ask me before an auditorium of hundreds, sometimes thousands, a version of the question: "Why do so many brothers despise us and chase white women?"

Of course, I am always reluctant to speak for all black men, especially when it comes to something as personal and subjective—though obviously not without serious social overtones—as who one likes or loves. And many of my heroes—Quincy Jones and Sidney Poitier among them—married white women at a time when doing so bravely challenged the nation's apartheid. In the sixties and seventies, interracial marriage, whether intended or not, represented a rejection of white supremacist values and indicated that love was a matter between individuals, not races. Few could miss the heroic gesture of loving across racial lines. Those who did often risked their reputations and social status while enduring cultural stigma. In short, it was apparent that interracial romance was unavoidably interpreted in political terms.

But if we are honest, interracial love has rarely, if ever, been simply about love. It has always borne political implications. From the very beginning of the black presence on American soil, stereotypes have distorted relations between the races, including those involving sex. Black males were brought to this nation in chains to be studs. Their virility was placed in the service of slavery. Black females were raped at will; their wombs became the largely unprotected domain of white male desire. Their sexuality was harnessed to perpetuate slavery through procreation. Later, of course, many more stereotypes of black men and women flourished, from the docile Uncle Tom, the fiery "field nigger," the compliant "house nigger," and the uppity buck, to the nurturing Mammy, the sarcastic sapphire, the promiscuous Jezebel, and now, in our day, the sex-crazed lothario, the unrepentant rapist, the welfare queen and the hoochie mama.

These stereotypes revolve largely around sex—how black people have it, under what conditions, for what reasons, how frequently, and if it can be read as a symptom of their debased nature and perverted character. Hence, these stereotypes often expressed the stunted social perceptions of black identity put forth by a white culture that refused to own up to its heavy hand in their creation.

Moreover, white society was ambivalent about black sexual identity—they wanted their blacks highly sexed to support slavery and white male pleasure. Otherwise, they wanted blacks to be constrained, even sexless if possible. Black men were feared and envied for their mythically large sexual organs. White male sexual desire was linked to strengthening patriarchal culture. As a result, white men sought to exploit black female eroticism, and to minimize sexual competition by outlawing black male sexual interactions with white women. The rise of lynching and castration are tied to the white male attempt to control the exaggerated threat of black male sexual desire. Long after the demise of such vicious social acts, the strong taboo on interracial sex prevails.

While black men were being constructed as studs, and black women as inherently lascivious—basically it was guilt by association, since black women must be hyper-sexed to be able to satisfy the sexual desire of their men—white women were being projected as paragons of sexual virtue and placed on pedestals of purity. White female sexual desire, as much as possible, was segregated from public view. It was exclusively directed toward the bedroom of their white husbands, whose carousing outside the home—whether in the slave quarter or the whorehouse—was for the most part exempt from ethical scrutiny. There was minimal sexual contact between black men and white women during slavery. However, during reconstruction there was a noticeable increase in these relations, although interracial marriages remained rare.

Anti-miscegenation laws prohibiting interracial marriage between whites and people of color existed in forty states until 1967, when the U.S. Supreme Court struck down these laws as unconstitutional in the landmark—and aptly named—*Loving v. Virginia*. Moreover, after emancipation, vicious sexual stereotypes served in part as a smoke screen to divert attention from how white men sought to prevent black men from enjoying the privileges of economic stability, middle-class status and the freedom to raise their families. Still, the white woman defined the norm of beauty for the culture. She remained the prized erotic possession to be fought over by black and white men. Black women were largely excluded from this economy of desire, except in the crudest fashion.

This history must be kept in mind as we ponder the sexual

fault lines in black America, and the tensions between black men and women around the perception that black men are aggressively marrying white women. Interracial marriage among black men and white women has risen dramatically in the last few years. Nearly eight percent of all black men between the ages of twenty-five and thirty-four who were married in 1990 married nonblack women, compared to just four percent for white men in the same age cohort who married outside their race. Region, occupation, and education play a huge role in determining the interracial marriages of black men. In the Pacific Northwest, thirty-two percent of black men marry white women; in California, it's twenty percent; in the Rocky Mountain states, its thirty percent; and in the New England states, nineteen percent of black men marry white women. Military service hikes the numbers for black men marrying women outside their race, as fourteen percent of black males in the military are married to nonblacks.

By contrast, only seven percent of black men who didn't serve in the military married nonblacks. More than ten percent of black men who complete college marry outside of their race, compared to only six percent for black men who didn't complete high school. And for black men who have attended graduate school, the number jumps to thirteen percent who marry nonblack women. In fact, black men with graduate school experience are thirty percent more likely to marry outside their race than even black men with a college degree. Overall, more than 200,000 black men are married outside their race, mostly to white women.

On the surface, despite the soaring rates of intermarriage for black men, that number might not seem particularly disturbing, but from the perspective of educated black women, it represents a significant draining of the pool of available black men from which to choose a potential mate. As more black men go to prison, die early from crime or from AIDS, are severely unemployed or underemployed, or choose an alternative sexual lifestyle, the numbers of compatible black men begin to significantly diminish for educated black women. And given the hostility that black men without higher education often harbor toward educated black women, the numbers of black men available for black women dwindle even more.

Young black women face a crisis in available black men unlike that faced by their grandmothers, who found marriageable black men in relatively plentiful numbers. The GI Bill altered the educational and employment landscape for black men of the post–World War II generation. Black men who had been closed out of white-collar and professional jobs found new opportunities beyond the school teaching to which they had been formerly relegated. While black women, especially in the South, held many of the teaching jobs, blue collar jobs were at the time a far better source of income, including waiting on tables in five-star restaurants and hotels, jobs that many college educated black males took, along with serving as Pullman porters.

In the South's segregated black schools, black men held most of the principals' jobs. For those black men who didn't go to college, especially since it was tough in the rigidly seg-

regated job market for black men to reap benefit from higher
education, they went to work immediately after high school
in the jobs that college-educated men coveted as well. Under
Jim Crow, the educated and uneducated alike met and mixed,
and black women enjoyed a much larger pool of available and
socially attractive black men from which to choose a mate.

Today, not only are the economic opportunities severely
shrunk for black men who don't obtain higher education, but
the overwhelming majority of black students who attend college—eighty percent of them—are matriculating in predominantly white schools. In contrast to black students of earlier
generations who attended historically black colleges and universities, black students now have far greater access to white
culture, tastes, opportunities, values and goals. And they mix
with white peers far more frequently than black students at
black colleges and those black youth who end their education
at high school.

The situation I have just outlined has in its own right negatively affected the prospects of black women finding a mate.
But when one takes into consideration the persistence of the
belief that white women are the ideal embodiment of beauty
in our culture, and the prize that *all* men seek, the situation
for black women is even more dismal. They not only fight
against trends in the economy, employment and education,
but they fight a far more elusive opponent: the mythological
eroticization of a standard of beauty that by definition
excludes them from competition. Furthermore, black women
are subject to stereotypes among black men about their being

"difficult," "demanding," "bossy," "full of attitude," "aggressive" and the like, ruling them out of play as possible mates, often by the relatively small pool of highly educated, or highly achieving, black men.

Thus, when black women express anger at being abandoned by black men in favor of white women, they are neither being irrational, unfair or unduly hostile. Rather, they are taking stock of an abominable cultural condition over which they have little control. When highly educated or visible black men consistently make choices of partners or mates outside of the race, it appears to be far more than coincidence or the capricious stirrings of affection. In fact, it hardly seems to be arbitrary at all. Rather, there seems to be an undeniable wall of separation between desirable black men and the educated and beautiful black women they are turning away from in droves. White women are often unconsciously elevated as the erotic payoff—the sexual reward—for those black men who seek elevated status in our society, or alternatively, who want to cement their position as outstanding men.

Hence, the spurning of black women cannot be considered an exclusively personal or private choice of black men in an erotic and emotional vacuum. In light of the factors that drive this trend, it must be seen as part of a deeply rooted, if often unconscious, process of pursuing the emblem of beauty and status from which black men have been historically barred. I am not suggesting that all black men who pursue or marry white women are the victims of an unconscious adoration of white standards of beauty. But it is difficult to ignore the compelling evidence that it is often more than happenstance or coincidence that drives interracial relations between black men and white women.

Of course, it is hardly a one-way street. Many white women find black men desirable too, obviously for purely personal reasons—as is the case many times with the black male attraction to white women—but also for more complex social reasons as well. A black female student at George Washington University, where I had gone to lecture, explained to me her theory about why many black men and white women are magnetized to each other.

"See, Professor Dyson, I think it has to do with the ideals both black men and white women represent," the beautiful brown-skinned woman said to me in a circle of black female students. "White women are allegedly the ideal expression of beauty: blonde hair, blue eyes, keen nose, thin lips, big breasts, and flat behind. And black men are the ideal expression of the ultimate physique: muscular, dark and handsome, sexually aggressive, and of course, having a large sexual organ. So naturally, when they get together, it's pretty explosive. It's the meeting of two ideals." That certainly was part of the answer, although neither the student nor I would reduce the complexity of erotic and interpersonal attraction to sheer physical chemistry. It also has to do with the way that chemistry is determined by deeply held social beliefs about features that we are told are attractive and those we are told we should avoid or that we can live without. Too often, those beliefs are shaped by racial considerations, driven by troublesome and often unexamined assumptions about white and black women that pass for common sense, but which, upon reflection, turn out to be little more than projections, stereotypes, or scapegoating.

For some black men, having a white woman or wife amounts to enjoying a level of liberation from erotic or social restrictions that is downright intoxicating. For some, it involves the complicated choreography of racial revenge, as they seek—as I once heard it explained of a black nationalist who justified his relationships with white women—"to punish their fathers." For others, having a white wife or woman is a way into the club of white patriarchy, as if to say, "I've got what it takes to snag one of your women, now let me have some of your power."

Of course, such a move might backfire, only increasing the likelihood of white male resentment, perhaps retaliation. But sometimes, in the strange machinations of the patriarchal imagination, the pursuit and capture of the white ideal of beauty signifies to white men a level of erotic and social competence that augurs well for transracial alliance in the business world. A black woman wrote to me about how her "sons' biological father (nothing more) married a woman who was thirty years older than him, just so he could move up in the ranks of his job and have a 'trophy white wife.' Then he proceeded to have children with other women while he stayed married to his security blanket." Of course, one might argue that this is merely the sour grapes of a woman who lost her man to a white woman. Still, her belief that some black men prize white women as stepping-stones is not far fetched.

Some social scientists have pointed out that members of a stigmatized social group, or those bereft of prestige, often trade characteristics when choosing a mate. That might mean that black men have a better chance of winning the affections of a white woman if they offer, for instance, higher socioeconomic status in return. In fact, white women marry up more often when they marry a black man than when they marry a white man. A black man has higher socioeconomic status to offer in exchange for the elevated esteem he might achieve, in his own eyes, or in the eyes of those he seeks to please, by marrying a white woman. Interestingly, black men marry down more often when marrying a white woman than when marrying a black woman.

This research may support the perception of many black women that many white women seek only those black men who are well educated, or whose high visibility and social status are compensation for the status conferred by white womanhood. Professional athletes and entertainers, among others, are noteworthy for a high, or at least, visible degree of interracial partnering and marriage. Many black women resent the fact that they are precluded access to such men because they do not offer the status of white skin, blue eyes or blonde hair. Nor do they simply cater to the unreasonable demands of the black male star or prominent figure, as some black women contend is true of many of their white female counterparts.

There is, too, a great deal of hypocrisy involved in the spurning of black women by well-known black men. For instance, some black men claim that their preference for white women—besides the fact that they are, according to these men, devoid of the bitterness, harshness, and drama of black women—has to do with the relative ease with which they yield to the sexual desires of black men. The irony, of course, is that if black women gave in easily, they are marked as "hos," and if they refuse black men's sexual advances, they are often seen as "bitches." By contrast, many white women are rewarded for the same behavior with permanent partnership or marriage. Further, many of the white women who aggressively pursue high-profile black men are viewed as appropriately assertive, endearing and supportive. On the other hand, black women who are equally aggressive are viewed as "gold diggers" and materialistic hoochies.

Perhaps one of the greatest furors among black women in recent memory was sparked when an outraged white woman—she signed her missive "Disgusted White Girl"—who was engaged to a black man penned a letter to Jamie Brown, editor of the popular gossip magazine *Sister 2 Sister.* Disgusted wrote to Jamie to "challenge some of your Black male readers," saying she was engaged to a good-looking educated and loving black male, and that she didn't understand "a lot of the Black females' attitudes about our relationship." Disgusted wrote that her man "wanted me because the pickings amongst Black women were slim to none. As he said, they were either too fat, too loud, too mean, too argumentative, too needy, too materialistic, and carrying too much excess baggage." Disgusted said that before she was engaged, she was "constantly approached by Black men, willing to wine and dine me and give me the world. If Black women are so up in arms about us being with their men, why don't they look at themselves and make some changes."

Disgusted said that she was tired of the dirty looks and snide remarks she got, that she "would like to hear from some Black men about why we are so appealing and coveted by them. Bryant Gumbel just left his wife of 26 years for one! Charles Barkley, Scottie Pippen, the model Tyson Beckford, Montel Williams, Quincy Jones, James Earl Jones, Harry Belafonte, Sidney Poitier, Kofi Anan, Cuba Gooding, Jr., Don Cornelius, Berry Gordy, Billy Blanks, Larry Fishburne, Wesley Snipes…I could go and on." Disgusted admonished black women not "to be mad with us white women because so many of your men want us. Get your acts together and learn from us and we may lead you to treat your men better."

Then she challenged black men and appealed to an unstated compact that has been seemingly forged by many black men and white women, when she confidently wrote, "If I'm wrong, Black men, let me know." This hurtful diatribe exposed the racial logic and, unwittingly, the unconscious white female privilege that work against black women, and to white women's advantage. By arrogantly lecturing black women about their shortcomings, Disgusted failed to account for the elevated status she enjoyed—and the exaggerated value she had conferred on her—because of her white skin and the social and historical meanings of white female identity.

But it isn't just the famous or visible black man who is the object of white female desire. In 1995, seven black female students at Brown University started in their dormitory a "Wall of Shame"—which listed the names of the black males who were dating white women—when they became angry that many of the black males on campus favored white women while spurning their affections. It would be easy to make these and other black women look frustrated, irrational, jealous, foolish, or plain loony when they point to the pathological behavior of their black men avoiding or stigmatizing them. And yet, the trends suggest that increasingly, black males in college are doing just that.

As a result, perhaps, college-educated black women are increasingly turning to white men and others outside the race in seeking companionship. Black women are often more constrained in the choice of partners or mates by a profound sense of racial loyalty. Between 1960 and 1980, the number of black women married to white men was relatively static, inching from 26,000 to 27,000. By 2000, it had grown to 80,000, and the number is bound to increase with the crisis of available black men only getting worse for the foreseeable future. To be sure, there is the possibility of the romanticized white male suitor—the one capable of providing life's best, unlike the bulk of struggling black men, or the white man who fits the bill of what is sexy and romantic in ways that black men are rarely permitted—playing an equally problematic role in the black female imagination as the idealized white woman plays for black men. And as with many black men, simple attraction to the opposite race might be in effect. For the most part, black women are perceived as coupling with white men out of necessity more than preference.

A recent spate of articles, in *Essence* and *Ebony* magazines, and in newspapers like the *Atlanta Journal and Constitution*, has commented on the phenomenon. The *Journal* article, entitled "Could Mr. Right Be White?" raised the ire of journalist Nathan McCall. The article quotes twenty-nine-year-old Melanie Robinson, a black woman who has dated three white men, as saying that black men take black women for granted since the numbers favor men, and that white men are "more romantic and willing to go on dates like walking in the park or visiting a museum." Robinson also wishes that black men would do more than offer to take her for a drink or go to "Red Lobster for all-you-can-eat crab legs on Monday."

In a letter to the newspaper, McCall wrote that he found the article "appallingly racist and typically shallow." McCall argued that it's "one thing to say that some black women date white men because there is a shortage of available black men," but quite another to "suggest that the very group that created and perpetuated that shortage—white men—are also the most sensitive and romantic people on God's great earth." He suggested that it would have been as easy to find women to "testify that white men are insecure, and that given a dating choice between an all-you-can-eat crab legs special and an evening at the museum, white men will opt for Red Lobster every time." McCall concluded that he was thankful for shows like *Jerry Springer* and *Ricky Lake*, because, as "insane as their

230 MICHAEL ERIC DYSON

programs are, at least they demonstrate that human frailties are as much a reality for whites as for anyone else."

Perhaps the most recent controversy involving a white man enjoying the pleasures of black female companionship erupted around the film *Monster's Ball*, starring Halle Berry as a waitress who becomes involved with a racist sheriff—played by Billy Bob Thornton—who executes her convict husband on death-row before falling in love with her. The film includes an extended and explicit sex scene where Thornton's character makes love from behind to Berry's waitress. Many blacks were torn when Berry won the Oscar for her powerful portrayal: they were rooting for her to be acknowledged for her superior skill, but reluctant to praise a part that even indirectly suggested that her character's sexual liaison was a reward for hating black people and executing her husband, played by Sean "P. Diddy" Combs.

A few weeks after the Oscars, actress Angela Bassett—whom Berry had graciously mentioned by name in her acceptance speech as one of "the women that stand beside me"—criticized the role Berry played even as she was careful to praise Berry for her performance. Bassett said, "I wasn't going to be a prostitute on film," and that "I couldn't do that because it's such a stereotype about black women and sexuality," concluding that "Meryl Streep won Oscars without all that." Bassett said that she loved Berry's performance, and that she didn't begrudge Berry her success, but that it "wasn't the role for me." Bassett said that she wanted an Oscar, but "for something I can sleep with at night." The issue of stereotypes

is extremely important, especially for black women in a powerful medium like film involved sexually with white men. But
so is the freedom to choose roles that stretch the boundaries
of sexual propriety and challenge the limitations imposed on
black female sexuality.

In her acceptance speech, Berry challenged the stereotypes
of how a black woman who has been honored by the powers-
that-be should behave. Instead of being safe, Berry was bravely political. She gave the millions who watched around the
globe not only a sorely needed history lesson, but also a lesson
in courageous identification with the masses. Berry tearfully
declared that her award was for "every nameless, faceless
woman of color" who now had a chance since "this door has
been opened." Berry's remarkable courage and candor are
depressingly rare among famed blacks with a lot on the line:
money, prestige, reputation, and work. Many covet the lime-
light's payoffs, but cower in light of its demands.

Even fewer speak up about the experiences their ordinary
brothers and sisters endure—and if they are honest, that they
themselves too often confront—on a daily basis. To be sure,
there is an unspoken tariff on black honesty among the privileged: if they dare cut against the grain, they may be curtailed
or cut off from reward. Or they may endure stigma. What
Berry did was brave and generous: on the night she was being
singled out for greatness, she cast her lot with anonymous
women of color who hungered for her spot, and who might
be denied for no other reason than that they were yellow,
brown, red, or black. Her achievement, she insisted, was now

their hope. Her performance that night was a stereotype buster.

No matter how you cut it, sex between the races is a complicated affair. Many black men honestly love white women, and many black women honestly love white men. But the history of traumatic interaction between the races shapes the patterns of love and sex across racial lines. As a social taboo that has been shattered, interracial sex is a healthy and edifying occurrence. As the symptom of the attempt to escape or avoid intimate contact with the women who have loved and nurtured our race, it can be a sign of utter self-hatred, and hatred of our group's most powerful and loyal members. One of the most vicious legacies of white supremacy is the belief that our women are not beautiful, desirable, intelligent, and worthy of our love.

The factors that rob black men and women of more love between us—imprisonment, early death, educational disparities and self-destructive habits such as snobbishness, skin-color bias, the preference for bad boys, and worship of white standards of beauty—can be combated through conscientious response to our plight. There are millions of black women from every walk of life who simply want, like every other group of women alive, to be wanted and loved by the men who issued from their mothers' wombs. To dishonor that wish is the seed of our destruction.

17

Terror/Isms

"Ladies, are you ready?" asked the beautiful woman with glowing caramel skin adorned in a flowing white African robe. "Let's get ready to rumble!" she exclaimed, repeating the famed phrase from boxing announcer Michael Buffer as she excitedly turned three hundred and sixty degrees in place as if to punctuate her point. Rev. Marcia Dyson was in the pulpit of St. Luke Community United Methodist Church in Dallas, Texas, preaching her first sermon on Mother's Day, 1999. It was thrilling to witness her confidence, and the ease with which she negotiated the protocol of an ordained minister. I couldn't help but reflect upon my wife's long and difficult pilgrimage to this place of triumph as a woman of God and a noted spiritual writer.

Marcia was born in 1951 into Chicago's profoundly segregated South Side. Her father, Clarence Dukes, had been born in 1911 in Birdsong, Arkansas, the youngest of four children, before he migrated with his family to the nation's second largest city. Marcia's father, known in his neighborhood as "Duke," became quite a gambler, betting on horses, dogs, boxing matches, and even policy, or "playing the numbers," which was the ghetto lottery, so to speak. Duke worked in the yards of the Illinois railroad. Marcia's mother, Rosa, was born in 1921, in Brazil, Indiana, near Terre Haute. She moved to Chicago when she was seventeen, living with her Aunt "Sis." Marcia's mother cooked, cleaned the house, ran errands, and soon began "writing policy"—she took down the numbers that folk selected and gave them to her aunt, who ran her own numbers station. Rosa eventually went to work for a bigger policy operation, run by a man named Buddy, and was able to rent a room across the street from her aunt on her thirty dollars a week salary.

Marcia's parents met at Buddy's policy station in 1948. Two years later, they had two daughters, and got married thirteen months before Marcia's birth. But in 1953, Duke left the family. He was tired of the crying babies, and resented having to spend his money on milk, food, and diapers, and not being able to come and go as he pleased. After Duke fled, Rosa took a job at a restaurant, working as a short-order cook and waitress. Duke told Rosa that he was moving to a nearby hotel, when in truth he moved in with his girlfriend. It was by accident that his family discovered where he lived. Duke had gone grocery shopping in a local store, and requested that his two boxes of food be delivered to his home. Not realizing that he had moved, the deliveryman brought the groceries to Rosa and the kids. A few minutes later, her father stormed into the house, removed the groceries, and angrily departed, only coming back sporadically to visit his daughters. The few times he saw the girls, he repeatedly avoided telling them where he lived, despite their urgent requests. It hurt little Marcia's heart not to know where the man she loved so dearly lived. It was perhaps even more painful for him to refuse to take her home with him. To his baby girl, it was exceedingly painful not to be able to spend time with Duke, the man who helped bring her into the world but who couldn't be present to help her understand it, or to show her affection.

When Marcia entered kindergarten, she was often accompanied to her half-day, afternoon session at school by her neighbor's older children, Paul and Shirley, who came home to eat lunch. One afternoon, Shirley inadvertently gave Marcia a jolt when she casually pointed out "Mr. Duke's" house on the way to school. Five-year-old Marcia made up her mind right then to pay a visit to her father. That night, she wet the bed, the first time in her young life that her bladder had leaked beyond her control.

The next morning, her heart was pounding in anticipation of making a determined detour to her Daddy's house. In a powerful essay, "Is My Daddy Here?" in the book *Fathersongs*, edited by critic Gloria Wade-Gayles, Marcia gives a poignant account of that fateful day.

"My heart was beating fast," Marcia writes. "As I approached Fifty-third and Princeton, I thought my heart was going to jump out of my chest. I withdrew the picture of Daddy's house from memory bank. That's it. I saw the house. I stood back to see if any lights were on. They were not. I approached the house with 'teeny-tiny' baby steps and sat on the steps of the porch for a half-hour. I watched trains as they passed on the nearby railroad tracks. I watched birds take flight and soar high in the air. I watched the old woman, who lived across the street, watch me. I tried several times to get up the nerve to ring the bell." After questioning whether her father actually lived there, she worked up the nerve to see. "I wiped my running nose on my gray-flannel poodle skirt and rang the doorbell." To her surprise, a strange woman answered Marcia's ring.

"Who are you looking for?" asked the bewildered woman behind the screen door.

"My Daddy, I want to see my Daddy," Marcia told her between sobs. Marcia writes that the "door opened and I stared at the woman's face. She was not pretty. Her leathery reddish-brown complexion reminded me of building bricks. Her goldish-brown hair was tied in a head rag, and she wore a faded house dress."

"What is his name, baby?" the woman asked.

"Clarence Earl Dukes," Marcia replied.

"Who!?" the woman said in disbelief.

"Clarence Earl Dukes," Marcia loudly repeated.

"What is your name?" the woman asked in an irritated voice.

"Mar-see-uh," she enunciated clearly.

"He is not here, but I will tell him you came by," the woman calmly stated as she shut the door in Marcia's face.

When that door closed, it seemed to have also closed the door of her father's presence in Marcia's life. She and her two sisters—Beverly and Elaine, who were born ten months apart—were stair-steps in the birth order, since they were born in quick succession. Before they became best friends, they were, like most siblings, in each other's hair and at each other's throats. Rosa eventually met "Doc," a tall, brown, and handsome podiatry student who became her husband and their beloved stepfather, although Marcia and her sisters loved him as their father. He watched over them with care and bathed them in his unfailing love. Still, the void in Marcia's soul from Daddy-deprivation was huge, since she longed for the affirmation of the man who helped to birth her.

When Marcia began to date, Doc was nearly apoplectic. The second oldest girl of the trio, Elaine, had gotten pregnant at sixteen and had eloped to Idlewild, Indiana, where parental consent for marriage was unnecessary. That broke Doc's heart, and Marcia had resolved to stay the course, graduate from high school and make him and Rosa proud. With Beverly attending Bethune-Cookman College, Marcia was the only girl left, and Doc and Marcia had even more time to bond.

Marcia was determined not to repeat Elaine's history, and at fifteen started a "Virgins Forever" club that had only one other member. She walked stiffly, so as not to sway her hips. She tucked in her behind so that she wouldn't attract the attention of onlookers. She studied hard and became an honors student. She even converted to Catholicism at fourteen—she had already been a Baptist at five, and a Methodist at seven, the only one of her sisters to be baptized—and began to date a tall, very handsome young man named Kirk, who, unlike Marcia, was part of the middle class.

"You have to watch that boy," Doc warned Marcia. "He has those funny looking eyes," referring to Kirk's beautiful hazel-brown peepers. Marcia continued to date Kirk, and three years later chose to renounce membership in her own club because in her mind she had met the man she would marry. When she made sixteen—as black Chicagoans say—Marcia made yet another religious commitment, one more radical than all her other choices combined. Marcia joined the Nation of Islam under the Honorable Elijah Muhammad, whom she eventually met, and who, along with his wife Sister Clara, invited Marcia to live with them, since her parents were mortified by her choice of faith. In fact, they asked the much-maligned Kirk to talk some sense into their daughter about this "dangerous cult." Marcia had to sneak out of the house in mini-skirts, only to change in a nearby restaurant into the long dress she kept hidden in a brown paper bag before attending the Mosque. Within a year and a half, Marcia had left the Nation. She had a conversation with the Black Muslim head after reading the *Autobiography of Malcolm X*, a big taboo in those circles. Marcia talked with Muhammad about the contradiction between asserting the black man's superiority while acknowledging that the inferior white man had gained the upper hand. When Marcia relentlessly questioned the leader, they mutually decided it would be best if she departed the faith.

Marcia's quest for spiritual and political liberation wasn't over. When she was a college sophomore at the University of Illinois in Chicago, Marcia announced to her family that she would marry Kirk under "Black Law." Marcia had renounced Western values and political ideologies for The Revolution. She had convinced Kirk to join the radical nationalist group the Topographical Center, which promoted self-empowerment, self-defense, and a healthy critique of the government. Marcia and Kirk had followed his brother Jimmy into the group, and now they sought to imitate Jimmy again by marrying without the sanction of the racist government or church. Doc was perplexed and outraged.

"What do you mean the legal system is nothing?" Doc challenged his youngest sweetheart. "What does 'the man' have to do with you getting a license?"

"You and Mama should come down and hear Brother C1 speak," Marcia countered, referring to the leader of the revolutionary group she and Kirk had joined. "He could explain all of this to you."

"Who is this C1 character putting this s—t in your head?" Doc demanded. "What does the f—g Topographical Center have to do with you getting married so young anyway?"

Despite Marcia's explanations about black revolutionary struggle—that white racism led to black oppression, that the rules of democracy were unfairly applied to blacks, that black people should actively seek to combat the forces that undermine their lives—Doc and Rosa just didn't understand. Marcia tried to tell her mother that the philosophy she was spouting was deep.

"Deep?" Rosa retorted. "Girl, you're full of crap." Since Rosa had spit that same line at me years later for what she thought was my ignorance, I could testify to how withering it might have been to her daughter. But Marcia persisted, hanging with the Topographical Center for nearly five years and over the objections of her parents, becoming Kirk's common law wife, which, Doc feared, would make Marcia common. In a way, he proved to be prophetic, and although Marcia and Kirk remained together for fifteen years—during which time they had a son, Mwata, now a physician, and Maisha, an actress in Los Angeles—it was a marriage marred by Kirk's cruelty and abuse. If her father's abandonment had been a kind of psychic terror, then Kirk's harsh treatment of Marcia had been an emotional one.

When I met Marcia in 1989, she was a thriving public relations specialist and a vice-president of a successful black Chicago firm. She had already worked for Jesse Jackson as chief of staff for Operation Push's International Trade Bureau, helping to develop the bureau's publication, coordinating conferences, helping to plan economic development for Third World countries and the Caribbean, and strategizing to bolster local businesses. She approached me as I stood along a wall in her church, Trinity United Church of Christ, after the close of a Friday night revival service.

"Hi, I *really* appreciate your work," the lovely young lady who I took to be several years younger than me stated. I immediately took notice, since most of my published work at that time had appeared in left-wing magazines and religious journals with painfully small circulations.

"You do?" I asked, impressed by her knowledge of my writings, some of which she cited. "You and my mother and a few other folk, but I'm glad to know that somebody is digging my work."

Her enchanting and transcendent beauty rushed me in a generous flood of wholesome images as she spoke to others who intermittently interrupted our conversation to say hello. Years later, in an assignment for her acting class at Spelman College, Marcia's daughter Maisha poetically captured her mother's distinct attraction.

Her deep-set cinnamon brown eyes twinkle like stars in the night. They are shielded by her flirtatious long and lovely lashes. Her button size nose always made me wonder if she could inhale as much air as I could. She has a warm smile, with voluptuous lips that hide her teeth, which gleam like the sunshine. As she grins, deep concave dimples are revealed on the surface of her honey golden face. She has auburn hair, as coarse as sheep's wool, yet as shiny as black patent leather shoes. Her petite size, five-feet-two-inches in height, and a fully developed body, tops off her appearance as a Nubian baby doll.

Marcia was breathtakingly fine, but I couldn't trace the voluptuous form her daughter lauded—nor, to me, her greatest asset—beneath the smart navy blue pants suit that draped her diminutive frame. But all that changed when I met her again a week later. She was adorned in a bluish purple wool gabardine dress, with a wide black collar that flared almost to the shoulders, tulip lapels, and a zippered front, falling a couple of inches below the knee, reminiscent of the finest of fifties-style clothing. (I was soon to discover that vintage purple clothing suited Marcia well. Her wardrobe also featured a forties-style purple satin suit, with a tapered waste and padded shoulders, wide lapels, with intricate black beading on the collars and pocket flaps, and a straight skirt that dropped just below the knees that featured a modest split in the back.) I was able to see her graceful gams, two of the most sensuous legs I had seen that were both sturdy and shapely. But most important, I was able to glimpse her glorious gluteus, a spherical wonder of taut flesh to which I would later devote passionate poetry.

As Marcia and I became friends, long before we became lovers and spouses, I discovered the depth of her brilliance. She is unquestionably one of the most intellectually curious human beings I have ever met. She is interested in quantum physics, social criticism, Brazilian society, Christian and Jewish mysticism, international finance, liberation theology, contemporary fiction, cosmology, spiritual discernment, feminism, domestic violence, the theater, juvenile justice, ancient philosophy, evolution, astrology, film noir, paranormal phenomena, environmentalism, homelessness, neurosciences, mathematics, and a whole lot more. She reads incessantly, thinks critically, and is constantly stimulating me intellectually. When I taught at the Chicago Theological Seminary, she sat in on my classes, and proved to be my most scholastically aggressive interlocutor. In my home, Marcia is the most incisive and insightful intellectual.

After we were married, Marcia began to act on her deep yearning to speak, preach and write about the plight of women. Besides her essay in *Fathersongs*, Marcia paid homage to Doc in "I'll Call Him Daddy," a personal essay she published in Brooke Stephens' edited volume, *Men We Cherish*. Marcia also moderated a provocative roundtable on sexuality and spirituality, entitled "Can You Love God and Sex?" for the February 1999 issue of *Essence* magazine, where she serves as a contributing writer. The roundtable featured scholars, ministers, psychologists, and gurus like Iyanla Vanzant, Linda Hollies, Delores Williams, Kelly Brown-Douglas, Ava Muhammad, Darlene Powell Hopson, and Emilie Townes. The panel addressed the cultural sources of sexual shame, sex and self-esteem, rape, sexual abuse and recovery, the search for God, the sharing of wisdom among black women, and developing a healthy self-concept.

It was in two other *Essence* articles that Marcia addressed issues that are critical to the black church. In May 2002, Marcia wrote an essay, "The Houses of Worship Our Mothers Built," which addressed the persistent barriers to ordaining black women, despite their overwhelming majority in the black church. She discussed how many more "Black women are formally trained in divinity, but their path to the pulpit remains blocked by men—and women who believe it is reserved 'for men only.'" Marcia examined the shallow arguments advanced by those black ministers who appeal to tradition and a narrow interpretation of the Bible to justify their ongoing sexism.

Given the problems that prevail in black communities—including families in crisis, the epidemic of AIDS, the criminalization of men and children—Marcia argued that the "talents of Black women preachers could be put to good use healing our communities," making it senseless to "turn our backs on these powerful resources." Arguing that the black church in America has "historically been an incubator for Black male leadership when it could assert itself nowhere else," Marcia suggested that the broadening of the cultural influence of black men lessened the cultural need to view the pulpit as the preserve of black men. She contended that the black male preacher's unjust "Sunday-morning dominance could become a threat to our spiritual health if it prevents us from fully appreciating that the feminine is also an important aspect of the divine."

But nothing else she has written has been as widely cited and controversial as Marcia's May 1998 feature, "When Preachers Prey." Marcia's article addressed a subject that is cloaked in taboo in religious circles: the sexual relations between male clergy and female parishioners. Written in the aftermath of the Henry Lyons debacle—where the leader of the nation's largest and most influential black church organization, the National Baptist Convention, was sent to prison for financial malfeasance, and who had engaged in extramarital relations with at least one woman—"When Preachers Prey" went full throttle at the sexual hypocrisy that swamps many of our churches. But Marcia's article was not a simple tirade against a sexually sinful male clergy, although she was bravely critical of the duplicitous sexual practices of ministers who condemn sexual sin even as they succumb to its temptations. She wrote, for instance, that "too many times I've seen preachers exploit [their] power and even take it for granted, as if it were an entitlement—sometimes preying on vulnerable and lonely woman, at other times seeking out accomplices in sexual misconduct who are quite willing or, at best, self-deceived."

Marcia's article was also self-critical—she confessed having been the preacher's prey and indulging "in the same corrupt delusion I've since seen many of my sisters use to justify an illicit relationship." She also made a distinction between those clergy who get caught up in a relationship out of emotional needs and seek forgiveness for their sin, and those who make a sport of bedding women with heartless abandon. Marcia criticized the double standard for males and females that prevails in the black church, where churches condemn teenage girls "for out-of-wedlock pregnancies" while "the (usually older) men who impregnate them are overlooked and hence implicitly excused." While she excoriated male clergy for their abusive practices, Marcia also cast a critical eye at those women who seek out sinful trysts.

In suggesting ways for "imperfect humans [to] avoid dangerous liaisons and unholy alliances," Marcia suggested that sisters learn to trust each other for their personal and spiritual needs; that women must stop projecting their needs for companionship onto married ministers; that churches must develop reasonable guidelines to address sexual misconduct by pastors and other members; and that Christians should seek to live up to the ideal expressed in the Old Testament book of Micah: to "do justice, love mercy and walk humbly with God." Marcia's article reaped a firestorm of controversy in local congregations, radio stations, and television programs across the nation, as folk debated the critical issues Marcia had courageously and honestly confronted. I was proud of how she handled herself with poise and dignity as outraged traditionalists and irate offenders alike assaulted her. Her article was one of the most heavily responded to features in the history of *Essence*. As we traveled across the country, hundreds of people thanked Marcia for her bravery in finally naming a problem that needed to be confronted.

If Marcia addressed clergy abuse with extraordinary eloquence, she was equally spectacular in clarifying the moral and political stakes of 9/11. In an online interview conducted exactly a month after the terrorist attacks, Marcia—introduced as "one of our nation's foremost religious figures and spiritual writers"—brilliantly historicized the *terrors* that the United States has imposed and endured. When asked if there was a way to handle the terrorist attacks other than fighting back, Marcia mentioned the valiant efforts of Mohandas

Gandhi and Martin Luther King, Jr. She also suggested that issuing an immediate call to arms, without comprehending the full scope and nature of the tragedy, was not only premature, but also potentially destructive. "During the Oklahoma bombing, which was perpetrated by Americans—fanatic, zealous Christians—that response [to go to war] was not given," Marcia said. "If it had been, we would have had Americans fighting Americans. Initially, we thought that it was perpetrated by our Arab brothers and sisters; but once we found out otherwise—that it was one of our own—the proper legal channels of investigation and discovery were made."

Marcia also argued that ignorance about United States foreign policies kept many citizens from comprehending our negative perception in many parts of the world. She also linked the amnesia about American-bred domestic terrorism to our failure to account for the distrust of American promises of peace and justice in the past. Referring to the heinous events of 1921 in Tulsa, Oklahoma, where more than 600 black citizens were burned, lynched, and murdered in an all-black town by white citizens, Marcia shed light on the political and moral connection between these two events of terror. "It was the first act of terrorism by Americans against Americans. Only these Americans, whose land was destroyed and whose economy was ruined, were well-to-do black folks. We don't find in our history books the outrage of the American government, a national consensus about this egregious event, an outpouring of comfort by the American Red Cross, a change in legislation, or a manhunt by our govern-

ment agencies for the perpetrators of this crime." Marcia said
that in light of this injustice, blacks might have been expected
to seek an eye for an eye and to retaliate violently against
whites. Instead, these blacks read the Scriptures and appealed
to their moral vision and the hope of God to see them
through. "The only strength, the only hope that we rest on, is
our faith in God, and the belief that justice will prevail for
those that live righteously."

Marcia was not being politically naïve, and said, "I understand that we have to defend ourselves," and that "this
mess...needs to be cleaned up and responded to." But she
pointed out that a small group of people who committed a
crime should not be used to indict an entire nation. When she
was asked if 9/11 was an instance of our political policies
coming back to us with a vengeance, Marcia responded,
"That's simplistic." Citing the American involvement in
Afghanistan before 9/11—funding freedom fighters, Bin
Laden among them, to stave off Russian invasion, and the supply of more than $40 million to eradicate the growth of
poppy fields—she raised an intriguing question. "Now, are the
chickens coming home to roost because we're willing to fund
freedom fighters—but not real democracy in Afghanistan—or
to protect our oil interests? Or are they coming home to roost
because American people who are drug users suffered because
we didn't stop the drug trafficking? America now has a
decrease of heroin coming into its borders, because we
stopped the planes, and we stopped the production. But we
could have done that before."

In response to a question about what the nation should be doing to prevent passivity in the face of possible misconduct by America in the war on terrorism, Marcia said that our nation shouldn't be self-righteous, bigoted, or narrow-minded. And then she offered a profound compassion for the victims of American capitalism and materialism the world over, those who understandably view our consumerism as evil. "The ground zero site of the World Trade Center may be devastating to Americans, but those people live in a country whose landscape is ground zero. We have not been…sensitive to the needs of others, unless we were exploiting their needs and pain for our benefit."

Marcia pointed out that we could love our country best by being critical of its unjust policies and affirming the need to distinguish between enlightened patriotism and blind patriotism. Enlightened patriotism advocates the view that Americans must offer critical support of the nation, affirming its good practices and criticizing its destructive ones. Blind patriotism, she argued, supports the nation regardless of its disloyalty to its stated goals of democracy, justice and freedom. But blind patriotism is little more than the obscured half of the Janus-faced terror that we are fighting. "We can become just as fanatical as any terrorist group that uncritically exclaims that their way of being and doing and knowing the world is the only way." Marcia argued that true patriotism meant that American citizens would become educated about our democracy, and that perhaps one of the hopeful outcomes of our disaster would be enhanced engagement with politics.

It is that kind of moral passion and hunger for social justice that led Marcia to the ministry. When she stood to give her first sermon, I knew that she was at home. I also knew that she had found the perfect way to help heal other people who are victims of all sorts of terror—domestic, racial, sexual, economic, and political. Although she is my wife, she is also my wise teacher and spiritual counselor. And as she continues to explore her God-given genius, I know she will continue to be a gift to the world.

VII. The Anatomy of Black Beauty

18

I Read It in a Magazine

Although I had once briefly visited the Johnson Publishing Company headquarters in Chicago—whizzing through the historical eleven-story building with a small group in February 1990 for a special program during Black History Month—this trip was altogether different. I was set to visit with Linda Johnson Rice, the dynamic diva who sits atop the cosmetics business and publishing empire, including *Ebony* and *Jet* magazines, built by her father, the legendary John H. Johnson. I was the subject of a *Jet* story about my move from Chicago's DePaul University to the University of Pennsylvania, in Philadelphia. It was a thrill to appear again in the magazine's pages. (In the past, I had contributed to *Ebony* and *Jet* as an expert on one issue or another.) My friends and I enjoyed a running joke shared by millions of blacks: you don't really *exist* as a black person until your name or face turns up in *Jet*. I was happy to have my existence confirmed.

It has become a tradition for black celebrities to pass through the offices of the only black-owned business building in downtown Chicago, and one of perhaps three such buildings in any downtown area in the entire nation. In a sense, coming to the Johnson Publishing Company headquarters for well-known blacks is like competitors in the Apollo Theater's famed amateur night rubbing the mythic tree stump before they take the stage. It is both a good luck charm and a sign of solidarity with those who have come before. I was literally on my way out of the city to take up my new duties, and before I left, I had to get a closer glimpse of the famous digs of a venerable black institution. I was just glad to be a cultural critic and social commentator whose views were taken seriously by magazines read in half of all black homes. Next to having your face peer from the front of a cardboard church fan as it is being furiously waved on a hot Sunday by a pew-dwelling sister, this was as good as it got for black circulation.

I was especially delighted to have an audience with Rice. I had admired her from a distance for many years, following in the press her rise through the ranks of the family business, and hearing nothing but praise for her extremely sharp mind and her down-home style. If Rice's life seemed charmed, it didn't begin that way. "I'm extremely fortunate," Rice has stated. "I was adopted when I was three and a half years old. It was the luck of the draw. There isn't a day that goes by that I don't think about that." It seems that Rice was bred to one day

become the head of the largest and most successful publishing company in the world, and the only black female CEO of
a top five business on the BE 100, *Black Enterprise* magazine's
list of the top one hundred black-owned companies. She
began frequenting the family business—her mother, Eunice,
is secretary-treasurer of the company, and heads the *Ebony*
Fashion Fair, an annual traveling fashion extravaganza through
which the company has donated nearly $50 million to black
charities—at the tender age of six. By seven, she was traveling
with her mother to a European couture show to select clothes
for the fashion fair. She was soon wrapping a feather boa
around her head and walking like a model; her early exposure
to fashion turned her into a self-confessed clotheshorse and
primed her to develop a vibrant sense of style.

When Rice graduated from the prestigious secondary
University of Chicago Laboratory School, she took a B.A. in
journalism from the University of Southern California, before
being named vice-president and fashion editor at *Ebony*, and
later, adding to her title assistant to the president. Rice
returned to school and collected an MBA from Northwestern
University's Kellogg Graduate School of Management in
1987, and was promoted to president and chief operating officer of Johnson Publishing Company at twenty-nine years old.

Even before she became president, Rice remarked on the
racial progress made by a new generation of black entrepreneurs. "We are young, independent, intelligent blacks who are
as good as young, independent, intelligent whites," Rice said.
"We are no longer tokens. At least we don't think of ourselves

in that respect." Rice also reflected on the social constraints on female executives and the pioneering role of feminists in clearing a path for the women who came after them. "Thank God for all those women who asserted themselves [in the '60s and '70s]," Rice said. "They helped set a pace of respect, and I think this is the key. The feminist movement through the late 1970s set up the idea in men in business that women deserve parity and equality at all levels. It's established now that we are intelligent and worthy of respect. And this has allowed us to be more feminine, instead of constantly having to display our strength."

Rice saw no contradiction between feminism and femininity, since performing well at work created a climate of acceptance that allowed her to express her female identity. To her they were flip sides of the same coin. "I don't see feminism and femininity as two separate things," she said. "I see them as one thing. In my work, I don't spend much time considering my femininity. I come to work each day, do my job, and I'm well respected. It may be because I've grown up with the people here, but my being a woman is not an important issue."

Still, Rice acknowledged that patriarchal practices occasionally interrupt the flow of gender equality. "Sometimes when you're dealing with an old-boy network, as in the television industry, those men don't want to bring a woman in on everything that is going on. Then I have to be extremely assertive. Otherwise, I don't give it much thought." Rice viewed her feminine presence as a political goad to awareness for men who can't reconcile beauty and intelligence in a female executive. "I have found that using my femininity is a plus at times with men who may think, 'Oh, she's attractive but perhaps not very bright.' When they find that you're attractive and you also know what you're doing, they're impressed with that."

Two years into her duties as president and chief operating officer, Rice spoke about the opportunities for young black business people, saying that they had "learned how to acquire capital, how to put together business plans, and how to start enterprises." But barriers remained. "There is still some discrimination in lending practices, and certain bank officers will have petty prejudices. A black entrepreneur has to be equally if not more prepared than a white to get his fair share of loan money."

Rice also anticipated the phenomenal success of figures like media mogul Cathy Hughes, founder and chairperson of Radio One, Inc., the largest black owned and operated broadcast company in the nation. "In the 1990s blacks could do very well in franchising, including starting their own. You'll also see more and more as broadcast journalists and as owners of radio and TV stations." But she also urged black entrepreneurs to extend the legacy of black progress by employing poor and working-class blacks as well as able professionals, foreshadowing the magnificent efforts of Earvin "Magic" Johnson to establish lucrative businesses in the inner city that employ thousands of blacks. "Black entrepreneurs owe it to themselves and to their heritage to tap the labor pool in the inner cities and hire other blacks—whether as a shipping clerk or a general counsel." Rice has put her money where her

heart is by hiring blacks at her company, and by contributing
to a variety of charities, including the Boys & Girls Clubs.
One evening at a posh fundraiser for the agency, Rice took a
breather from the caviar puffs and the cold rounds of duck
pâté to observe that there were "so many black boys and girls
who directly benefit from the Boys & Girls Clubs," noticing
that when one visited "communities like Henry Horner
Homes [a Chicago housing project]," that "kids are learning.
They're thriving at the 'club.'"

Rice's business acumen has often fused with her racial
awareness. For instance, in the spring of 1993, *Ebony* teamed
with Spiegel, Inc., the nation's largest mail-order catalog company, to produce *E Style*, a catalog featuring clothing designed
especially for black women's bodies. *E Style* included clothing
ranging from casual, career, and evening wear to hats, shoes,
and other accessories. "Spiegel has done its homework," Rice
said, speaking of the *E Style* catalog. "What they've done is
take a random selection of women with different body types
and analyzed them, so that when the clothes are manufac-
tured, they fit the needs of black women." But there were
black critics who argued that it was offensive to target black
women for clothing designed specifically for their bodies,
contending that it reinforced stereotypes from which blacks
for decades had tried to escape. But Rice argued that her aim
was to "give African-American women what we believe is not
out there now: clothes that will fit their bodies, in colors they
like, at affordable prices. The key is to service a market that has
not been serviced to its full potential." Ever conscious of the

racial politics of aesthetic choice, Rice revealed an edifying purpose behind the *E Style* catalog. "We didn't want everyone in the catalog to have fair skin and long hair. We wanted to show the range of what black women are about. And the age range. And the size range."

Rice's politics weren't limited to magazines or catalogs. In 1992, Rice participated in President Bill Clinton's economic conference in Little Rock. In1994, she traveled with Vice President Al Gore and first lady Hillary Rodham Clinton as part of the predominantly black forty-four-member official U.S. delegation to the historic presidential inauguration for South African President Nelson Mandela. And in 2000, she and three other black women resigned from the board of Chicago's Museum of Contemporary Art because they concluded that the museum's diversity efforts were progressing too slowly.

More recently, Rice crossed rhetorical swords with former CBS *This Morning* host Bryant Gumbel. In a commencement address at the 2001 Howard University graduation, Gumbel declared that the graduates were "entitled to a rich life," but that the status of blacks would not change "if all you're going to seek is a superficial *Ebony* magazine view of life—one that accentuates only your cars and your clothes." Gumbel's remarks drew first blood, and the ire of Rice, who retaliated swiftly. "We're glad that you found time to visit Black America, but we regret you were not better informed," Rice wrote in a letter to Gumbel that was reported in the press. "We don't visit Black America, we live here." Rice was obviously referring to the belief of some blacks that Gumbel is insufficiently connected to the mainstream of African-American thought and culture. She was incensed as well by Gumbel's apparent ignorance of the trajectory of Johnson Publishing Company's history of addressing serious social issues through its magazines. "I find it appalling," she said. "He's obviously misinformed and probably has not picked up a copy of *Ebony* in some time…We have chronicled every important historical event in the African-American community over the past 56 years." Ironically, *Ebony* had included Gumbel in a spread entitled, "The 55 Most Intriguing Blacks of 2000."

Rice's argument about the racial importance of her company's magazines is supported in the history surrounding the founding of *Jet* magazine. *Jet* appeared in 1951, the same year that *Negro Digest* ceased publication. *Negro Digest*—subtitled a "Magazine of Negro Comment"—featured articles by luminaries ranging from Langston Hughes to Carl Sandburg. When it appeared, blacks who were severely underrepresented in nearly every way and sphere in America welcomed *Negro Digest*. After a decade, however, *Negro Digest's* circulation dropped to 15,000, giving way to *Jet*. Unlike *Negro Digest*, *Jet* focused on black marriages, deaths, and news from the social world. Until *Jet* was regularly published and available, black life was invisible to most of the nation.

Moreover, *Jet* provided a common frame of reference for blacks who were separated by class and region. *Jet* also featured profiles of black achievers to combat negative stereotypes of black identity while providing a weekly chronicle of the struggle for black progress and liberation. When *Jet* published a picture of Emmett Till's mangled and bloated body in 1955, it horrified and galvanized blacks across the nation to fight with more determination for racial equality. Its brief articles and short number of pages ingeniously anticipated the episodic character of consciousness—and the shrunken attention span—of the postmodern MTV era. But it also addressed a more substantive issue: barely literate blacks just emerging from the South who needed information quickly and simply. With a one-million circulation, *Jet* has survived to become the longest-running weekly digest-sized magazine in the nation.

When blacks in the 1960s clamored for an outlet for more politically relevant reflections, Johnson launched *Black World*, edited by a doyen of the Black Arts Movement, the militant Hoyt Fuller. *Black World* had a circulation of 100,000. Publisher John H. Johnson finally closed the magazine, but not because he was offended by Fuller's politics. "[Fuller] gave everybody hell, including me," Johnson remembered. "And I let him give me hell, so I know there were no restrictions on what he did or printed. We lost 2 million dollars on it." When *Black World* shut down, demonstrators gathered in front of the Johnson Publishing Company's headquarters. Johnson brought the protesters inside and offered them coffee and recorded their names. When he checked with the subscription department, he discovered that none of them were subscribers. "How can you tell me what I need and then not support me?" Johnson queried.

I had all of this history in mind when I made plans to visit Johnson Publishing headquarters.

"You've never met Ms. Rice?" Clarence Waldron, the author of my *Jet* profile, asked in amazement.

"No, I sure haven't, and I'd love to hook up before I leave town."

When Clarence called back to say that Linda Johnson Rice wanted to meet me as well, we arranged a time for our rendezvous.

As the cab dropped me at the impressive, sand-toned contemporary building at 820 South Michigan Avenue, facing the calmness of Lake Michigan and the beauty of Grant Park, I looked up to see the famous JPC letters mounted in script along the top of the headquarters' face. On the ground, two lovely ladies greeted me on their way out of the front doors for an early lunch.

"Hello, Professor Dyson," a tall, luscious caramel sister sweetly intoned. "I am such a fan of your work."

I was hoping the "Damned, you fine" phrase punching my brain hadn't escaped my lips. I even repressed my next reaction, the only slightly less cheesy, "Thank you, and as I gaze upon your feminine form, I'm a huge fan of God's work." Instead, I settled for "You're so kind."

I had barely darkened the lobby door when a security guard was equally generous.

"I see you on television all the time, and I love the things you talk about," she said, her magnificent skin shining in ebony clarity.

"That's very nice of you to say," I replied, thinking to myself that I was already enjoying my visit and I had been here less than a minute.

As the male security guard called for Clarence Waldron to retrieve me from the lobby, more women—beautiful, vivacious, glowing, confident, short, tall, light, dark, medium, voluptuous, wispy women—filed in and out of the building. I didn't realize just how dominant gorgeous black women are in the Johnson Publishing Company headquarters, or else I might have beaten a path to their door years before. Sure, I always turned first to the *Jet* "Beauty of the Week" centerfold when I fetched the magazine from my mailbox—if my wife was near, I turned to the obituaries, what *Jet* genteelly calls the "Census," since her presence killed any hope of fully appreciating that week's sister, even as I tried to conjure my feminist conscience to quell my guilty pleasure. But I had no idea of the smart, sexy, and spirited sisters who bless that space. I was already quietly chanting hallelujah and Handel was nowhere to be found.

When Clarence arrived to take me upstairs, he was, thankfully, not alone. After we exchanged greetings, he introduced me to his stunning companion.

"Michael Eric Dyson, this is Margena Christian, an Associate Editor at *Jet*," Clarence stated.

"Ms. Christian, how are you?" I joyously retorted.

"Just fine, Reverand Dyson, it's good to meet you."

Oh, right, *Reverend* Dyson. That woke me up—a little bit. But I was vibing off the spirit of black female *presence*, reveling in the splendor of the varied colors that rim the black rainbow. I was in church, all right, but it was the Cathedral of Sweet Sisters The Divine.

Margena is a five-foot-two-inch chocolate charmer, a graceful young lady whose gray dress silhouetted her curvaceous frame with dangerous precision. Her beautiful brown face is punctuated by a warm and delightful smile, and her long black hair flows to her back with an assertive authenticity that shouts, "This ain't no weave!" We talked about our love for rap music: how it has changed over the last two decades; how it receives a bad rap when it often sends a positive message; who counts among the genre's best lyricists (Rakim, KRS-One, Talib Kweli, Common, Mos Def, Chuck D, Lauryn Hill, 2Pac, Nas, and more); who had the greatest flow (Biggie, Snoop, and Jay-Z among others); and who was the most influential (2Pac hands down).

"I saw you preach at Trinity," Margena let on, informing me that we were members of the same Chicago church. "You threw down, and rapped as well. You have a nice flow yourself."

Of course, that deserved the warmest hug I could summon. After my spontaneous show of affection, we all headed to the elevator. Our car stopped first at the third floor, which houses the Fashion Fair Cosmetics department, opening onto a landscape of bronze pulchritude. It might as well have been a Frank Capra sketch of office life with a serious tan. The sight was majestic, as black women of every hue, height and hairstyle streamed through the halls. As the elevator doors closed too quickly, I sighed and looked Clarence Waldron in the eyes and gave him that black male "boy there are some amazing women in this place" look that he readily acknowledged with a wide grin.

When we got to the seventh floor, Clarence, Margena, and I toured their working area, where I met yet more intelligent and beautiful sisters. Because Clarence and Margena had to attend a brief meeting—I was a half-hour early—they deposited me in the gracious hands of the company's librarians. The head librarian, Pam Cash, I was shortly to learn, is a scrupulous bibliophile, a full-figured and dynamic brown-skinned sister full of warmth and knowledge. Another librarian, Dona Robertson, a vivacious and buxom dark-skinned woman, recalls the striking, angular beauty of opera diva Jessye Norman. The third librarian, Kelly Spurlin, a comely light-skinned young lady, was that day celebrating her birthday, which called for yet more hugs for her and her comrades in cataloging and enlightenment.

I parked at Pam's desk, and we established an immediate rapport as she discovered that I was writing a book about my love for black women.

"You know, *Ebony* has done some great articles on various aspects of black women through the years," Cash proudly boasted.

She delighted in using her encyclopedic powers to recall relevant articles that have appeared in the Johnson publications. I was about to discover why Cash has been called a valuable "information specialist."

"Follow me," Cash enthusiastically commanded. We headed for the files and then scoured the legendary archives. Cash thumbed through the cards as only a true manager of information can, and generated a list of articles she could show me on the spot. She hunted quickly and purposefully through the long aisle containing old *Ebony* magazines, and soon we had an impressive stack of paper that testified to her claim of her company's commitment to chronicling love for sisters.

"Here's an interesting one," Pam said. "It was written by Duke Ellington."

The famed bandleader's paean to the fairer sex was entitled, "The Most Exciting Women I've Known," and appeared in the April 1952 issue. Besides Eleanor Roosevelt, all the women he named on this occasion were black. The Duke liked Marian Anderson—"think of her, straight and tall and groomed," he wrote, asking us to picture "the ease with which she tilts her magnificent head, arches her priceless throat and sends forth her richness and warmth which has all the color and richness of a rainbow or sunset." Ellington also praised legendary entertainer Josephine Baker's "supple, gold and autumn-brown body" that swayed with the very restraint which is abandon," while lauding dancer and choreographer Katherine Dunham, "who is as famous for her skill as an artist as she is for the attraction she weaves for men who are accustomed to feminine luxury." The world-famous composer greatly admired singer Ivie Anderson, who "immortalized" his song *It Don't Mean a Thing If It Ain't Got That Swing*. "She made people look up to Negro women," Ellington wrote, adding that she "had a very live, militant social sense," and a "way of tackling 'problem' situations by herself and 'on her own.'"

Duke wrote that he knew "few more exciting women" than educator and civic leader Mary McLeod Bethune, who "throbs with powerful magnetism as surely as an organ throbs with beautiful sound." Ellington wished that her fans would realize that pianist Hazel Scott—who was then married to Adam Clayton Powell, Jr., and who possessed "wonderful shoulders, a pretty petulant mouth and an awful lot of talent"—also "plays a wonderful tune of intelligence and awareness of what is happening in our times." Finally, the great performer Lena Horne, who "had a *café au lait* complexion," and "a throaty, pulsing voice" and "a lovely body, young and eager," also excited the Duke, but for more than her good looks. "There are several Lenas, all exciting," he wrote. "There is the Lena who makes every individual she encounters, great or small, fellow entertainer or autograph hound, feel important because of the way she greets, meets and accepts him. There is the Lena in conversation, incisive, determined and thinking on her own. There is the Lena who can seduce the mind, who can advertise to the world that her people can be beautiful, inside and out."

Pam showed me a powerful article by *Ebony* editor-in-chief Lerone Bennett, Jr., who is also a brilliant intellectual and historian. Named simply, "What Is Black Beauty?" the November 1980 essay was published a decade after the "Black Is Beautiful" slogan had rung in the heads and hearts of black

America. Bennett argued that there are three reasons that whites, and some blacks, fail to give "Black beauty its due." (*Ebony* capitalizes black as a sign of racial respect equal to that of the white race). First, black beauty is "often disguised by poverty, nutritional inadequacies, and intolerable burdens." Next, black beauty is "appraised almost always by White standards alien to its genius." Finally, black beauty "is often forced *to doubt itself* and to disguise itself by the cruel and artificial standards of a society which says always and everywhere that Black is bad and White is good."

Drawing on the vast outpouring of letters and photographs from *Ebony's* thirty-fifth anniversary tribute to black women, which Bennett suggested was the basis for "a group definition of Black beauty," he asserted seven propositions for black beauty. One, black beauty "is evolving and cannot be defined with finality," and when black folk enjoy power and resources, we will we be able to "nurture and sustain" our beauties "and define and defend them." Two, black women are beautiful "just as they are, with the noses and the hair and the shapes that God gave them." Three, "Black beauty is *Black* beauty," because it must be appraised by standards we generate from within the race. Four, black beauty "is beauty defined by its relationship to a black base." Hence, blackness is characterized by an "ecumenicity of colors," including black, cream, and brown. "What draws all these colors into the Black continuum and makes them relevant to Black beauty is the way the black base colors, shapes, and *blackens* the brown and cream and gold."

Five, "Black beauty is a synthesis of external and internal factors and cannot be defined a priori by physical factors alone." (Bennett quoted Hegel in his first point; now he uses another philosophical term in his argument, without fear of being called highfalutin' or dubbed an egghead. I must confess that I find that a manifestation of extreme black beauty!) Six, "Black beauty is Joy," since it rests in how a black woman "laughs, the way she calls a bluff, the patented, wholehearted, wholebodied way she moves." In supporting his point, Bennett—at "the risk of chauvinism or worse"—quotes a choice line of poesy, apparently the work of Julian Bond, that I must confess I missed: "Look at that gal/ Shake that thing/ We cannot all be/ Martin Luther King..." Finally, black beauty is "in the soul of the Black beholder." As Bennett eloquently phrased it, "There are elements of beauty in every Black woman that speak with particular force to particular men who were called by their Creator to testify to the beauty of that particular combination."

Along those lines, Cash showed me a three-page spread, from January 1950, featuring headshots of well-known black figures with a bikini-clad model at the center of the first two pages. The headline read, "What Men Notice About Women." Weighing in were celebrities like singer Billy Eckstine ("large flashy eyes"), heavyweight champ Joe Louis ("soft, graceful hands"), Urban League head Lester B. Granger ("intelligence and a sense of humor"), entertainer Nat "King" Cole ("carriage and attire"), performer Earl "Fatha" Hines ("a strong sense of understanding, breeding, and good manners"), and comedic actor Eddie "Rochester" Anderson (perfect "ankles" and "calves just right—tapering into lovely hips and a perfect bust").

The model's photograph was marked with lines radiating from her different body parts and features to register the results of a poll of one hundred men to determine what they noticed about women. The percentages prove in some measure an intriguing consistency in what attracts black men to black women: hands, 1%; ankles, 2%; hair, 2%; eyes, 3%; legs, 7%; lips, 8%; bust, 31%; and hips—46%. This was long before hip-hop's preoccupation with hind parts and its admonition to beautiful young ladies to "back that thang up," but it seems as if their forefathers, stoked by jazz and rhythms and blues, were in complete agreement. A March 1978 reprint of a September 1956 article counseled black men about "How to Handle Beautiful Women," proving that the subject still held fascination more than two decades later. The five rules include self-assurance, the ability to hold a conversation instead of gaping at a woman's beauty, the careful selection of compliments, being oneself, and the suggestion to be "firmly masculine, yet gentle."

In March 1979, *Ebony* ran a story on the "Problems and Pleasures of the Tall Woman," addressing the difficulties of finding clothes and a man who was not intimidated by women six feet and taller. The article caught my interest because it featured a sweet, happy photograph of six-foot Phyllis Hyman, the supremely gifted but underappreciated chanteuse who slumped into depression and took her life eleven years later. I had caught Hyman in concert at Hampton University's 1992 homecoming, and had even had a memorable encounter with her at an *Essence Awards* after party in New York City in 1990.

"I love your music, Ms. Hyman," I had assured her that evening as I looked up to her gorgeous mocha-colored face with those incredibly shapely lips and baby-doll eyes carved in an almond mold.

"Do you baby?" she asked me as my yellow skin flushed rouge. "Then come here."

She pulled me close to her ample chest, which loomed large in a midnight black gown with a furiously assertive décolletage. As my face landed barely above her softly fleshed breasts—which I had seen on page a decade earlier when she posed nude for a men's magazine, the memory of which caused me shame and pleasure—I felt at home in her hug. After we posed for a couple of photos, we spent the next hour chatting and generally carousing in gleeful abandon. When I learned of her death five years later, I grieved at the loss of a singular talent and beautiful though troubled soul.

Two articles highlight *Ebony's* commitment in the 1970s to bringing sophistication and scholarly depth to the issues confronting black women. Joyce Ladner's August 1975 essay, "The Women," with its revealing subtitle, "Conditions of slavery laid the foundation for their liberation," is a brilliant, engaging survey of the progress of black women over a 200-year span of black history. Ladner, a pioneering black sociologist, and the former interim president of Howard University, argued that "the black woman has been one of the most creative, resourceful, and enduring forces in America." Ladner contended that while the "conditions of slavery" forced the black woman into servitude, they may have ironically "laid the foundation for her true liberation long before there was movement." Because she was compelled out of necessity to work in the field, to be a nursemaid, cook, seamstress and nurse, the black woman "became a versatile untiring laborer who could not afford the luxury of concentrating on a single task. Out of this tradition she forged her own identity, set her own pace, and established precedents that are now being followed by women all over the world."

Ladner referred to Deborah King's notion that black women are subject to "double jeopardy"—being the victim of both racial and gender oppression—she argued that black women, unlike their white counterparts, have had to master their economic domain as breadwinners and caregivers for most of their history. Ladner charted the progress of the black freedom struggle and the quest for equality through the efforts of courageous black women, including abolitionist Harriet Tubman, novelist Frances E. W. Harper, teacher and poet Charlotte Forten Grimke, anti-lynching crusader Ida B. Wells Barnett, folklorist Zora Neale Hurston, Mary McLeod Bethune, suffragist Mary Church Terrell, entrepreneur C. J. Walker, civil rights activist Rosa Parks, activist Gloria Richardson, freedom fighter Fannie Lou Hamer and a host of other pioneering women. Ladner concluded that despite the "relative achievement that can be projected for the future, one must remember that, while the heroines of the race shall continue to be commemorated, it is the average women who, unsung and unnamed, will be the supporting cast."

Lerone Bennett, Jr.'s "No Crystal Stair: The Black Woman in History," whose title is borrowed from a line in Langston Hughes's famous poem of a talk given by a mother to her son, traced in the August 1977 issue the valiant role of women in the struggle for black self-determination. Bennett proposed that "to understand what the Black woman has become and what she is becoming one must walk with her a little while on the steep and tortuous stairs that made her what she is." Bennett measured the downward spiral of black women from "the great height of the African tradition which revered mothers and gave a relatively high status to women in general," to the slave trade that "ended all that and plunged the ancestors of contemporary Black women into a maelstrom of brutality and horror which lasted for more than 400 years." Bennett argued that slavery damaged the relations between black men and women, and that "because of the sexism of an age which believed that women, Black and White, should be seen and not heard, the pioneer Black social movements were led by men." Bennett said that, despite these barriers, black women often outstripped the men in fighting for freedom.

Bennett also argued that in the Reconstruction period, black women "had the first opportunity to explore the suppressed possibilities of Black femininity." He identified three responses: the attempt to legalize relations that had gone unrecognized in slavery; the adoption of new dress codes, where black women for the first time wore jewelry and fine clothes; and the mass withdrawal of black women from the fields, since such work dishonored the women and children of black families. Bennett discussed the deadly effect on black communities of white supremacist terror, including lynching. Bennett pointed out that between 1882 and 1927, ninety-five black women were lynched, the most heinous example being the murder of pregnant Mary Turner, who was lynched and burned. While Turner was still alive, a knife was taken to her womb to cut loose her unborn baby, which cried feebly before a member of the lynch mob crushed its skull. Turner's sin in the eyes of the mob was that she had protested the lynching of her husband. Bennett concluded his article with a discussion of black women liberators, activists and entrepreneurs—from Bethune to Madame C. J. Walker—whose heroic deeds have advanced the race. But Bennett was aware of the unsung heroines who populated the army of black liberation. He said that what "these women accomplished at the top of the structure was duplicated on a lower level by the battalion of Black women who nurtured and sustained the Black church." Bennett lauded as well the "major vehicle of Black female expression in this period," the National Association of Colored Women, which "co-ordinated the work of Black women and supported a wide range of social and philanthropic activity." He also praised Ida B. Wells and Mary Church Terrell, cofounders of the NAACP.

Just as I finished scanning Bennett's article, Waldron reappeared.

"Ms. Rice is ready to see you now," he stated as he gestured for me to follow him.

"Ms. Linda Johnson Rice, this is Michael Eric Dyson," Clarence said as he introduced me to the striking head of this $400 million empire.

"Yes, of course, how are you?" Rice said as I entered her domain. "Please have a seat."

I greeted Rice with a warm embrace, and took a seat across from her and Waldron at a table in her recently renovated office with a spectacular view of Lake Michigan.

"I have seen pictures of you, and you always looked great," I said to Rice. "But those pictures don't begin to capture your true beauty."

She sported a fitted, purple designer suit that sinuously traced her extremely voluptuous frame. As beautiful as Rice appears in photos, they don't nearly communicate her breathtaking sensuality and her magnetic charm, pouring through her playful eyes and warmly radiant smile. Her beige skin shimmered, set off by impeccably coiffed reddish brown hair. In a company of bright, beautiful black women, it only made sense that Rice would so richly embody their sumptuousness in the most extraordinary way.

Her captivating good looks reminded me of an article I had read about an outfit Rice had worn fifteen years before. "Carlotta Alfaro whipped up Linda Johnson Rice's va-voom little gown, which had a layer of dotted sheer chiffon on top but still bordered on the illegal." While her suit was tastefully wrought, it nonetheless revealed a handsomely sculpted figure that, if not illegal, was surely worthy of a warning ticket. A year before that article appeared, Rice revealed the raison d'e-tre of her style. When her coworkers suggested that Rice purchase a few suits now that she was a vice president of her father's company, she followed through—with purple and red suits.

"I like bright colors," she said. "I cannot dress in a carbon-copy way. I have always been a person who is an individual, and what I wear is a reflection of my personality. I could never get up and put on a uniform."

As we chatted about the virtues of Chicago and Philadelphia, about a couple of my books, and about the nature of black intellectual life, I was struck by Rice's warmth, intelligence, and unpretentious spirit. Upon parting company, I thanked Rice for taking seriously the challenge to extend her father's legacy into the next century, and doing it with grace and élan.

Clarence rode with me down to the lobby, and just as we were saying good-bye, a former student from Spelman who had enrolled in my course at Brown University during a semester's exchange spotted me.

"Professor Dyson, how are you?" Ingrid Larkin, a volup-tuous, light brown beauty who conjures thoughts of songstress Jill Scott, called to me.

"Hey, Ms. Larkin, it's good to see you," I replied, as I gave her a hug.

"Now you know I should be mad at you," Larkin playfully chided me. "You gave me the only 'C' I got at Brown. But I'm not upset. I loved your class because it made me think hard about a lot of important issues."

"Then I've done my job," I said.

As I left the building, I was more than a little impressed with the job that Johnson Publishing Company had done over more than fifty years of covering the lives and stories of black America. The thought that so many talented and beautiful sisters would now guide the company into the twenty-first century under Linda Johnson Rice's leadership gave me a feeling of indescribable pride.

19

In Praise of Older Women

For a brother of my generation, this was heaven. My wife and I had come to Maxine Waters's birthday party in a Los Angeles hotel on the Sunset Strip to give her a present. Instead, I got the biggest gift.

It was a beautiful, crisp California night, and the 2000 Democratic National Convention had monopolized the city for nearly a week. When I got to Maxine's party, I was flowing off the adrenaline of constant political engagement, strategy sessions, television appearances, speeches, and panels. I was ready to let my hair down. As I was soon to discover, I would have more help than I could ever wish for.

Marcia and I greeted Maxine and gave her well wishes, scooped up some food from the elegant buffet, made our rounds of saying hello to various guests and politicos, and took our seats to eat. We were famished from the day's grinding activities, and I nearly inhaled my food and quickly went back for more. Marcia ventured out on the back balcony of the hotel as I fixed on the tasty victuals. Before I knew it, she burst back into the room and issued a stern warning.

"Look, I know you're about to lose your mind," she said with an impish grin. "But I'm about to introduce you to the thrill of your life."

"What is it?" I demanded with raging curiosity.

"And when you get back there, I don't want you to act a complete fool," Marcia continued, ignoring my burning question. "I have already warned them that you will have little self-control."

"What, Marcia, what is it?" I insisted. But she simply smiled, took me by the hand, and led me out onto the balcony. As soon as I stepped into the cozy back chambers, I was in a haze. Sitting there, in one group, in one spot, in one moment in time, were many of the black women I had fallen in love with while growing up. I had followed them on television or through recordings. I had also read about them and, I must confess, fantasized about being their suitor, or at least their dashing date for a ritzy premiere or a smashing party.

There, in the center of the table, sat fifty-six-year-old Denise Nicholas, or, as I first knew her from 1969–1974, Ms. Liz McIntyre on the television series *Room 222*, one of the first shows to feature black actors in the lead. She also played Olivia Ellis in the short-lived 1978 sitcom *Baby, I'm Back*. And, of course, from 1988–1994, she would star on *In the Heat of the Night* as Harriet DeLong, one-half of the most visible interracial couple on television, opposite Carroll O'Connor. Denise Nicholas was then, and remains to this day, one of the most breathtakingly beautiful women I have seen or met. Her striking, big hazel eyes shone brightly as ever. Her smile was as incandescent as it was when it gleamed at me from the small screen. Her smooth, yellow skin glistened in the night's warm glow. Her hair was just as full of body as I remembered it in photographs, and on the silver screen in the company of Bill Cosby and Sidney Poitier in 1975's *Let's Do It Again* and 1977's *A Piece of the Action*. I had been in love with Denise for so long that I felt we must be old friends. Actually, when we later got the chance to talk, it felt like we'd known each other for years. Besides the false familiarity created by television, I suppose I felt so close to Denise because I heard when I was growing up that she used to live around the corner from my ghetto house on Detroit's west side. I couldn't believe that a star so bright had escaped the gravitational pull of social misery that clouded our neighborhood sky. But there she sat, in regal repose and with the grace of a self-possessed queen.

Next to Denise sat fifty-six-year-old Mary Wilson, one-third of the greatest girl group in the history of music, *The Supremes*. I was on a roll with childhood idols and imaginary lovers drawn from my hometown. I always had a huge crush on Mary because she was a pretty chocolate doll, an adorable chanteuse with a golden pair of pipes—although she never got full credit for her talent—and a face and figure as comely as her vocal gifts. Mary was still a chocolate dream, her pretty face radiant and full, her beautiful eyes alive and sparkling, her

hair large and lovely, her lips wet and pouty, her figure, like
Denise's, fetching and eye-grabbing. I also liked Mary because
she was the group's griot, its truth-teller, and a politically sensitive scribe who penned books, made music, and mounted
her own career long after the great Diana Ross flew the coop.
I liked it that Mary proved she, too, was great and gritty. Her
earthy sensuality and her quick mind were true assets in making her a diva who couldn't be dismissed.

There, literally sitting pretty at the table, was fifty-four-
year-old Judy Pace, a drop-dead gorgeous scoop of dark
chocolate dessert that I often tried to reach through the
screen to consume whenever her stunning visage was captured by the cathode ray tubes of our modest black and white
television. Judy appeared at least once on the television series
Ironside, at the side of her real-life husband, actor Don
Mitchell, whom I envied almost to no end for his ability to
kiss her sweet lips on screen and at home. I imagined scenar-
ios where Don had to leave the country for a long spell, and
that Judy and I were able to spend time together. Alternatively,
I fantasized that Judy and Don broke up (they eventually did),
and that she had stumbled across me while healing her
wounds on a Detroit beach. (I had to keep the fantasy local,
since I could press my charms to full effect on my home territory. I'd know which fast-food restaurant we could hit, and
what neighborhood haunt we could frequent. My fantasies,
like my foreseeable future, were working class). I hungered for
more of her face and form when I was growing up. I soon
concluded that had her skin been lighter, Judy might have

won the greater fame I thought she deserved. When I saw her that night, she was as riveting a figure for me as she had been on television and in magazines. (In 1971, *Ebony* appropriately summarized her charm in the article "Judy Pace: The Thinking Man's Star.") Judy's face was just as magnificent, her cherubic cheeks, dazzling smile, piercing eyes and shock of hair all testifying to her ineffable youthfulness, the same as with Denise and Mary. And like them, she remained a sensuous presence and a vitally alive woman whose appeal, like that of many women who are just beginning to soar into mature womanhood, was undiminished by time.

Next to Judy sat sixty-six-year-old Nichelle Nichols, striking in her radiant beauty, preserved just as if she had stolen a secret from the other worlds she visited weekly as Lieutenant Uhura on the wildly successful *Star Trek*. Long before talk of the digital divide, and the questionable role of black folk in technology, and the images of black intelligence being divorced from the domains of science, Nichelle Nichols was a valiant, vocal disclaimer, even if by fictional association. (Why shouldn't it work for blacks, like it works for white guys who admit, "I'm not a doctor, but I play one on TV?") Nichelle's pretty mahogany face beamed in the night's blackness, her eloquently coiffed and shimmering silvery hair, bright smile, shapely figure, and twinkling eyes adding luster to her mellow but vibrant personality. I used to watch for her every week, tantalized by her short skirts, her impressive legs, and her striking eyelashes—which are still in full effect. Nichelle's sexual appeal is almost against the laws of this world, which, I fathomed, is why she was sent into outer space, in search of a planet that could handle her otherworldly charm. Even as I shared space with her on earth, I was sent back into my child-hood fantasies about intergalactic intimacy—that is, if it could happen in my backyard. I had to be in school each day since I didn't want to miss the teachers I had crushes on.

And next to Nichelle sat one of the most mercilessly sexy women in the world, a fifty-five-year-old woman from whose every pore there screamed a sensuality so intense that I had to remind myself that I wasn't in a private dream where I might range freely over my imagination without censure. Freda Payne is still insanely fine, as fine as she was when I'd spot occasional clips of her on television performing her monster hit, "Band of Gold." Ever since I had read in *Jet* about Freda marrying Gregory Abbott, a man eleven years younger than her—and a man who was working on his Ph.D. in English at Stanford, before he dropped out and who, years later, after they had split, had one big hit—I believed that if we ever met, I might have a chance with her. Of course, I harbored the same fantasy about Diahann Carroll, who had married a man whose age difference was even greater than the one between Freda and Abbott. I read about them in *Jet* as well. In fact, he had been an associate editor at the magazine, and I hoped one day to get a job at *Jet* doing anything, since that seemed to be the common denominator that linked my fantasies for Freda and Diahann. Later, when I began my doctoral studies at Princeton, I still nurtured the fantasy that Freda might even find me even more attractive than Abbott, since it looked like

I wouldn't have to drop out of school to pursue my career. Maybe actually getting that Ph.D. would help me out, not only on the job market, but also with one of my enduring fantasies.

The thing is, I had Freda's *Ebony* spread from January 1973 emblazoned on my brain. I had made love to her so often in my mind that I was afraid that if I ever met her, she might sue me for abandonment. I hardly needed the magazine anymore (although I hope I never lose it), since I could conjure the lay-out page by page. First, she appeared on the cover, with her long, black flowing hair swept back, her arched eyebrows neatly drawn on, her eyelashes accented in sharp strokes, and her mouth slightly ajar with only a shadow creeping through her luscious, orangeish lips. Freda's regal nose was in perfect symmetry with her almost hidden ears, and her perfectly manicured and long, painted nails capped fingers on hands that were each curled in a glistening, sensuous pose. Her flower print bikini swimsuit—composed of burnt orange, brown, tan and chocolate colors—featured a low-cut bottom and a top that barely contained her gently heaving bosom, with her shoulders wrapped in a cover-up. On the inside, on pages 118–119, Freda rested, slightly elevated, on her right arm, leaning in repose in a Peter Max-like psychedelic, multi-colored print bikini and a sarong. On the right side of page 119, at the top and bottom, Freda appears, respectively, in a lime green bikini, whose trunks featured adjustable side-ties, with her arms swung in the air, and in a multicolored floral print one-piece with a halter-neck maillot and a matching cover-up.

On page 120, Freda was featured in two shots: at the top, she struck a sexy pose, slightly propped on her elbow in a yellow wool blend cover-up with two buttons, and at the bottom, she wore a one-piece sea velvet maillot in violet nylon, with a halter neck and elastic back strap, and a yellow and blue head-wrap. Finally, on page 121, Freda was featured in side-by-side poses. The far right pose was a near duplicate of the cover. And for her sexiest pose yet, on the inside right, Freda sported a red knit bikini, with a halter neck and triangle bra, whose trunks featured a cord tie that gently and sensuously fell over her left thigh, as if she and the suit could come unraveled at any moment with just a gentle tug. She has a smile on her face, coy and cute, and her arms are stretched up and behind her head, showing her amazingly svelte and curvaceous frame to full—and noticeably glistening—effect.

This history of desire was locked deep inside me as I smiled at Freda. She was still incredibly fit and trim, and if possible, even more voluptuous now than when she appeared in *Ebony*, with an ironing-board flat stomach and wickedly proportioned shape. Her face was still quite beautiful, with clean, angular features, and a smile to light the world, at once coquettish and fully woman. Of course, her "Band of Gold" anthem, when it first came out, was years beyond my comprehension, although I would learn in bitter increments its lessons as I ploughed through two marriages, being left, and leaving in turn. And I recalled the plea she made in song for the troops in Vietnam to be brought home, a political cry dressed up as a successful and memorable single.

When I was able to open my mouth—or should I say speak, since my jaws had been dropped since I walked into the room—I uttered greetings to each one, sharing my long-standing love for their crafts, careers and curves. They were so good-natured, even ribbing me for my apparent, uncontrollable desire.

"Yeah, you are just having too good of a time, aren't you," Mary Wilson winked at me with knowing flirtation.

"Oh, yes Ma'am," I sheepishly grinned as I admitted what was already obvious to them all.

I took pictures, several of them actually, and made sure to position myself near each delightful diva for individual shots as well. And I hugged each of these sweet, soulful sisters whose sharp minds and beautiful bodies were still alluring after all these years.

My love for these women reflected a trend in my own life. I have always been attracted to older women. My three wives have been older than me—my first wife, Terrie, by eight years, my second wife, Brenda, by eleven years, and Marcia by seven. I have at times dated women who were as much as thirty years my senior. I think women don't even begin to approach the peak of their intelligence and appeal until they ripen into fifty-five- or sixty-year-olds, and then they can coast for another decade into sensuous senior-hood. Although I surely find younger women beautiful and charming, there is something irresistible about sisters who are seasoned, who wear their experience like subtle perfume, who know what they want and when they want it, who are familiar enough with

frailty to forgive its tracks even as they march defiantly into
the best years of their lives with a surer grasp of their own
sexuality and spirituality. The two go hand in hand, and the
mature woman knows that her body is a portal to her spirit,
and that sex is more than surrender of flesh; it is communion
of hearts and souls.

I thought about this as I basked in the afterglow of my rendezvous with this dream team of ebony pulchritude. But one
more delightful spin awaited me before I departed.

The music at Maxine's party—herself a prime example of a
woman only beginning to reach her peak—was slamming,
and somehow, as a gesture of God's grace, I got the chance to
dance with Freda Payne. I couldn't in all good conscience
allow this opportunity to pass me by. When Freda stood, I was
astounded at how well proportioned she remains. I had seen
her in *Sprung*, and in Eddie Murphy's *Nutty Professor 2: The
Klumps*, and knew that she was still beautiful, but in person,
her form defies gravity. Her shape puts women half her age to
shame, with a body hand carved by God—and her hard work,
I'm sure—into a voluptuosity that is thrilling and breathtaking. Her bosom is pleasantly ample, and her snug chocolate
scooped neck, three-quarters length sweater with its neckline
trimmed in fur, and her skin-tight, snakeskin slacks, revealed a
torso as taut as a Marine's bed.

When we got on the dance floor, I thought I might show
Freda some of my suave moves, darting here, jumping there,
scooting over, ducking under, raising up and gyrating with just
enough juice to let her see me work whatever mojo I had.

But the moment we hit the floor, Freda was a flurry of acrobatic activity: she twirled, gyrated, twisted, and moved her body with such electrifying sexiness that it was all I could do to watch. And then the thrill of my night came, suddenly, unexpectedly, during our third and final dance: Freda bent her head down to the floor in perfectly symmetrical, ram-rod straight fashion, with her splendid backside seemingly rising to my face as her hands nearly scraped the floor. I was flabbergasted, moved, disturbed, bothered, as the erotic swirl of her movement sent me crashing into sensual overload. I was done, done-in, undone, overdone. I knew it was time for me to leave. I didn't want to embarrass myself by reverting back to the magazine memories that had stoked a fire for Freda for nearly thirty years. So I after I hugged her, I left the floor, and soon after, the hotel.

But I was floating on a cloud of sheer nostalgia that materialized into a reality that exceeded my wildest imagination. Denise, Mary, Judy, Nichelle—and especially Freda—helped me to fulfill my fantasy of being in the loving presence of beautiful black women who the clock might have suggested were getting older, but who apparently never bothered to listen. And they each brought a black boy thirty years before— and a black man now—the sort of joy that lasts a lifetime.

How to Love Black Women
A Sermon

Today, I want to turn your attention to the letter of Ephesians, the fifth chapter, beginning at the twenty-first verse, and several verses following. I'll be reading from the New International Version.

Submit to one another out of reverence for Christ. . . . Husbands love your wives, just as Christ loved the Church and gave himself up for her to make her holy, cleansing her by the washing with water through the word, and to present her to himself as a radiant church, without stain or wrinkle or any other blemish, but holy and blameless. In this same way, husbands ought to love their wives as their own bodies. He who loves his wife loves himself. After all, no one ever hated his own body, but he feeds and cares for it, just as Christ does the church—for we are members of his body. "For this reason a man will leave his father and mother and will be united to his wife, and the two will become one flesh." This is a profound mystery—but I am talking about Christ and the church. However, each one of you also must love his wife as he loves himself, and the wife must respect her husband.

I want you to think with me from the subject, *How to Love Black Women.*

By all accounts, there is a crisis in black male and female relationships. Beyond the differences that men and women often have, a great deal of the problem has to do with how black men think about black women. A lot of that thinking is rooted in narrow notions about how we believe God has set up a hierarchy where women fall beneath men in the natural order of things. But I think it's long past time that we reexamine our beliefs and come up with different ideas about how things work, and how we should behave in light of what we learn. Now I'm not suggesting that these different ideas I'm speaking about are new. In fact, there's been a great deal of provocative thought about gender going on for quite some time, but we haven't often adopted the best of this thinking in our churches. I think it's time we started.

So let me make it plain. This sermon is not a neutral activity. It is an act of rhetorical and theological resistance. It is an attempt to challenge the kind of thinking and behavior that causes black women to suffer. Consider this sermon an act of interpretive warfare, since I'm doing battle with how we've used the Bible to justify some terrible beliefs about black women. We get awfully upset—and rightfully so—with how hip-hop culture demeans and degrades sisters. We are outraged when a rapper resorts to epithets to disrespect our women, and despite my great love for hip-hop, I'm sympathetic to that critique. But at the same time, we permit some destructive ideas to flourish in the church. These ideas are harmful because they influence how we act, not only in church, but also in our homes and schools. We've got to find a new way to behave so that our children inherit a more positive future.

I'll concede right away that sexist ideals and patriarchal notions ring through many of the texts of the Bible. But thankfully, the Bible offers helpful ideas about how human beings should treat one another when they've been redeemed by God's love. When God's love inhabits your heart, you act differently. You seek to translate God's love into social justice. And since charity—or love—begins at home, then justice begins there, too. A new understanding of black male and female relationships that can truly help our communities should flow from our churches. I believe that the black church is still the greatest institution black folk have, and we've got to work hard to keep it that way. That means we've got to move beyond the spiritual apartheid we practice. Seventy-five percent of the black church is made up of women, and yet they rarely have access to the central symbol of power—the pulpit. We've got to stop dragging our feet and begin to acknowledge just how important black women are to our churches— and to our mosques, temples, ashrams, and sanctuaries of all sorts. We must also realize just how important black women are to our success and survival as a people.

Now before I get to the real substance of the text, I want to argue that black male and female relationships are framed by at least three factors. First of all, the long legacy of slavery continues to affect our identities and our family structure. I'm not suggesting that we make a general appeal to slavery to explain everything that's wrong in black life. But I am suggesting that the kinds of relationships we developed in slave culture, under extreme oppression, shape how black men and women relate to one another. The second factor that affects our relationships is the steadily deteriorating material conditions of black America. We are under assault in our communities from economic, political and social forces. When crucial resources are scarcely available, black men and women often turn on one another in a form of cultural cannibalism. We eat away at each other's psychic strength and personal esteem instead of feeding off of one another's love and support. Instead of feasting on each other's downfalls, we should be collectively destroying the forces that destroy us. Finally, role expectations have shifted, and the social status of women has changed in this so-called post-feminist era. The rules of gender have been transformed. As a result, the way men and women relate to one another is very different from twenty years ago. I want you to keep these factors in mind as I interpret this text in favor of those whose voices it has suppressed.

It is both ironic and subversive that I've chosen to preach from this passage in Ephesians. Why is it ironic? Because this text has usually been used to silence the very voices I want to speak about this morning, the voices of women. Historically, this passage has been manipulated to deny authority to three groups—wives, slaves, and children—reinforcing racism, sexism, and ageism. And no matter how much you try to fiddle around with the text, or to suggest it as a product of its own times, which it certainly is, there is no denying that it has been used to quiet the speech—and really, to segregate the bodies—of women in the church. It's subversive that I've chosen to use this text because I want to reread the fifth chapter of Ephesians in light of our own freedom struggles, and to see it through the lens of our suffering and salvation. I want to enlist this text in an effort to liberate us from the gender beliefs that have poisoned our communities.

Now the first thing that the writer of Ephesians suggests is that there ought to be mutual submission between men and women in reverence of Christ. The first way I want to suggest that black men can love black women is to promote this principle of mutual submission. We usually concentrate on the latter verses of this chapter that urge wives to submit to their husbands. We also use these verses to legitimate our patriarchal fantasies and formulas. We appeal to them to justify our male supremacist rule and to suppress black women's voices. The problem with such behavior is that it doesn't acknowledge the fundamental humanity of women. Neither does it underscore the dignity of personhood that all of us want to promote, a belief that black people, in fact, *have* historically advocated. We have helped this nation live up to its ideals because we have fought for freedom from all tyrannies and terrors. Black women have been a defining force in our liberation struggles, so we shouldn't seek to oppress the very sisters who valiantly helped to win our freedom as a people, and *as black men*.

Mutual submission means that we act in a way to enhance the interests of each partner in the relationship. I think it's extremely significant that the text links reverence for Christ to mutual submission. Already, the text topples the notion that men should rule over a woman's life, or direct her domestic agenda. We are taught in the most liberating moments of our black religious history that nobody has ultimate authority over our lives but God. That means that we're suspicious of all forms of authority, particularly those that masquerade as substitutes for God's Word.

Now don't get me wrong; I'm not suggesting that we shouldn't submit to any authority. I'm arguing that the authority to which we submit must be one that we agree on, one that we ask questions of, and one that is democratic. Otherwise, authority can be used to undermine equality. We've got to understand that all of us are children of God, and that nobody has the right to determine our destinies or to limit the expression of our gifts and talents. Mutual submission means that we love one another based on mutual respect for one another. Mutual submission is dictated by the needs of the relationship and shaped by love for our partners. Our love relationships should be flexible. That means that black men have to surrender the pose of patriarchy and the strut of sexism. We've got to affirm women as agents of God's gifts and graces. Women can offer us the richest possible dimensions of God's love and leadership. In our homes, that means that we've got to listen and learn from our women as we shape our relationships. Mutual submission means that we respect one another, encourage one another, sacrifice for one another, and stand up for one another, even against harmful ideas we've supported over the years.

A lot of black men are afraid to love our women with this kind of holy abandon. We fear that it will keep sisters from recognizing the hurts that black men face. But nothing could be further from the truth. In fact, black women have been among the most vocal and progressive advocates for black men. They have helped us to find solutions to the problems that plague us. For instance, who was way out front on the issue of the prison-industrial complex that affects the million black men locked away, many unfairly, and to warn us about the injustice of incarceration? Angela Davis. And who edited the book that rigorously explored the cultural claim that black males are an endangered species? Jewelle Taylor Gibbs. And who sang a song about the destructive images of black men in the culture and praised us for our moral beauty and our strength? Angie Stone. So loving a black woman doesn't mean that we surrender our pride as black men. Nor does it mean that we divert our attention from our social distress. It means that we have enough sense to realize that one of the reasons we suffer is because we ignore the wisdom of our women. We don't have to disrespect or dominate our women to feel like real men.

Black men must be careful not to justify our ugly treatment of black women by pointing to our pain. We must avoid what the scholar Barbara Christian calls "the oppression derby," where groups argue over who has suffered the most. Black men can't pretend that our oppression is worse than black women's. Neither can we take solace in our suffering as a way to excuse our brutality toward our sisters. We cannot have a hierarchy of pain. If it hurts, it hurts. All of our pain is legitimate and real—if it *is* legitimate and real. So let's not waste any more time structuring a totem pole of catastrophe where we cut our niche of misery deeper or higher than black women's. After all, to switch metaphors, we're in the same bed. Instead of cutting each other's throats, let's rub each other's feet, massage each other's backs and heal each other's wounds. If mutual submission is tied to reverence for Christ, that means there is a spiritual foundation to our relationships. Therefore we've got to nurture spirituality through tender care and gentle regard for one another. In a world where black women are battered by negative half-truths in the media, and ambushed by brutal put-downs from their own children in entertainment, the least we can do is to wrap sisters in the healing garments of reverence and respect.

The writer also says that we must love our women as Christ loved the church. What kind of love did Christ have for the Church? Well, first of all, it was an empowering love, the kind of love that encouraged people to be themselves. In other words, Christ was the kind of lover who permitted the members of his family to freely express their talents and gifts. That kind of love is empowering because it breaks down artificial social barriers to self-expression. It also urges us to move beyond harmful habits and traditions. As black women have taught us, that kind of love encourages us to claim our own voices. It gives us the liberty to learn to speak with power and confidence.

Black men must not be frightened by the ways women learn to speak. And we shouldn't be intimidated by the strength and intensity of our women's speech. Some women will have been deprived of their voices for so long that they will want to shout when they finally speak honestly and freely without having to lie about what they feel or want. We must not be afraid to listen to them speak. We should even encourage them to take voice lessons—which, in this case, means that they gather with other women who encourage them to clearly and courageously express their beliefs. Practice, indeed, makes perfect.

There are many ways to speak our truths. We must be true to how God has blessed us to express ourselves. Now that sounds simple, but it's much harder to achieve, particularly when men think that women's voices are in competition with our own. Our voices must supplement, not supplant, one another. That doesn't mean we can't challenge each other, but it does mean we shouldn't silence each other. Given the vicious history of patriarchy, men have been largely at fault in suppressing the speech of black women.

Christ also had a sacrificial love. That meant that he was willing to pay the price, and to do his part, in sustaining his relationship to the church. Now this is no easy thing. Sacrificial love is demanding, often inconvenient, and surely time consuming. And it can be life changing. I think it means that black men must be willing to sacrifice at least three things. First, we've got to sacrifice our investment in patriarchy. What I mean is that we can't lean on male supremacy to resolve conflicts or settle disputes in our homes. Instead, we've got to appeal to reason and to prayer, to negotiation and to consultation, to iron out our differences. Second, we've got to sacrifice the unfair privileges we've gained by being men and seek to share power and responsibility with our partners. We've got to be willing to argue our case, but also to hear a case argued, as we make critical decisions that affect our relationships.

Finally, we must be willing to sacrifice our beliefs about *women* and honestly encounter the *woman* that stands before us. No two people are alike, and no two women behave in the same manner. Now we can't be foolish and reject what experience and common sense have taught us. But we must subject our biases to Cross examination—which means we view our beliefs and behavior in light of Christ's sacrificial love for us. And if Christ was willing to forgive our sins and to forge a new relationship with us based on his redeeming love for us, then surely we can seek to emulate that love in our relationships. We can't begin our sentences with, "All women…" It is better to say, "In my experience, women…" It is even better to say, "Women are distinct individuals, and I want to know who you are…" In the final analysis, sacrificial love is not just something that happens in dramatic moments. In some ways, it might be easier to surrender one's life for a loved one than to do the daily and difficult work of making a relationship work.

But Christ's love was also demanding. Nobody gets a free ride, so to speak. Each of us must pay the toll and be responsible for our relationships. I believe that our best selves are nurtured in an environment of expectation. Love, after all, has to do with acceptable requirements and reasonable demands. Of course, what's acceptable and reasonable is determined by each relationship. This is tricky, because some people appeal to this idea to justify their perversions and abuses, or to sanctify their exploitation of another person. We should have nothing to do with that kind of behavior. Still, we should not fit our relationships into a preexisting mold. In the end, if you love your partner, you will demand their best, and make sure that they do the same for you. We must take it upon ourselves to do all that we can to sustain love and nurture affection.

But a demanding love means more than simple declarations of selfish desires. We must demand only what we deliver. If we're not willing to give it, we can't expect to get it. Christ gave up his life for us, which is why he can demand we do the same. Now doing the same thing doesn't mean we do things the same way. For instance, since none of us is the Savior, we can't redeem the world through a cosmic act of sacrificial love. But we can act sacrificially, and unselfishly, in our own relationships. I may not be able to do for my partner what she can do for me, or vice versa. For instance, perhaps I can cook and she can sew. A demanding love doesn't mean that she cooks for me because I cook for her, or that I stitch her hems like she stitches mine. Demanding love is not a demand for similar gifts. It is a demand for a similar willingness to share one's gifts.

Finally, the writer suggests that we love our partners as we love our bodies. Now that's a deep concept for many reasons. Howard Thurman said that the time and place of a person's life on earth is the time and place of her body. The body is the primary means by which we experience the world around us. Through the body, we express our God-given identities. Embodiment is a crucial notion to Christian theology. We say that God took on flesh and became a human being—not an idea, a cosmic principle, a theory, nor a political abstraction. That's why we must treat the human body with respect. All bodies deserve love and protection—gay bodies and straight ones, colored bodies and white ones, female bodies and male ones, foreign bodies and American ones, poor bodies and rich ones, imprisoned bodies and free ones. All human bodies are important because they are the product of God's imagination meeting up with human circumstance. We make love, God makes babies.

When you love a woman like you love your body, it is the deepest love possible. It is a love for the other tied directly to self-love. It is interest for the other linked to self-interest.

Healthy Christians have a high regard for the body. We should not be ashamed of our bodies, but proud that they bind us to our God and our loved ones. Unfortunately, we have often pretended as if the body wasn't there, that it wasn't important to our identity, our celebration of life and our worship of God. This is why we don't teach our children about sex. That's also why we deny that a healthy sexual identity is critical to enjoying our earthly existence. We often repress our sexual identities in an unhealthy fashion. Even God depended on the body to communicate divine love. We are embodied creatures, and we men should do as the Bible says: love our women as we love our bodies. If we appreciate our bodies, we'll appreciate our women's bodies.

But the flip side is true, too. If I dislike myself, if I dishonor myself, if I hate myself, I will dislike, dishonor, and hate my partner. If I refuse to take care of myself, I threaten the quality of my relationship. If I hate myself I damage the person about whom my partner deeply cares. If I fail to appreciate the gifts God gave me I deny their expression to my partner, and perhaps, the world. If I have a low estimation of myself, I obviously believe my partner's judgment of me is distorted. That is a weak foundation on which to build any enduring relationship. That means that black male self-hate is hatred of black women. But even more important—and this is especially relevant to a hip-hop culture that assaults black women's identities while exploiting their bodies—black male hatred of black women is ultimately self-hatred. So the "bitch" we black men really hate may be staring back at us in the mirror.

The beauty of this passage for black men is that we are given theological license to affirm our black women's bodies. We have a holy obligation to acknowledge the beauty of God's creation in black women's unique shapes, sizes, and styles. That's good news, because black women, like black men, have been attacked and exploited since they arrived on American soil. Their hair is said not to be silky enough, their lips not thin enough, their noses not slim enough, their hands not smooth enough, their feet not soft enough, their waists not trim enough, their skin not light enough, their breasts not firm enough, their hips not straight enough, their frames not sleek enough, their eyes not blue enough, their teeth not white enough, their necks not long enough, and their behinds not small enough. Despite such vicious treatment, black women have managed to hold on to a relatively healthy view of themselves.

Recent studies suggest that black women feel healthier about their bodies than any other population, including white women, who, despite centuries of idealization—or perhaps because of it—feel they have to constantly nip, tuck, tighten, and flatten themselves. Black women in the main have no such anxieties, which is a miracle in itself. This point was recently brought home to me when I discussed hip-hop culture on a *Vibe* magazine "Big Willie" panel that included, among others, my dear friend Jean Riggins, the brilliant sister who heads Universal Records, and who has a beautiful pecan complexion and an earthy sexiness that is alluring. The panel also featured Star Jones, whom I had met before when we hung out together with Colin Powell and Chris Rock before Janet Jackson's concert at Madison Square Garden. But I was mostly kicking it with the General and Rock, and missed an opportunity for Star-gazing.

But on this day, I *scoped* Star Jones. She is an electrifying force of hard-to-miss black woman. She is smart as a whip, and she is also astonishingly beautiful. As fine as she is on television, it still doesn't do this trained lawyer justice. She has impeccable walnut-colored skin, big, beautiful, almond-shaped eyes framed by eyelashes that beat like butterfly wings against the wind, a brilliant and infectious smile, sweetly succulent lips, and a smoldering sensuality that floods her pores and radiates a confidence that is contagious. With her Payless shoes, no doubt, she was trouncing every stereotype of black female identity. In fact, she had locked Aunt Jemima in the closet, tossed Mammy into retirement, and brought out the vivacious, full-figured black woman completely at home with her body and her undeniable beauty. What black men must do is create a world where more Star Joneses can emerge, where more black women not only accept themselves, but also *celebrate* their God-given beauty.

We have a Biblical mandate to laud our lovely women. We should love black women's skin, in whatever shade it comes, from vanilla vitality to chocolate charm, from mocha mist to espresso elegance, from beige bliss to almond effect, from tan tint to blue blaze, and from cream comfort to black beatitude. We should love black women's noses—broad or pointed, snub or extended, fine-lined or bluntly drawn. We should love their eyes—black, brown, hazel, green or blue—and their lips, whether pouting, pursing, protruding, huge, small, voluptuous, streamlined or luscious. We should love their feet—long toes or short, painted nails or nude, and whether they are broad, flat and thick, or thin, fleshy and narrow. We should love their breasts—whether tiny or enormous, whether sagging or taut, and whether they fit into A or D cups. We should love their hands—manicured or untouched, long fingers or short pointers, and acrylic nails or natural. We should love their faces—made-up and plain ones, oval-shaped and banana-like, ellipses and concaves, high foreheads and low brows, and fleshy ones and tight ones. We should love their legs—long, lean legs and thick, short legs, shapely legs and skinny legs, and legs that are clean-shaven and legs with hair. We should love their hair—natural, dreaded, locked, kinky, nappy, permed, curly, straight, silky, jagged or wiry. I love black women's hair so much I wrote *Black Hair Poem* to celebrate it:

> *Your hair is a wonder to be*
> *hold*
> *when thick*
> *locks*
> *my gaze into bushy abandon*
> *I swim in your serpentine swirls*
> *down to my nappy roots*
>
> *To say I love your*
> *Hair*

Is to comb through a million black contradictions
where unruly myths coil
in wiry self-hatred

Your hair makes me hair-hungry
Starved of bald-faced lies told to us
when we were little more than buckshots
on some hateful tribe's headlines
splashed in ugly black across
newspaper's graying, dulling white

When I look at your hair
I see streaked mirrors of broken selves
littered in your mane
The fragments of a continent's hurts
strung purposefully around your curls

When I feel your hair
I feel mostly me
A tender-headed ache of snipped desire
Reaching for what should have never been
hated or sheared
A self perfectly formed in fuzzy fullness

And finally, I think we should celebrate a crucial feature of
black women's bodies. I believe that God, when searching the
divine imagination for what shape the world should have in
order to flow through the universe with grace and gravity,

simply looked at the heavenly design for the black woman's behind and concluded, "that will work." Even if you don't agree with me that there is cosmic consistency between black women's behinds and the structure of our planet, there can be little denying that black women's behinds inspire homage to the God who created them. I believe that black women's derrieres are the signature of a God who stands behind her work—that they are the fleshy, formidable fruit of God's love for all of us who love black women. We should celebrate the black woman's behind—fat or fatter, big or bigger, huge or huger, and of course, flat ones, skinny ones, lean ones, drawn-in ones, and high and low ones, too. In the end, so to speak, the black woman's gluteus *maximus* is a joy to be held.

The love of black women is indeed a divine gift. It is also our privilege and responsibility to love black women. We owe it to our children, and to their children, to embrace our women—our mothers, our sisters, our daughters, our aunts, our grand- and great-grandmothers, our wives and our lovers. By blessing them, we bless ourselves. Black men owe it to Harriet Tubman to love Tamika; we owe it to Sojourner Truth to love Shenita. We must love every kind of sister there is: the other-abled and the physically fit, the healthy sister and those who suffer illness, the living and the dying, the professional woman and the working-class sister, the welfare denizen and the CEO, the bourgie sister and the around-the-way girl, sisters with terminal degrees and sisters working in airport terminals, and many more beside. When we love black women, we love ourselves, and the God who made us.

Index